What Your Colleagues Are S

The beauty and power of this book is moving the debate away from the nature of teacher questions to the wonderful process of questioning. This process involves more than the teacher; it begs for questions moving learning forward, not reinforcing facts; it asks for questioning for exploration, excitement, extending, evaluating, and engagement. Renton opens the possibilities for questioning to improve learning and he provides so much advice to advance a pedagogy of questioning.

—John Hattie
**Laureate Professor, Melbourne Graduate
School of Education, Australia**

In a world awash with misinformation and bogus certainty, we all need a questioning attitude to what we hear, read, and see. Good teachers ask questions that develop this attitude in their students. This book is the detailed guidebook to being a questioning teacher that every educator needs. Read it—and don't forget to question it too.

—Guy Claxton
Prof of Education Kings College, London, UK

Thinking skilfully will be the most critical life skill needed by pupils as they become adults in the volatile, uncertain, complex, and ambiguous world they'll inherit. By systematically posing some very relevant and searching questions to his readers within *Challenging Learning Through Questioning*, Martin Renton has done what he encourages teachers to do: to act as a guide towards deeper thinking through purposeful and insightful questioning.

Using practical examples, he artfully deconstructs the learning process and demonstrates how, by making a clear link between the knowledge, skills, and understanding they are seeking and the questions they ask, teachers can encourage deep enquiry and thereby promote learning.

Martin has provided us with a highly readable masterclass into the seemingly simple and yet deeply layered process of questioning.

—Geoff Moorcroft
Director of Education, Isle of Man

The ability to craft effective and meaningful questions is sometimes overlooked and underappreciated. Questioning is a skill that needs to be cultivated and honed. This book challenges the reader to move beyond the simplicity of *who, what, when,* and *where* questions to more critical and analytical questions of *how* and *why.* How do we craft better questions? How do we elicit engaged and thoughtful responses? This book provides a roadmap for how to facilitate dialogue and advanced thinking.

—Brent Raby
Assistant Superintendent, West Aurora District 129, Illinois, USA

If you are ready to approach questioning as a powerful process that has the potential to transform learning, you need this book. *Challenging Learning Through Questioning* is a game changer. Renton has delivered a must-read, practical pedagogical guide to questioning that will not only challenge your current notions about the practice but will simultaneously show you how to hone this essential instructional skill. What you will encounter is a systematic approach and countless strategies, derived from Renton's own practice, that can be implemented immediately to facilitate deeper levels of thinking, reasoning, and learning for all. I highly recommend this essential guide to questioning for all educators looking to make a significant impact. Don't miss this opportunity to learn from one of the best!

—Sarah Callahan
**Executive Director of Curriculum, Instruction, and Professional Development,
East Rochester Union Free School District**

This is an informative and practical guide on how to develop good thinking and deeper learning using effective questioning in the classroom. It enables you as a practitioner to reflect and engage your students in developing higher-level dialogue. Throughout this book, Martin gives a series of strategies that enables you to facilitate your student's journey by coaching them out of the comfort zone into the learning zone. And who would have thought silence could be so varied and purposeful?

—Jennie Carter

Growth Mindset and Learning Disposition leader

Highweek Primary School, Newton Abbot, UK

As a professional development provider, I value resources that provide a clear connection to learning while supporting adult learners in their journey to shape practices that have the greatest impact on student learning, and this book does both very well. The strategies and concepts that are detailed in the book are focused on using questioning in a way that extends learning rather than evaluating learning, which is often the focus of current questioning practices. The strategies are introduced at various levels of complexity, allowing for the reader to enter where they are comfortable while still having room to grow.

The approaches suggested in this book are slight adjustments to what educators are already doing—not complete shifts in practice. The questioning suggestions and the examples shared will resonate with all educators, regardless of experience, interests, or background.

—Carmen Bergmann

Asst Superintendent, Regional Office of Education #17

Bloomington, USA

This book is a must read for any classroom teacher who is looking to develop and deepen their questioning on a day-to-day basis in the classroom. Martin approaches this from the perspective of a practitioner, meaning that the book is full of strategies and tips that can be transferred directly to the classroom. This is also a must-read for any senior leadership team that is serious about improving questioning in their school.

—Richard Paul

Headteacher, Greatfields Secondary School

London, UK

Martin presents us with a fascinating insight into our understanding and use of questioning, providing us with a powerful opportunity to reflect on the quality of questioning that takes place in our classrooms.

Martin's book is packed with strategies and ideas on how we can use questioning to become an integral part of the learning process. It's a rich resource, that will support quality, long-term change, enhance teachers' questioning skills, and effectively promote deeper learning to have maximum impact through increased student engagement.

Never has silence been so powerful.

—Judy Martyn

Headteacher, Highweek Primary School

Newton Abbot, UK

In *Challenging Learning Through Questioning* Martin Renton clarifies the importance of using questioning in a purposeful way and as a core teaching tool. Renton challenges myths like labelling questions as "open" or "closed," and instead presents "questioning moves" as stepping stones to effective questioning and learning. An important, well-written, and well-researched book with new perspectives (like The Taxonomy of Silence). It will definitely make you question your own use of questions in the classroom and help students become more thoughtful thinkers. What more could you ask from a book . . . ?

—Bosse Larsson

Freelance Consultant, Sweden

Martin has captured the essence of his exceptional teaching practices in this book. It is an eloquently written book that offers both insight and practical ways of supporting teachers and their learners to make progress. His book highlights that we can all develop our questioning skills to support our learners to think deeply and meaningfully. After all; it isn't what we ask but what we do with what we hear that matters.

—Leonie Anstey
Freelance Consultant
Victoria, Australia

At Søndervangskolen (DK) we have worked closely with Martin Renton for a number of years to develop a shared mindset and language for learning. Together we have built a professional culture where teaching staff coaches and leaders develop teaching and learning with a focus on questioning, active learning, collaboration and challenge. In the book *Challenging Learning Through Questioning* you will find the same combination of resources—theory, examples, strategies and tools—that has supported our learning and student learning. We find the "Reflection sections" really useful to ensure we focus on not only "Where are we going?" and "Where are we now?" but remember to reflect on "What's the next step?". This book will undoubtedly support our work with student learning in the future.

—Rani Hørlyck and Anne Katrine Kusk
School and Pedagogical Leaders
Søndervangskolen, Aarhus, Denmark

The 'Challenging Learning' series of books have been central to my leadership reading resources, and each one has proved a constant source of reference and development. This book is no different and will prove equally important in developing our teaching skills and the quality of learning for any school. Renton provides a perfect balance of theory and practical ideas to engage the reader and provoke reflection.

As educators, we would all suggest that our questioning is paramount and a skill we hold core to our work. However, this book pushes us to unpick the quality and reflect on the effectiveness of our questioning so we can improve the impact these questions have.

Each chapter provides clear examples that demonstrate the theory and top tips for making immediate improvements in the classroom. The exercises suggested make the book extremely practical and act as a tool for improving how we get the best from our learners. Renton's style is informative and entertaining, and although the focus of the ideas is based in an educational setting, the suggestions would develop any leader's approach to getting the best from their team. I look forward to sharing it with our school team and using all the ideas suggested.

—Jill Harland
Headteacher, Brudenell Primary School
Leeds, UK

Challenging Learning Through Questioning connects theory with practice to provide a thought-provoking resource for teachers. Martin's book provides practical tools and frameworks to help teachers engage students and deepen their learning. This is a valuable resource for teachers at all stages of their career development.

—Pippa Leslie
MA Education Professional Practice Programme Leader,
University of Cumbria, Lancaster, UK

Martin Renton provides experienced insights on how to maximise the effects of questioning in today's classroom. He shares practical examples and strategies that educators can easily implement in order to create the conditions for increased engagement and deeper learning. As a result of reading this book, I am learning how to ask better questions and sequence them in a way that will move learners toward the intended learning goals. Thank you, Martin, for this exceptional and unique contribution to the field.

—Jenni Donohoo
Freelance Consultant and Author, Ontario, Canada

CHALLENGING LEARNING
THROUGH
QUESTIONING

Challenging Learning Series

The Learning Challenge: How to Guide Your Students Through the Learning Pit to Achieve Deeper Understanding

by James Nottingham

Challenging Learning Through Dialogue

by James Nottingham, Jill Nottingham and Martin Renton

Challenging Learning Through Feedback

by James Nottingham and Jill Nottingham

Challenging Mindset

by James Nottingham and Bosse Larsson

Challenging Learning Through Questioning

by Martin Renton

Learning Challenge Lessons, Elementary

by James Nottingham and Jill Nottingham

Learning Challenge Lessons, Secondary ELA

by James Nottingham, Jill Nottingham and Mark Bollom

CHALLENGING LEARNING
THROUGH
QUESTIONING

*Facilitating the Process of
Effective Learning*

Martin Renton

Foreword by James Nottingham

CORWIN

CORWIN
A SAGE Publishing Company

FOR INFORMATION:

CORWIN
A SAGE Company
2455 Teller Road
Thousand Oaks, California 91320
(800) 233-9936
www.corwin.com

SAGE Publications Ltd.
1 Oliver's Yard
55 City Road
London, EC1Y 1SP
United Kingdom

SAGE Publications India Pvt. Ltd.
B 1/I 1 Mohan Cooperative Industrial Area
Mathura Road, New Delhi 110 044
India

SAGE Publications Asia-Pacific Pte. Ltd.
18 Cross Street #10-10/11/12
China Square Central
Singapore 048423

Acquisitions Editor: Ariel Curry
Associate Content Development
     Editor: Jessica Vidal
Associate Editor: Eliza B. Erickson
Editorial Intern: Nyle DeLeon
Production Editor: Tori Mirsadjadi
Copy Editor: Melinda Masson
Typesetter: Hurix Digital
Proofreader: Emily Ayers
Indexer: Integra
Cover Designer: Janet Kiesel
Marketing Manager: Margaret O'Connor

Printed in the United States of America

ISBN 978-1-5063-7657-8

This book is printed on acid-free paper.

MIX
Paper from
responsible sources
FSC® C008955

FSC
www.fsc.org

20 21 22 23 24   10 9 8 7 6 5 4 3 2 1

CONTENTS

Chapter 5: Stay Silent (and Listen)   79

PART II: QUESTIONING AND CHALLENGE   95

Chapter 6: Thinking About Challenge   97

Chapter 7: Questioning Activities to Challenge Thinking   113

LIST OF FIGURES

THE CHALLENGING LEARNING STORY

By James Nottingham

I am absolutely delighted that *Challenging Learning Through Questioning* is the latest book to join the Challenging Learning library.

The series began in 2010 with the publication of my first book, *Challenging Learning*. It has since grown into a series of four books for teachers and leaders on dialogue, feedback, the Learning Pit, and growth mindset. There is also a book for parents (*Encouraging Learning*); one for early-years staff (*Challenging Early Learning*); and, more recently, two books sharing lesson ideas for guiding students through the Learning Pit (*Learning Challenge Lessons—Elementary* and *Learning Challenge Lessons—Secondary English Language Arts*).

The aim of all of our books is to challenge the way learning takes place as well as to make learning more challenging: hence the series title, Challenging Learning. You can find many reasons for this in our books, as well as in our consultancy work. These include the notion that we learn best when we step outside our Comfort Zone despite the contrary evidence that students are so often praised for completing tasks by staying *in* their Comfort Zone. Indeed, this is one of the reasons why I created the Learning Pit almost 20 years ago, and why perhaps it is so popular around the world—because it encourages *more* students to step out of their Comfort Zone *more* of the time.

Another example of Challenging Learning is to question the notion that feedback is one of the most effective ways to enhance learning. The problem is, when feedback is given too soon—often as a way to stop students from struggling with something—it can *get in the way* of learning because it brings them back into their Comfort Zone prematurely. Similarly, when feedback is given too late—as is so often the case when teachers mark students' work at the *end* of a task—it is rarely acted upon and therefore remains relatively impotent. Then there is the insistence of so many leaders to check that teachers have *given* feedback, rather than to look for evidence of *impact* of feedback—all of which gets in the way of learning.

Now there is this book, *Challenging Learning Through Questioning*, by my closest and longest-standing colleague and friend, Martin Renton. Within these pages, Martin shows how questioning can be one of the best ways to engage students and deepen their learning, and yet is so often used to close learning down, particularly as part of the "IRE" approach. IRE stands for *Initiate* (teacher asks a question); *Respond* (student gives an answer); *Evaluate* (teacher confirms or asks again). This IRE approach does little to improve learning; indeed, it could be argued that it does the opposite. Martin also suggests that silence rather than more questions can often do more to extend the impact of questioning, and that there is no such thing as an open or closed question. You will have to read on to find out more, but I'm sure you would agree that these are good examples of ways to challenge learning!

The term *Challenging Learning* doesn't just apply to our books; it also refers to our group of companies providing consultancy for preschools, schools, colleges, and school districts around the world. Currently, we have 30 employees in six countries: the United Kingdom, the United States, Australia, Denmark, Norway, and Sweden. Together we transform the most up-to-date and impressive research into best pedagogical practices for staff working with 3- to 19-year-olds. Martin is co-director of these companies, and now co-owner. The wisdom he has developed in helping to grow these companies as well as to design the pedagogical and leadership processes we use can be witnessed throughout this book. It makes the book so much the better, in much the same way as Martin's wisdom makes our Challenging Learning team so much better.

Enjoy the read and the ever-more-expert actions it can lead to.

With warmest wishes,

James Nottingham
October 2019

FOREWORD

By James Nottingham

This is the book we've all been waiting for!

I mean that in more ways than one: it has taken Martin a very long time to write, and so it is quite literally the book our whole team has been waiting for. Indeed, it has become a running joke over the last few years that our meetings have finished with predictions as to how far into the future it will be before "Martin's questioning book" is published.

However, I also mean it is the book we've all been waiting for in the teaching profession because, with it, we have the opportunity to transform everyday practice and deepen learning for everyone—staff and students alike.

Martin's determination to understand leading and learning, and his respect for context, is second to none. Every day, he engages with staff and students, in classrooms and in corridors, to better understand what they wish to achieve and how best to support their learning journey. Time and again, I have heard comments about how Martin has designed 'the best professional learning of our careers' or how 'Mr Renton has made me think and care about things I used to believe were really boring!'

Those who know Martin might suggest these responses are due in part to his wit and wisdom; those who don't know him might wonder if it is because of natural charm and good looks. And yet everyone who sees or hears him in action knows it is also due to the curious, respectful, and questioning approach he takes, be it with a group of 3-year-olds in kindergarten, a 17-year-old apprentice in college, or experienced members of staff who are trying to engage the hardest-to-reach students. That is why this book has been worth the wait: because it shares some of the best ways to achieve exactly that—being curious, being respectful, and taking a questioning approach that will deepen learning.

In mentioning the time it has taken Martin to write this book, I do not wish to imply that he has been prevaricating or hasn't prioritised his writing. In reality, he has spent the last few years—arguably the last 25 years—honing his messages, fine-tuning strategies, and revising his thoughts as he continues to work in schools, preschools, colleges, and school districts around the world.

At the same time, Martin has helped grow our company, Challenging Learning, from four of us in the North East of England to a 30-strong team in Australia, Denmark, Norway, Sweden, the United Kingdom, and the United States. He has also led the creation of a long-term process that builds a culture of organisational growth, shared ownership, distributed leadership, and collective efficacy that is now being used to significant impact in more than 400 schools, 100 preschools, and 30 colleges in 10 countries worldwide.

Regardless, though, of the reasons for the wait, you will see when you read this book that it has been worth it! Within these pages is the best of Martin's experience distilled for us all to use.

This book guides us through some of the very best ways to engage staff and students in questioning that will deepen learning, reasoning, and metacognition. It teaches us a series of steps and strategies we can all use to further enhance our skills of questioning. And it does all this in Martin's characteristically encouraging yet challenging, light-hearted yet serious-about-learning approach that he takes to life in general and pedagogy in particular.

It is now your time to read this book and try out the ideas, and I can assure you: it will be time well spent.

PREFACE

Here are some of the tools, models, and ideas that frame the *Challenging Learning Through Questioning* approach, all of which we will dig deeper into, to give you everything you need to refine and improve your questioning skills!

We will work through each of these in this book to build up your questioning expertise and experience, giving you guidance and reflection opportunities along the way.

The Three Essential Skills.

> Know Your Intent
>
> Plan Your Responses
>
> Stay Silent (and Listen)

These run throughout the book and are at the heart of improving your questioning techniques, ensuring your questioning is purposeful, your responses well considered, and you pay attention to what your students are saying so you can build on *their* learning.

The Challenging Path.

Source: Nottingham & Larsson, 2019.

It is only after the first student response that we can truly identify the nature and purpose of your questioning. Your basic structure for questioning should be 'IRE' (Initiate-Respond-Explore). So let's ensure the intention is to explore the challenging path.

Funnelling.

This involves refining the basic IRE structure so that you can plan more deliberately for progress in the Explore step.

Here you will follow up your students' first response with an Explain and Extend question, to widen possibilities and deepen the learning.

The Learning Pit®.

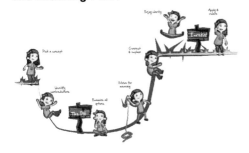

The Learning Pit® (Nottingham, 2007, 2010, 2017) is a metaphor for the cognitive conflict students feel when working through a challenge and grappling with concepts.

We show you questioning techniques to support your students at all stages of The Learning Challenge, including how to deliberately get them *into* the Learning Pit!

(Continued)

(Continued)

The IDEAR Framework.

Step 1:   Initiate   All initiate questions have value

Step 2:   Draw In   Does anyone else think the same?

Step 3:   Extend   Why do you think that...?

Step 4:   Abstract   What about [this example]...?

Step 5:   Reflect   So what do you think now?

This is a framework for planning and managing your whole-class dialogues.

Following the five steps of the IDEAR Framework will include *more* learners in *more* dialogue and get *more* language from more incisive, smooth questioning sequences.

IDEAR will get your questioning flowing!

Taxonomy of Silences.

Who would have thought that silence could be so varied and purposeful?

We will show you that talking is not always the best way to get your students thinking! This taxonomy demonstrates nine different ways to improve your questioning by saying nothing, in an environment of true collaborative inquiry.

We will use the phrases *questioning sequence* and *questioning moves* throughout this book to describe effective questioning.

What we mean is that the most effective questioning is based on a series of questions being asked that lead to a goal or position of intent, like stepping-stones crossing from one side of a river to the other. Each stepping-stone is a question, and students' responses are like the gaps in between. Each question is referred to as a move (like hopping to the next stepping-stone) and usually follows a student answer. A run of two or more questioning moves and student responses is referred to as a questioning sequence.

A basic questioning sequence involves a first question, a first response, and a follow-up question. This questioning sequence involves three steps, two of which are questioning moves.

Putting these moves together like this with the intention of building student understanding, skills, and attitudes in a culture of high expectation is what we mean by effective questioning.

Stepping-stones (like questioning) take you from one side of the river (your current position) to the other side of the river (the goal) in a series of moves. At the Heian-jingu Shrine in Kyoto, shown in Figure 1, the stepping-stones don't take you in a straight line from one side to the other; they keep you turning, to face a different way.

Each stepping-stone (move) adds to your view (understanding) and each turn adds something you haven't seen before (perspective) so that once you reach the other side, the journey was an experience, rather than a leap.

▶ Figure 1: **Stepping-stones at the Heian-jingu Shrine, Kyoto.**

Source: iStock/Marissa Tabbada

ACKNOWLEDGEMENTS

Martin Renton has written this book with the support of his colleague and friend James Nottingham, and with contributions from:

- Mark Bollom
- Richard Kielty
- James Nottingham
- Jill Nottingham
- Laura Taylor
- Steve Williams

All authors and contributors can be contacted through www.challenginglearning.com.

Martin would like to thank all those who have supported him in the writing of this book.

Family and friends; work colleagues in schools, colleges, and universities; the schools who feature in the book and those I have been lucky enough to work with across the globe; the students I have enjoyed teaching; the consultants I have worked alongside and, of course, all of my colleagues and friends at Challenging Learning—I owe you all a huge debt of gratitude for your constant support, inspiration, and infinite patience (especially where this book is concerned!).

I would also like to make a special acknowledgement to James Nottingham. As friends of 25 years, we have somehow managed to spend a quarter of a century not growing up! As a colleague for the last 11 years, James has challenged me to think differently, struggle, and take risks and, as a co-director of Challenging Learning, to strive for improvement. All of this has shaped how this book turned out and encouraged me to think about presenting questioning differently. Thank you for all of that, mate, and for still believing that this book would actually get finished, even when I'd given up on it myself! I should probably buy you a beer or two. (But I won't . . .)

I definitely need to say a huge thank-you to my family. For many weeks of the year, I am an absent husband and father, travelling to schools and districts across the world. And then when I am at home, I have my head buried in book writing! Thank you for being who you are, and for always being there. I couldn't have done any of the work that features in this book without you. Thank you, Katherine, Ben, and Toby, for making the home I love to come back to.

I also need to thank Ariel Curry at Corwin, who must be the most patient person in the world . . . ever! I know that getting me to complete this book has been like herding cats for you, so I appreciate all your support, your timely challenge, and your nurturing of this book from first baby steps to maturity and finally letting it loose in the world!

Soundtrack to the Book. This book was mostly written along to these three records:

Cream: *The Very Best of . . .*

Wardell Gray: *Memorial*, Vol. 1

Steve Hillage: *Fish Rising*

PUBLISHER'S ACKNOWLEDGEMENTS

Corwin gratefully acknowledges the contributions of the following reviewers:

John Almarode, Associate Professor of Education

College of Education, James Madison University

Harrisonburg, VA

Debbie Arakaki, Curriculum Systems Coordinator

Niu Valley Middle School

Honolulu, HI

Carmen Bergmann, Assistant Regional Superintendent

Regional Office of Education #17

Bloomington, IL

Michelle Liga, K–8 Technology Integration Specialist/Coach

Kingwood Elementary/Central Preston Middle

Kingwood, WV

Ainsley B. Rose, Consultant-President

Thistle Educational Development Inc.

West Kelowna, BC, Canada

Joan Taylor, Adjunct Professor

College of Education

University of Nevada, Reno

Reno, NV

Michele Thomas, Headteacher

Pembroke Dock Community School

Pembrokeshire, Wales, UK

ABOUT THE AUTHOR

Martin Renton is Challenging Learning's director of consultancy and evaluations. He is a highly sought-after keynote speaker, leader, facilitator, and coach.

Martin's excellent reputation is well earned. His core belief that professional development is not a 'quick fix' but a deep process of change has led to some very powerful effects in schools and colleges around the world. Teachers and leaders who have worked with Martin over an extended period of time refer to increased engagement, motivation, and progress for all students.

Martin ensures that all our Challenging Learning trainers blend theories of learning with active tools for the classroom, giving teachers and leaders the opportunities to put into practice new skills and approaches. The effect can be seen most dramatically in our long-term projects around the world. The most significant of these are in Sweden, Denmark, Norway, Isle of Man, Northern Ireland, Australia, and New Zealand.

Martin's knowledge of pedagogy and leadership is borne out of his experiences in schools and colleges as a teacher, leader, consultant, and coach. His early experiences as a nanny (2- to 9-year-olds), then as a teacher and leader in middle schools (9- to 13-year-olds), secondary schools (11- to 18-year-olds), and colleges (16+), have given him a comprehensive insight into how people learn from the age of 2 to adulthood. Martin uses these insights to challenge, inspire, and engage his audiences.

THE LANGUAGE OF LEARNING

The following terms are used in the following ways in this book.

ASK: An acronym for attitudes, skills, and knowledge, usually presented in the ASK Model.

Attitude: A tendency, preference, or 'disposition'. In the case of questioning, we try to encourage the attitudes of curiosity, perseverance, resilience, open-mindedness, and so on.

Challenge: An addition to learning that makes a situation more demanding or stimulating and is used to encourage students to learn more than they otherwise would.

Closed question: A term, often misused in classroom dialogue, that presupposes a specific type of thinking will result from a single question. Often called 'lower order' and thought of as 'bad'. Used to describe a question to which the respondent is expected to give short, factual responses and that discourages further lines of inquiry.

Cognitive conflict: Broadly defined as the mental discomfort produced when confronted with new information that contradicts prior beliefs and ideas, or when two existing ideas don't match.

Cognitive processing: The act of thinking something through.

Concept: A general idea that groups things together according to accepted characteristics.

Culture: The behaviours and beliefs that characterise a group of people. Used in the context of developing a positive culture for questioning, dialogue, and collaborative inquiry.

Dialogue: Both conversation and inquiry. Dialogue combines the sociability of conversation with the skills of framing questions and constructing answers.

Discussion: The action or process of talking about something.

Exploratory talk: Talk that is characterised by longer exchanges, use of questions, reflection, explanation, and speculation.

Funnelling technique: A structure for planning questioning sequences that move from the question to *initiate* to asking your students to *explain* and then *explore*.

IDEAR Framework: A structure for managing and planning whole-class questioning sequences.

Initiate: To prepare the ground for a questioning sequence with a first question. This can be any question, as all questions have value.

Inquiry: A process of questioning ideas, information, and assumptions and of augmenting knowledge, resolving doubt, or solving a problem.

IRE: An acronym to identify the basic questioning sequence in which the teacher *initiates* (I), the student *responds* (R), and the teacher then *evaluates*, or *explores* (E):

> **I-R-Evaluate:** A pattern of classroom talk to ensure that pupils remember what they already know.

> **I-R-Explore:** An updated version of IRE, demonstrating the intent to explore ideas in order to improve thinking, language, and understanding.

Know your intent: The purpose of your questioning. Why you are asking your questions and what you hope to gain by asking them. Shifts the focus from 'the questions asked' to 'the impact of your questioning on learning'. Your intention can be about expectations for engagement or understanding or link to the learning goals of the lesson.

Language of reasoning: The words, phrases, and concepts that structure thinking, discussion, or writing of any complexity. They help people think about everything else.

Learning Challenge: After he created the Learning Pit, James Nottingham designed a four-step model for encouraging students through the pit: (1) identify a concept; (2) create cognitive conflict; (3) construct meaning; and (4) consider the learning journey. He wrote about this in depth in *The Learning Challenge* (2017).

Learning Pit®: One of the most powerful and popular heuristics of learning to have emerged in the last 20 years. The Learning Pit®, created by James Nottingham, encourages learners to more willingly step out of their Comfort Zone and engage in questioning and problem-solving strategies.

Metacognition: Literally 'thinking about thinking', metacognition is an important part of dialogue and requires focussed questioning sequences. It encourages students to think about how they are learning, and how they might improve.

Minimal encourager: A short verbal or nonverbal indicator that signals to the respondents that they should keep talking and expand on their idea or opinion.

Open question: A term, often misused in classroom dialogue, that presupposes a specific type of thinking will result from a single question. Often called 'higher order' and thought of as 'good'. Used to describe a question to which the respondent is expected to give a longer response and share an idea, opinion, or reason.

Paraphrase: To restate what a student has said in a more direct form, in order to create a bridge into the next question.

Pause: The deliberate action of doing nothing, to create spaces in the questioning sequence that encourage further thinking, talking, and reflection.

Pit, the: A metaphor to identify the state of confusion people feel when holding two or more conflicting thoughts or opinions in their mind at the same time.

Plan your responses: Consider beforehand what your students might say when you ask a question and then work out what you will ask next to take them deeper.

PPE: An acronym for Pause-Paraphrase-Explore as a way to remember key steps in facilitating effective questioning sequences. Inserts into the IRE structure.

Questioning for Challenge: A questioning sequence that creates cognitive conflict in the respondents and encourages them to rethink their initial response and therefore seek clarity.

Questioning 'move': Following up a response with another question, in an attempt to elicit more from the respondent.

Reflection: Giving serious consideration to a thought, idea, or response.

Silence: The deliberate act of remaining quiet, to encourage processing-time for the respondent and to give yourself thinking time.

Socratic method: An approach to questioning based on the techniques employed by Socrates (467–399 BC), who encouraged his students to think more deeply, express their understanding more fully, and consider alternative ways to think about common concepts and accepted wisdom. In this book, the classroom adaptation of this approach is known as 'Questioning for Challenge'.

 | Challenging Learning Through Questioning

Taxonomy of Classroom Silences: Created by Martin Renton, this is a classification of educational processes in which the teacher leaves deliberate, purposeful gaps in questioning sequences.

Think-time: A period of silence before or after a response is given, which allows the respondent 'time to think'.

Understanding: The mental process of a person who comprehends. It includes an ability to explain cause, effect, and significance, and to understand patterns and how they relate to each other.

The root of the word *education* is derived from the Latin words *educare, educere,* and *educatum*. *Educare* means 'to nourish'; *educere* means 'to draw out'; *educatum* means 'to train'. The English word *education* is derived from all three.

INTRODUCTION

This is a book about questioning.

I was very careful in my choice of title for this book. Notice the emphasis: questioning, not questions. That *ing* may look small, but it is significant. It changes this from being a book about what to ask, to being a book about process. Questioning is a skill; it is a series of steps and strategies that facilitate good thinking. This book goes way beyond the idea of simply 'asking questions', and instead encourages you to engage your students in a process of deep learning and reasoning, facilitated by your high-quality questioning skills.

Effective questioning therefore does not have one single purpose, and it is not 'one-size-fits-all'. There are no magic questions that always work to make questioning effective.

I will be up front from the beginning and say that I do not believe that closed questions and open questions exist. At least, not in a dialogic sense. When the focus of questioning is on learning, there is no such thing as a closed question, and no such thing as an open question. There are only questions.

I may be overstating that belief, but it is very important that we get away from the tyranny of open and closed questions or, at the very least, just hold onto those notions *lightly*, as a way of considering our intention to extend questioning and explore learning.

The primary purpose of asking a question—any question at all—is to get an answer. What really matters in questioning is what you do *after* you have that answer. It is your response to the answer that will *close* a dialogue down or *open* up a process of learning.

This obsession with classifying questions as 'open' and 'closed' has led teachers to believe that specific questions will always lead to a certain type of response from students, and that asking a certain question in a certain way will lead to a predetermined outcome.

Of course, teachers can then very easily, and understandably, become disillusioned with open questions when they find that a perfectly formed 'open question' has much the same impact on the students as asking a closed question. If the intent is not there to *be* open, then whatever question is asked is more likely to lead to an evaluative step and close off the thinking, than when the intent is there to explore.

Teachers attempting to memorise banks of 'thinking questions' and rephrase their closed questions as open questions will make no difference at all to students' learning or to quality classroom dialogues, unless the intention shifts to follow up the students' responses with something more than 'well done'.

The questions we ask, then, can only be judged in the context of where they are placed in a sequence, and how they help move learning toward the intended goal.

We need to move away from the misguided notion that questions have any kind of character of their own and instead consider that questioning is only ever a process—a set of steps that can lead toward better thinking so that when linked together in a sequence, they can be seen to have closed down (evaluated) or opened up (explored) thinking and opportunities for better understanding.

Question*ing* can be open or closed; questions can't.

So I will try to refrain (as much as is possible) from using the terms *open* and *closed* in this book, and instead focus on the power of questioning moves, so we can look at questioning afresh and in a new light and ensure that student answers are followed up with the intent to explore learning further.

Researchers have consistently found that questioning is the second most commonly used teaching tool in the classroom. (You might not be surprised to learn that the most commonly used tool is 'teacher talk'!) However, just because we are using questioning a lot does not necessarily make it as effective as we'd like. John Hattie's *Visible Learning* meta-analysis (2009) reports that questioning has an effect size of 0.48, only marginally higher than average (the average effect size in a typical classroom is 0.4) in comparison to student *self-questioning*, which has an effect size of 0.59, and classroom dialogue, which has an effect size of 0.82.

Much of the research demonstrates that teacher questions tend to be focussed on the recall of information. Similarly, the questions referred to in Hattie's 0.48 effect size often just check for current knowledge. In this frame, each question we ask appears to stand alone as an isolated incident, so it does not form part of a well-considered sequence that contributes to effective learning.

To make questioning *really* effective, we have to consider it as a way of creating focussed classroom dialogue. The power of questioning lies in its ability to move your students forward in a purposeful and accessible way that gives them both time and a reason to think. When information moves at a pace they can process it at, and in a language they can understand (their own), they are more likely to engage cognitively, and so make better progress in learning.

It is important that you identify what you want the students to gain from your interactions so that you can construct the most appropriate questioning sequences for student progress in that situation.

Like feedback, questioning is not always used to best effect, and it does not always make a big difference to your students' learning. In this book, we aim to show you how to get the best from your questioning—to engage and challenge your students and encourage deeper thinking. To do that, there are two key things to remember:

1. **Questioning is a skill.** This means it is something you can practise, learn, and get better at. Throughout this book, we will encourage you to try new questioning tools and review your progress as you go. By the end of the book, you should notice a difference in the way you engage with your students and how you respond to them in dialogue.

2. **Questioning is a process.** It is a series of deliberate steps that strategically move your students toward the learning goal. Effective questioning facilitates better learning. By the end of this book, you will be making smooth and incisive questioning moves, encouraging students to go beyond their current understanding and into their Learning Zone.

To make your questioning more effective, we will focus on the following three essential skills throughout the book:

1. Know Your Intent
2. Plan Your Responses
3. Stay Silent (and Listen)

We will explore these three skills in more detail in the next chapter and encourage you to practise each of them in your setting. Throughout the book, we will guide you with tools and approaches for improving your questioning so that you can develop these three essential skills more fully and get noticeably improved responses from your students.

We will show you how high-quality questioning supports a culture in which students can flourish intellectually; where they not only are challenged, but *expect* to be challenged; where questioning supports progress and the development of a better learning language so that students develop the attitudes, skills, and knowledge they need to become lifelong independent learners.

Key focus areas are as follows:

1. The intention to explore

2. A focus on reasoning so that students demonstrate their thinking, explore their ideas, and share understanding with each other

3. The purpose and benefits of challenge

4. Creating techniques for challenge through questioning in the classroom

5. How to manage individual, group, pair, and whole-class dialogues using questioning, thinking tools, and strategic silences

6. How questioning models the process of good thinking, encouraging a culture of high expectations

BELIEFS ABOUT QUESTIONING

But just before we dive headlong into questioning skills and how to develop them, it is worth taking a moment to consider your current beliefs about questioning. Sometimes educational practices are borne out of habits, long developed and often unchallenged. These habits are reinforced through classroom behaviours, training days, and staffroom conversations. They create mental models, or mindframes, that drive the way we behave.

Consider this list of common myths about questioning that can often shape the mental models we hold and therefore become deeply held beliefs. How many of these do you hold? How many of these do you hear reinforced in your school or setting?

1. Closed questions are *bad*; open questions are *good*.

2. Teachers naturally question well.

3. Closed questions produce lower-order thinking; open questions produce higher-order thinking.

4. Open questions slow the pace of the lesson.

5. Open dialogue can go anywhere, and the teacher 'loses control' of direction.

6. Only the person answering is doing any thinking.

7. Challenge is for the most able students.

8. When students are struggling, they need the answer.

9. Once a student gets the right answer, stop asking questions.

10. For open questioning to work, there should be 'no right or wrong' answer.

All of these are myths. At best, they are untrue; at worst, they could actually be damaging to your students' learning. And yet we hear these repeated over and over in dialogue with teachers about improving quality of questioning in their classrooms. In this book, we want to reframe these myths so that questioning is more powerful and more beneficial to students' learning. To do that, each of the myths has been rephrased to reflect a mindframe that will impact positively on student learning, and on your questioning.

Challenging Learning Through Questioning

Mindframes that support effective questioning include the following:

1. **You can only judge a question in the context of the sequence in which it is placed.**

2. **Questioning is a skill that needs practice and refinement to do well.**

3. **It's not about the first question you ask; it's how you respond to the student's answer that really matters.**

4. **Effective questioning ensures appropriate pace for thinking.**

5. **The teacher is an expert facilitator of learning—guiding, prompting, and pushing the learners toward the learning goal.**

6. **The students answering are verbalising their thinking, but *everyone* should be internalising ideas (thinking) during effective questioning. Answering the teacher is not the only outcome of questioning!**

7. **Challenge is for everyone.**

8. **When students are struggling, help them find strategies to cope with difficulty, so they learn self-efficacy.**

9. **Hold onto answers lightly. Even if the students give the right answer, they can still be challenged to think beyond their first response.**

10. **There is often more than one possible right answer, or more than one way to reach the answer.**

These mindsets should drive your questioning actions and influence patterns of practice in your classroom. Your actions, in turn, will reinforce your values and expectations to the students.

How many of these mindsets do you currently hold? Which ones are jumping out at you as new or different? Which of these mindsets—if you held them right now—would make the biggest difference to your students' learning?

Throughout the book, we will provide you with tools and strategies that help make these beliefs a reality in your classroom, so that your questioning becomes ever more expert in guiding and extending your students' learning.

What this book *is not* about . . .

- Good questions versus bad questions

- Saying that any one question is 'better' than another

- Providing a magic bank of questions that 'work' whenever you ask them

- Asking pseudo-philosophical questions that will 'make students think'

- Creating novelty questions and challenges that fill time when the real learning is done

- Challenging only the most able

- Getting students to a predetermined right answer

And what this book *is* about . . .

- Reinforcing that questioning is an *integral part* of the *learning process*
- Increasing students' *understanding* of disciplinary *concepts* and *knowledge*
- Increasing *engagement* and *motivation*
- Increasing the likelihood that *thinking* will take place
- Increasing the likelihood that students will *struggle* and find new ways to *explore* their *understanding*
- Using questioning as a *core teaching tool*, practising it to increase your skill and effectiveness
- Using *questioning as feedback* to the students about your expectations for challenge, reasoning, language, and reflection
- *Modelling* the thinking that you want the students to be able to do

PART I
HOW TO QUESTION

What can a human teacher give to a student that technology can't?

Questions. Particularly questions to which no one knows the answers. If no one knows the answers, technology does not know either. Humans know how to ask questions.

—Sugata Mitra (2019)

QUESTIONING ESSENTIALS

Before you make any attempt to develop your questioning skills, it is important to consider why you want to do so. I hope you are reading this book because you are excited about impacting positively on your students' learning! That's the best reason to work on your questioning. Do it for yourself (for your own practice), and do it for the benefits that your students will get from that.

In the introduction, we talked about how questioning is both a skill and a process. It is not the act of asking a question in isolation, but the process of asking a series of questions that build on your students' responses.

But! Be warned. There are no simple fixes to improving questioning! Making questioning more effective requires practice and personal reflection to keep improving. I have been working on my questioning for almost 20 years, and yet every time I teach, I still feel I have something new to learn—a nuance to a familiar dialogue, a response I hadn't considered before, or a new way to phrase a challenge— each of which adds to my practice for tomorrow.

1.0 • THE THREE ESSENTIAL SKILLS

In terms of improving questioning, what really matters is why you are asking the question in the first place, and then how you respond to the answers the students give you. All questions can have value, if you learn to follow up on them with purpose and clarity.

So ask your students whatever you like, and phrase it any way you like. But then ask yourself, 'Once the students have answered my question, what will I do or say next to encourage them to keep thinking?'

That means asking a question, listening to the answer, and responding with another question in a series of deliberate moves. When you put these moves and responses together in a meaningful sequence, you will find that you are facilitating better learning. This is what we mean by 'effective questioning'.

Of course, getting those moves right takes time and practice. And like any other skill, questioning can be frustrating and exciting in equal measure, so reflection on action is key to developing your own questioning practice. We want to show you how to get the best from your questioning: to engage and challenge your students and encourage deeper thinking. To do that, there are three essential skills that you should constantly practise to improve your questioning techniques.

These essential skills apply to all the tools and approaches that follow in this book:

1. Know Your Intent

2. Plan Your Responses

3. Stay Silent (and Listen)

Think 'IPS': Intent-Plan-Silence. In this chapter, we will look at each of these three essential skills in more detail, but before we do, it is important to emphasise how closely linked these three elements are. In fact, they are all based on the same premise—that the most effective questioning is well considered and incisive, building on the last student response, placing emphasis on developing your students' understanding, and making your students think for themselves.

1.1 • KNOW YOUR INTENT

Arguably the single most important factor in improving your questioning is to ensure that you know why you are asking the question in the first place! As you ask that first question, you should have in your mind an idea of where the questioning sequence could take you, and what you would like the students to gain from the interaction. Considering the *impact* of what you ask is more important than just thinking about *what* you ask.

You should be clear about your reasons for entering the dialogue. Your intent can be expressed as a simple statement—for example, I want the students to give reasons for their answers; I want to challenge my students; I want to engage all of my students; I want the students to share their ideas with each other and with me; I want the students to be able to use [subject] language in context.

So before saying your first question out loud to the group, reflect to yourself, 'Why am I about to ask this?'

There are two common responses. The first is 'I don't know'. If that is the case—that you don't know why you are asking a question—then again reflect, 'Why ask it at all?' Quite commonly, when we don't know why we are asking a question, or we don't have any purpose in mind, the questioning sequence will look something like this:

Teacher: What is the capital of Scotland?

Student: Edinburgh.

Teacher: Well done.

Because the questioning sequence is unplanned, we get stuck on simply asking a question, and are unable to think of a relevant follow-up question, because we didn't know where we intended to go. So, only one student engaged in answering, and the questioning was over almost before it began. There is also very little opportunity for engagement, either from other students or in terms of extended thinking.

The second most common response teachers give to 'Why am I about to ask this question?' is 'To check students' understanding'.

Typically, a 'checking understanding' questioning sequence runs like this:

Teacher: What is the capital of Scotland?

Student: Edinburgh.

Teacher: Well done.

Look familiar? Now, there is nothing wrong with the idea of checking understanding. Indeed, it is important that we check students' understanding, and so we need to ask these questions. But what if this is the *only* reason you have for asking questions? If the question leads to very little engagement from other students in the group, or little engagement in thinking from the respondent, then you wouldn't want to repeat this pattern too often in the classroom, would you?

While checking understanding is important, it shouldn't be the only reason for asking a question.

So how might our questioning sequence look if your intention was to get extended responses from the students, engage more students in the group in the dialogue, challenge their thinking, or use subject terminology in relevant ways?

We could try it. Here's our sequence again, but this time with the intention of *getting extended responses from students*:

Teacher: What is the capital of Scotland?

Student: Edinburgh.

Teacher: How do you know?

The next student answer would require an explanation, or extended response.

Now let's try our sequence with the intention of *engaging more students in the group in the dialogue*:

Teacher: What is the capital of Scotland?

Student: Edinburgh.

Teacher: What do we all know about Edinburgh?

Or with the intention of *challenging their thinking*:

Teacher: What is the capital of Scotland?

Student: Edinburgh.

Teacher: Why Edinburgh and not Glasgow, when Glasgow is a
           bigger city?

Or with the intention of *using subject terminology*:

Teacher: What is the capital of Scotland?

Student: Edinburgh.

Teacher: So, what do we mean by 'capital city'?

Considering your intent encourages you to think about how you want the dialogue to go *after* your first question and after the students' first response.

The first question doesn't matter at all; it is only the way in to the process. So all questions have value at this stage; there is no such thing as a closed or open question. They are, simply, questions. It is only when you know what the intention was in asking the first question that you can see whether the process *opens up* a dialogue or *closes down* the sequence.

This is why we say that there is no such thing as a good or bad question. In our earlier examples, the teacher asks, 'What is the capital of Scotland?', which many observers would classify as 'closed' and therefore 'bad'. But it is not until you see the teacher's response to the students' answer that you can define the intent and recognise that the purpose of the question is not to close the students down but to open the dialogue up— to other students, to challenge, or to the development of language.

So it is not the question itself that makes a difference. We need to reframe the notion of 'closed question' and 'open question', which implies a bank of magic questions exist somewhere, waiting to be found and unleashed on our unsuspecting learners. Instead, we need to emphasise that questioning involves a series of steps. It is the goal you have for asking the question, how you respond to the students' answer, and whether that response moves you toward your intended goal that will determine whether your questioning has been effective.

We can only judge the quality of a question in the context of the sequence in which it is placed, and the effectiveness of that sequence in moving the students toward the intended goal.

Knowing the intention of your questioning therefore increases the likelihood of impacting positively on your students' learning.

1.2 • IDENTIFYING YOUR INTENT

When you consider the questioning sequence you are about to embark on, there are a number of different ways you can identify your intent. In 1.1 we considered broad statements as a way of framing what you want to achieve. These are a simple and accessible way to start to think about the impact of your questioning on your students.

To help identify your purpose in a more structured way, these five frames are a useful guide for planning your questioning steps. The five frames all imply 'progress toward' a goal so that your questioning can help students to develop:

1. Knowledge

2. Understanding

3. Skills

4. Attitudes

5. High expectations

Each of these frames is expanded in Sections 1.2.1–1.2.4 so that you can really start to consider the different intentions behind your questioning and begin to plan your questioning sequences to have a more focussed and visible effect on progress. This is in part because you will need to create a shared language with your students, with which you can all express the progress being made, in terms of not only knowledge and understanding, but attitudes and skills as well.

In *Challenging Learning Through Feedback* (Nottingham & Nottingham, 2017), we talked about how Learning Intentions (goals) are best expressed in terms of what the students will 'know', 'understand', or 'be able to do' by the end of the lesson. Your questioning should emphasise these and reinforce progress toward the goal.

1.2.1 • Identify Your Intent: Knowledge . . .

Effective questioning around a knowledge goal is often best used to check whether students remember a fact or know the basic information. This kind of diagnostic questioning allows you to gauge the current level of learning the students have.

For example, if your Learning Intention is 'to know the first five presidents of the United States in the correct order', then at the start of the lesson, ask your students if they can name the first five presidents, and to record their answer. If your students can't name them yet, then you have pitched your lesson at the right level and you can teach them the presidents, with your usual exciting and well-planned activities. Throughout the lesson you can ask, 'Who was the first president?' and 'Who came next?' and at the end of the lesson ask the students, 'Who were the first five presidents of the United States?' If they can answer this question, then your students have demonstrated progress from the start of the lesson to the end.

This kind of questioning is often referred to as closed questioning. And it has, unfairly, acquired a bad rap. Questioning with the intention of checking knowledge gained, and therefore progress, is absolutely fine when used purposefully; it is, in fact, a really useful tool to help diagnose your students' current position and their subsequent progress toward a knowledge goal.

So, don't demonise recall and diagnosis; it has a valuable role to play in generating the platform of language around key facts or subject terminology from which you can build new learning.

But two words of warning: First, do check that you have diagnosed the current knowledge of *all* your students, and not just one! Often when we ask a knowledge-based question, only one student answers (you know who they are!), and then it is easy to make the assumption that if one of your students can answer the question, all of your students will know the same answer. Often, this is not true! So try to avoid the 'one-student-represents-all' trap.

And second, this is not the only intent of questioning! Make sure there are other reasons for questioning your students too.

1.2.2 • Identify Your Intent: *Understanding* . . .

Asking questions such as 'What is the capital of Scotland?' is not really checking understanding. It is checking recall of a fact—checking *knowledge*. Knowing and understanding are not the same. You can know many separate and individual facts. But it is only when you can explain how these facts are similar and different, and how they affect each other, that you can be said to understand something. Understanding, therefore, can be seen as more conceptual and is the result of knowing how and why separate facts are connected.

For example, I may be able to recall all the parts of a flower, and label a diagram, because I *know* the names. But I can't be said to *understand* it until I can explain their functions and how they interrelate. I need to create meaning from the separate elements.

As your students work, the intent of your questioning should now be to seek longer answers from more students and encourage them to demonstrate their knowledge of *how* and *why*. In short, the purpose of your questioning is to place more demands on your students' thinking.

The outcome of effective questioning should always be the development of your students' thinking. Knowing your intent means knowing what type of thinking you want your students to engage in so you can plan to ask questions that engage them in that thinking.

So, if your lesson goal was 'to understand how plants reproduce', then your students would need to be able to do more than just name the parts of a flower. They would need to explain how each part functions, how the seeds are carried or dispersed, and the process of pollination. This will help them move from knowledge (the parts of a flower) to understanding (the concept of reproduction), which requires some key thinking skills:

Explain

Give reasons

Make connections

These thinking skills become the Success Criteria against which your students will demonstrate that they have understood how plants reproduce. So if, for example, they can *explain* how pollination happens, they will have shown that they understand that part of the process. You can read more about Success Criteria in our sister publication, *Challenging Learning Through Feedback* (Nottingham & Nottingham, 2017).

To stick with this example of pollination, let's consider how that might look in a lesson. First, you can check for current knowledge (as in 1.2.1) and ask your students simply to name the parts of a flower.

To build on this and move to understanding of concepts, ask if anyone can explain the process of plant reproduction. It is a good idea to get all students to write down a first response so that you can return to it later and hopefully demonstrate progress. Set up your lesson with your usual exciting and engaging activities to help the students learn how reproduction takes place, and as they work, intervene in groups, with individuals, and as a whole class with a questioning sequence such as this one, recorded from a conversation between a science teacher and a Grade 6 student (looking at a diagram as they talk):

Teacher: Can you *explain* what the stamen does?

Student: It's where pollen is produced.

Teacher: So what does the anther do?

Student: It . . . creates . . . erm . . . pollen . . . as well?

Teacher: So are the stamen and anther the *same*?

Student: Erm . . . no, the anther is part of the stamen.

Teacher: Does the stamen have other parts?

Student: Yes, the filament.

Teacher: So can you *explain* the *connection* between the stamen, anther, and filament?

This extended questioning sequence is based on key thinking words: *explain* and make *connections* (including how something is the same or different). This ensures that the student not only knows the names of the parts of a flower but is demonstrating a better understanding of how the parts relate to each other and what they do. The questioning sequence drew that out and encouraged the student to use subject-specific language to answer the final question in the sequence, and the explanation was a lot clearer as a result, as you can see here:

Student: The stamen is the whole thing [points to the diagram], but it has two parts: the filament, which is this long, thin bit which has the anther on top, and the pollen is made in the anther. So overall, it's made in the stamen. But the part it's made in is the anther. Which is here [points to diagram] on top of the filament.

Questioning should enhance the learning activity and accelerate progress toward the learning goal.

Focussing your questioning sequence on the thinking skills that demonstrate understanding allows your students to process the terminology of your subject and rehearse subject-specific language. For this to happen, you can purposefully plan your questioning sequence to encourage these thinking skills to take place and intentionally create opportunity for your students to apply them and be ever more active participants in the dialogue.

The earlier science example shows how you can respond to your students' answers by encouraging them to explain, give reasons, and make connections, and therefore use the subject language that demonstrates understanding of a concept, rather than simply 'checking for current knowledge'.

In this way, the questioning sequence here is more 'open'. This does not make it better than the questioning in 1.2.1. It is just different and serves a different purpose. Effective questioning is more about getting a balance of different types of questions that promote different types of responses from your students, for different reasons, than it is about assuming that one type of question is always better than another.

1.2.3 • Identify Your Intent: *Skills and Attitudes* . . .

Knowledge and understanding goals both deal with learning the 'what'; they refer to *knowing* facts and *understanding* concepts, respectively, so they have an information function. Creating a Learning Intention which states that 'by the end of the lesson your students will be able to . . .' generates a clear focus on the development of skills and attitudes. It is about learning 'how' rather than learning 'what'.

As you start asking questions in this frame, be aware that your intent should be to elicit *how* the students are working and ask questions that extend their skills and attitudes. The trick here is to assume that the key knowledge will be learnt as a result of the skill and attitude being applied.

For example, you might want your students to 'be able to research the causes of the Second World War'. The temptation is then to teach the students the causes of the

Second World War. But resist this! With the learning goal of 'being able to', what you actually want your students to learn is 'how to research'. So your usual activities will engage your students in the process of researching, while your questioning steps should then hone their researching skills:

Teacher: What have you found out so far?

Students: [Responses.]

Teacher: Which do you think are *significant factors*?

Students: [Responses.]

Teacher: What was it *in the literature* that made you think these were important?

Students: [Responses.]

Teacher: Can you find anything in *another text* that agrees with that idea?

In this way, the questioning is focussing on some of the skills needed to research well. To make that explicit, give your students opportunity at the end to discuss, or write down, some of the skills they learnt to be more successful at researching. Even in the short example just provided, we can see the skills of *selecting significant factors, giving reasons from text*, and *using a supporting source*.

Teaching students *how* can also relate to attitudes or dispositions as well as skills. Attitudes can be a minefield to work with at first, because we rarely practise the vocabulary associated with them and so often dismiss them as 'soft skills', or as simply 'good attitude and bad attitude'! However, attitudes play a key role in our ability to access learning, and so using your questioning to focus on the way we learn can have a significant impact on your students.

One of the key attitude developments you will notice in your students when working on questioning sequences is the attitude of open-mindedness and the will to be reasonable. At first you might think your students are quite defensive about their ideas, concerned about being wrong, and unwilling to accept that other students' responses can have as much value as their own. So, in extended questioning sequences, encourage your students to use stems like 'I agree with [Student X]'s opinion because . . .' or 'I think that [Student Y] made an important point when they said . . .'. This encourages a culture of shared information, and your questioning can then support the development of open-minded attitudes:

What was your first response?

What did you hear that added to your idea?

What did you hear that was different from your idea?

What might another person add to that?

What would be worth investigating further?

How has your first response developed?

The intent of the questioning is to focus on helping the students learn to be open-minded, so deliberately plan your questioning sequence to include questions that focus on listening to others and adding to their understanding—possibly even leading to a change of mind!

As you work more with questioning and encourage students to talk, you will notice how your students are thinking and what their attitudes to learning are. Questioning is a useful tool to encourage thinking. It makes the process of thinking visible, encourages different types of thinking at different times and between different people, and allows reflection on thinking to take place. For this reason, specific types of thinking and attitudes for learning should always be part of the purpose of questioning and progress within it and, therefore, be a specific intention of your questioning sequence.

1.2.4 • Identify Your Intent: *High Expectations . . .*

Questioning sequences do not just live in the moment. During any questioning sequence, there is the immediate effect of checking knowledge, encouraging thinking, developing a skill or attitude, and helping students move forward in their learning. But questioning also has a more lasting effect as it models a process of thinking and can therefore create internal dialogue.

When purposeful questioning sequences are used regularly and consistently, your students begin to recognise the patterns and are therefore more likely to predict next steps. So, if your current questioning predominantly runs as in our earlier example—

> Teacher: What is the capital of Scotland?
>
> Student: Edinburgh.
>
> Teacher: Well done—

then students begin to expect that pattern. They think that you value knowing the right answer, so if they know it, they will say it, and receive their 'well done'. If they don't know the answer, they can't take part and will try to opt out of the game. The more you repeat the same type of questioning, the more it reinforces their idea about what you value and what has meaning in your classroom. In this instance, the students will come to believe that you value knowing the right answer.

Your questioning sets your culture of expectation.

When you consistently use questioning sequences that focus on process—for example,

> Teacher: What is the capital of Scotland?
>
> Student: Edinburgh.
>
> Teacher: So, what do we mean by 'capital city'?—

the students begin to expect a follow-up question, so they know they have to extend their answer. They also know you might ask others in the group to share their view, opinion, or reason, and so they begin to mentally prepare for your questioning.

When your students are not only challenged in the moment, but come to *expect* to be challenged, you create a culture of high expectation.

This means that your students will predict questioning sequences, think through likely challenges or extensions, and mentally rehearse the language of reasoning needed. This type of thinking happens internally or in smaller groups ahead of your questioning, and it is this pre-thinking that encourages better learning and engagement.

Developing questioning skills also models the everyday practice that you want your students to exhibit too. Once students have adopted the culture of high expectation, you will start to notice that they will start to use the same questioning sequences with each other as you use with them. In this way, questioning becomes part of the shared language of your classroom.

Of course, the more your students predict your next question, the more they can prepare their responses, and so the more you have to develop your questioning to keep extending their thinking, which in turn places further demands on your questioning skills! This is why we consider questioning to be a skill and process that you never stop learning. And it's what makes it such an exciting aspect of teaching!

Knowing your intent is the first step in developing the three essential skills of questioning:

1. Know Your Intent
2. Plan Your Responses
3. Stay Silent (and Listen)

Now we will have a look at the other two essential skills.

1.3 • PLAN YOUR RESPONSES

As we discussed in 1.1, many teachers set off with a question without knowing their intention and without an idea of what they *could* ask to get there, and so the question sequence usually ends up closing off too early, or is well intentioned but without purpose. What we have to try to remember is that while the intention to check knowledge quickly and move on can be easy to administer, it is not the only way to question; and questions that encourage students to think, give reasons, and explain their understanding won't always come to you on the spur of the moment.

To ensure that your questioning is focussed and working toward your intention, you will need to consider the dialogue beforehand so that the sequence happens by design.

This doesn't mean that every question you could possibly ask should be written down in a lesson plan; there is no need to go that far. And actually, when teachers do that, they often can't remember all those questions in the lesson anyway, so they don't use any of them! But it is worth thinking a sequence through and having just one or two possible questions and examples ready to use in the lesson.

To do this well, you will need to think ahead to the dialogue. You know your students, so you probably predict what they are likely to say when you ask a question. Use this power of prediction to help build a possible questioning sequence in your mind. Write some of your ideas down to help you remember them in the lesson and stay focussed on your intention. Your plan could be something as simple as this:

I ask [this question].

A student might respond with [this or this].

So I ask [this question] next.

And that's all it needs to get your questioning going. For example, let's use this frame to plan a sequence. If your intention is 'to get *more* students involved in answering', you might plan a series of questions and possible student responses, as follows:

I ask:	What is a proper noun?
A student might respond:	The name of something.
So I ask:	Can someone give me an example?
A student might respond:	Tom.
So I ask:	Can someone give me another example?
A student might respond:	Chicago.
So I ask [to the group]:	What do these two things have in common?

If you change your intention so that you are now looking to *challenge* the students' thinking, then your planning steps would include questions and predicted student responses, like this:

I ask:	What is a proper noun?
A student might respond:	The name of something.
So I ask:	A 'table' is the name of something. Is it a proper noun?

In this example, you can then look for who thinks *table* is and isn't a proper noun; engage all of your students by doing a hands-up, or do a Think-Pair-Share first. This will tell you who understands and who has any misconceptions. Your questioning moves can then encourage your students to refine the first definition of a proper noun, to say that it is *the name of a specific person, place, organisation, or thing, and always has a capital letter.*

This simple sequence only planned the first few steps in the dialogue. You can plan for as long or as short as you wish, and of course, longer sequences get easier to do the more you practise with them. In the early stages of developing your questioning sequences against an intention, you can plan just one or two short steps to help get you started. When you try them, reflect on the impact of those steps on your students' thinking, and on your understanding of their current level of learning. In the next few chapters, we show you some frameworks for helping plan your questioning.

In 1.2.1 we suggested that you get your students to write down their first response (or you can write it for them), and then at the end of the questioning sequence, or at the end of the lesson, you can ask them to rewrite their definition in light of their learning. This is a clear way to show your students the progress they are making and help you all to see how the questioning moved their thinking forward (also see 1.2.4 on high expectations).

I was talking to a colleague about questioning, and she told me about an example she had seen just that week, of how thinking about your questioning sequence beforehand can help create an opportunity for better learning.

She told me that she had recently had a group of student-teachers thinking about how they might teach 'shape' in a maths lesson to elementary children. In one example, the student-teacher had shown a picture of an equilateral triangle on the screen in the classroom and then asked, 'What shape is this?' One of the children answered that it was 'a triangle'.

Perhaps not surprisingly, the student-teacher then said, 'Good, that's right', and the questioning sequence closed down.

My friend had asked the group to think about the same activity, showing the image of the triangle on the screen, but this time to have a clear intention in mind when asking their first question. The intention she gave them was *to try to engage as many students as possible in giving an answer so that they practise the language needed to talk about shapes.*

With that intention in mind, she asked her student-teachers what question they might ask to engage as many students as possible and get them to practise the language of shape.

Tentatively at first, but then with increasing confidence, they came up with suggestions:

What does this look like?

How many sides does it have?

What can you see on the screen?

What can you tell me about this image?

How would you describe this shape?

If this was a picture, what would you tell someone else about it?

How do you know it's not a square/circle?

Once they had a few of these ideas, they then began predicting what the children might say in answer to the questions. They began listing:

It's got three sides.

It's very big.

All the sides are straight.

One side is flat (horizontal), and the other two are diagonal.

All the sides are green and quite thin.

All the sides are the same length.

My friend described how she could see the penny drop when her student-teachers realised how much the children would be using the language of shape to answer the question, and of course, a lot more children would be able to join in and offer up their ideas to the group.

She then extended this activity by adding a picture of an isosceles triangle, then a square, and adding questions:

How is this shape similar to the last one?

How is it different?

Is it still a triangle?

Why do you think this is called a triangle?

What makes a square different from a triangle?

In this example, you can see how the questioning sequence supports the intention of involving more than one student and develops progress in the language of shape. Here's how that questioning sequence could look in the way we described in 1.2:

Teacher: What shape is this?

Student: A triangle.

Teacher: OK, so how would we describe a triangle? What does it look like?

Student: It has three sides.

Student: All the sides are straight.

Student: One side is flat (horizontal), and the other two are diagonal.

Student: All the sides are green and quite thin.

Student: All the sides are the same length.

Teacher [shows isosceles triangle]: So what shape is this?

Student: A triangle.

Teacher [checking for misconceptions]: Does *everyone* think this is a triangle?

Teacher: How is this shape similar to the last one? How is it different?

Students: [Extended thinking.]

The key to planning your questions is to make sure that you know your intent and build from there. Once underway, listen carefully to what your students currently know and don't know, and then having considered the dialogue beforehand to predict what questions you might need, ask a question that you have prepared so that the ensuing dialogue works toward your intent.

Questioning should enhance the learning activity and accelerate progress toward the learning goal.

1.4 • STAY SILENT (AND LISTEN)

It is perfectly natural that teachers who want to improve their questioning first look to what questions they can ask. However, asking a question is only one part of the process. And as we have said already in this book, the questions themselves are less important than what the students say and then how you respond to that.

So, an essential skill in developing your questioning is to learn not to speak! This is a simpler step to implement than learning and designing questions, as you can do it straight away, but it is also quite a difficult skill to master; knowing when to stay quiet, when to listen, and when to speak is fraught with nuances. Especially if you are used to being the focal point of a lesson with all eyes looking at you for information and answers!

Remaining silent is a key 'move' in facilitating learning. These 'moves' mean not just asking a question, but listening to the answer and responding with another question, with the intention of moving the respondents forward in their thinking and their language. Students will say what they know, and what they know is based on how they think. If you can learn to listen to what your students say, you can also learn to understand how they think.

If you know what you want to get out of the dialogue that follows your first question (know your intent), it is important to listen to where the students are now—to find out what language they know and don't know, what reasons they think exist, what misconceptions they have, and how they respond to new ideas or challenges. Doing this means shifting the balance of responsibility in the classroom so the expectation is on your students to talk to learn, and on you to listen, so you can design the learning more effectively.

The purpose of staying silent, then, is to listen, and to give the students space to think—sometimes before they answer your question, but often *during* their answer! You can find out more about the power of silences in Chapter 5.

"If we want students to talk to learn . . . then what they say probably matters more than what the teacher says" (Alexander, 2006, p. 26).

So, get comfortable with silence, and don't always fill the gaps!

1.5 • REVIEW

This chapter has covered the following main points:

a. Questioning is a skill and a process, based on a series of 'moves' rather than asking a single 'question'.

b. There is no such thing as a closed or open question. There are only questions. What matters is the reason you have for asking the question, and how you respond to the answer your students give you.

c. The three key essential skills in developing your questioning are:

   1. Know Your Intent

   2. Plan Your Responses

   3. Stay Silent (and Listen)

d. Know Your Intent is the first of the essential skills in improving your questioning and is arguably the most important, as without knowing the purpose of your questioning, you are likely to struggle to create meaningful, incisive dialogues that move the students' learning forward.

e. The purpose of your questioning can be expressed as a statement, such as 'to engage more of the class in the dialogue' or 'to encourage your students to give more reasons'.

f. Questioning without purpose is often short or doesn't lead anywhere. The most effective questioning should enhance the learning activity and accelerate progress toward the learning goal.

g. The purpose of your questioning can also be identified within these five key frames:

Knowledge	This frame involves diagnosing what students know and identifying what they need to consider next to move forward.
Understanding	Questioning in this frame helps students think at a conceptual level, on how and why knowledge is connected and explained in the context of subject-specific language.
Skills	Questioning here focusses on *how* learning takes place and ensures students can apply knowledge and understanding.
Attitudes	This frame focusses on developing the habits of good thinking, such as open-mindedness, reasonableness, and resilience, which are made explicit in learning through questioning.
High Expectations	Creating a culture where your students are challenged and *expect* to be challenged means your questioning sequences model the thinking you want your students to develop.

h. To ensure your students make progress, you will need to consider the dialogue beforehand so that the sequence happens by design.

i. Learning to stay silent at different times during a questioning sequence encourages your students to think more and say more and allows you to listen to what and how they understand the concepts of the lesson.

1.6 • REFLECTION

Consider the frames we have created so far in developing questioning, and reflect on where you are now. How often are you aware of your intent before you start questioning? How often are the students aware of your intent?

Have a go at expressing your intent as a statement, such as 'to get the students to talk for longer'.

What do your students currently expect when you ask a question? Do they expect to be challenged? Do they all expect to take part and give extended reasons for their thinking?

Rather than assume what your students might think, try asking them. What is questioning currently like in your classroom? How much do the students have to think? How often do they feel challenged? For how long do they typically talk when answering?

What next?

Practise identifying your intent ahead of a lesson. Think of a question you are likely to ask tomorrow, and establish what you want the purpose of it to be.

Try to express your intent in relation to one of the five frames: knowledge, understanding, skills, attitudes, or high expectations.

In the first instance, don't worry too much about planning the follow-up question to your student answers; just see if you can identify what the intention of your questioning could be and see if that changes the way you view your questioning in the lesson.

You could also have a go at staying silent. What happens when you ask a question and then say nothing at all for 5 seconds, 10 seconds, 20 seconds? What impact does it have on the students? What effect does it have on you?

What happens when a student gives an answer and then you stay silent? What impact does silence have on the student? Does the student then offer more, or less, to a dialogue? What effect does it have on you? Try to use the silent time to consider your next question.

After the lesson, ask yourself:

- **Did my questioning take the students to where I wanted them to go?**
- **Was my questioning more purposeful as a result of knowing the intent?**
- **Did my questioning encourage the students to talk more or think more?**
- **Was there a focus on knowing or understanding?**
- **Did my questioning focus on specific thinking, skills, or attitudes?**
- **What did my questioning sequence model for my students, and what did it say about my expectations?**

Remember to identify your intention *before* the questioning episode, and ideally before the lesson. Don't try to decide what the purpose of your questioning was *after* the questioning sequence. Considering the dialogue beforehand is key!

Ask questions to find out something about the world itself, not to find out whether or not someone knows it.

—John Holt (Holt & Farenga, 2003, p. 163)

THE BASIC QUESTIONING SEQUENCE

In this chapter, we will look at common patterns of questioning behaviours in classrooms and, in light of the essential skills we considered in Chapter 1, consider how we might develop these patterns to focus on a process of thinking and therefore impact positively on your students' learning.

Throughout this chapter, we will focus on questioning steps—that is, a series of moves that form sequences—and not on individual questions. Each question is just one step in the process and should be viewed as part of a whole, rather than on its own.

Try to hold on to the idea of knowing your intent throughout the chapter so you can reflect on how the patterns we describe connect to the purpose and values of effective questioning.

2.0 • THE IRE PATTERN

I am often in the very privileged position of being asked to observe lessons, especially when working with teachers on questioning. Observing learning in the classroom should always be considered a great way for both parties (the observer *and* the observed) to learn. And it is observing questioning sequences and the impact of questioning on student learning that has really helped me to develop my practice beyond what I could achieve without those professional conversations.

One of the patterns of questioning practice that I observe frequently in classrooms is what we call IRE:

Initiate

Respond

Evaluate

In real terms, the IRE pattern looks very much like the questioning sequence we saw in 1.1:

Teacher: What is the capital of Scotland?

Student: Edinburgh.

Teacher: Well done.

Of course, this applies in many different subject areas. See Figure 2 for a few examples that represent typical IRE sequences I see regularly.

▶ **Figure 2: Some typical examples of IRE patterns in different subjects.**

	English	Maths	Science	Music	History
Initiate	How do you make a text more persuasive?	10% of 10 is 1. What's 20% of 20?	If I accelerate, what am I doing?	What's the interval between the first two notes of this melody?	Who was the first roman emperor?
Respond	Put lots of reasons in.	2 . . . no, 4!	Going faster.	Fifth.	Julius Caesar.
Evaluate	Good.	Ha! Well done!	Excellent, yes.	Perfect.	No!

2.1 • IRE AS CLOSED QUESTIONING

In the IRE pattern, the teacher poses a question, a student gives a response, and then the teacher evaluates the response (usually stating whether it is right or wrong). The purpose is to assess knowledge gained, and there is no intention to follow up, or to develop a dialogue. Once the response is given, the purpose of the Evaluate step is to end the questioning process, so it goes no further.

The IRE process can last less than 5 seconds (try reading an example from Figure 2 while watching the second hand on your clock!). The intention on the teacher's part is to check that the student knew the answer. There is no intention to continue the exchange, to challenge the response or open the dialogue for further cognitive function. But it is only when we get to the Evaluate step that we can see the intention of the sequence; this is not apparent at the Initiate stage.

If we return to the idea of the difference between questions and questioning, then we can recognise in this pattern why there is no such thing as an open or closed question. You need to see the whole sequence first before you can identify the intent, and therefore the type of dialogue engaged in.

As in this example:

I am back in the privileged position of observing a lesson. This time it's the English lesson in Figure 2. I am nestled at the back of the (imaginary) classroom listening to the early instruction. The questioning dawns (excitement rises):

Initiate: How do you make a text more persuasive?

Great! At this point, we are in good shape. For all intents and purposes, this looks like an open question—lots of possibility, no single answer—a big tick on the observer's sheet! Then a student answers:

Respond: Put lots of reasons in.

Excellent! We are still in good shape. This is a good response—it's one possible answer; the student has been listening; there's opportunity to build; they just need a few more ideas (come on, kids; come on!)—and the teacher says . . .

Evaluate: Good.

Ouch!

It's only after we see this third step that we can identify the nature of the sequence. The student already knew the answer, and when he said it, he received praise. So the process of thinking, talking, and learning ended, and the teacher moved on.

The Initiate question looked to be open, but the *sequence* was closed; the intention was to keep the dialogue short and therefore close it down *after* the first response.

We can only judge the quality of a question in the context of the sequence in which it is placed, and the effectiveness of that sequence in moving the students toward the intended goal.

I often see this questioning sequence unfold in a classroom in real life. At the first and second step, we look to be in good shape, but the third step often involves what I call 'missed opportunity'. When the first response comes in from a student, all the questioning possibilities seem to dance in the air just waiting to be plucked out and used to extend the dialogue, create more thinking, and share more language. But they often get missed in favour of Evaluate.

This is why 'Plan Your Reponses' (1.3) is so important. The more you have prepared and ready at hand to follow up your students' responses, the less likely you are to miss opportunities to engage your students in effective questioning.

2.2 • PROBLEMS IN IRE

This IRE pattern gives your students the impression that, when questioning, you are only interested in those who already know the answer, and this reinforces a culture of expectation.

For many students, the problem with the IRE pattern is that it forces them to decide whether or not to take part in the questioning sequence. Their decision is driven first by whether they know the answer or not, and second by whether they value extrinsic praise or not.

If they don't value your praise, they won't seek to please you with the right answer; they can leave that to those who want the praise.

And if they don't know the answer, they can't take part, so they often choose to opt out of the game—partly to save face but mostly, practically speaking, because they don't have anything to contribute! And the idea that your students could learn by listening to others giving the right answer doesn't usually hold water, unless you have explicitly let your students know that they should listen to the answers given and make a note (mental or written) to remember the facts.

Of course, this connects back to our idea of 'Know Your Intent' (1.1). If you want your students to learn facts by listening to others give the right answer, then you can, of course, tell them that.

To be most effective, however, questioning should demonstrate to your students that there is value in taking part; that they also feel valued taking part, in themselves and by their peers as well as by the teacher; and that questioning will contribute positively to their learning. The more your students see integrity in the questioning process, the more they will engage in it.

2.3 • RETHINKING THE *E*

If the intention of your questioning is to engage more of your students in talking and thinking, then clearly this pattern of Initiate-Respond-Evaluate won't create the culture of high expectations that we discussed in 1.2.4. Demonstrating integrity in questioning means rethinking IRE so that evaluating answers isn't the only outcome of questioning in your classroom.

A good way to do this is simply to change the function of the *E* in IRE. How might we act differently if the framework for better questioning became:

> Initiate
>
> Respond
>
> Explore?

In this framework, we change the *E* step in the sequence to try to open the dialogue and therefore create possibilities for engaging more of your students, getting your students to think, challenging their ideas, and modelling high expectations in learning.

The idea of Explore is the intent to go further than the first response.

Here's how it might look, using the example from Figure 2:

> Initiate: How do you make a text more persuasive?
>
> Respond: Put lots of reasons in.
>
> Explore: OK, that's one way. Does anyone have another idea?

Of course, there are any number of different questions we could have used at the Explore step to develop the responses further:

> Explore: What kind of language would work best for that?
>
> Are reasons and opinions the same thing?
>
> Can you find an example of a reason [in your text]?

Placing any of these questions in at the third step of the sequence would encourage students to explore their ideas and give more reasons, and get more of them involved

in the process. Initiate-Respond-Explore highlights the intent to develop an idea further and understand how the students are thinking beyond the first answer they come up with.

The Explore step doesn't use a set of magic questions either. They are not special questions; they are just connected to the response the student gave. Because the third step links to your students' answers, the dialogue continues the theme and therefore takes the students from a surface-level answer to deeper thinking.

Of course, you would expect to have intentions connected to your subject area, so the Explore step should help move your students' thinking toward that goal. For example, if your intention in history is for your students 'to be able to explain cause and effect', then your Explore step should feature opportunities for them to do just that.

An example of this could be as follows:

Initiate: When was the Battle of Bunker Hill?

Respond: 1775.

Explore: Who won the battle?

Respond: The British.

Explore: How would you describe the victory?

Respond: The British won, but only just. They lost a lot of men and officers.

Explore: If you were British, how might that affect your approach in the next battle?

You can see in this sequence that the Explore step doesn't end after one response. The teacher knows her intent (cause and effect) and has used each step of the process to move her students' thinking forward and open up the idea of cause and effect. The intent is clear, and the link between her students' responses and her next question shapes the resulting dialogue around the learning goal.

The teacher could then introduce the New York and New Jersey campaign and consider whether the approach taken by the British was related to the outcomes of the Battle of Bunker Hill. She could use a similar questioning sequence to explore the causal link between the Battle of Gloucester and the Burning of Falmouth. These questioning sequences intentionally move her students' thinking toward the goal.

Returning to the essential skills for questioning we outlined in 1.0, we can see how these are firmly embedded in the idea of Initiate-Respond-Explore:

Know Your Intent can be as simple as knowing you want to explore the idea further.

Plan Your Responses can be seen in the options you need to have at hand to follow up on your students' responses purposefully, and not miss opportunities. These prepared options allow you to create a meaningful sequence that continues the thinking and exploring after your students have given their answer.

Stay Silent (and Listen) means that you can connect the Explore step to the response your students gave.

Exploring ideas, concepts, or skills places emphasis on the *process* of learning. You can see how each of the examples encourages your students to think and talk about *how* and *why* as well as *what*. In terms of knowing your intent, the I-R-Explore pattern has the intention of focussing on the thinking behind the answer as much as on the answer itself.

To do this well requires you as a teacher to think about your questioning differently—that it might be the way you reach the answer that is more important than the answer itself. This change of emphasis is more likely to lead to longer-term transferable learning, than just knowing the right answer.

Here's an example from a mathematics arithmetic lesson. In this example, the teacher told his Grade 5 students that he would put a sum up on the screen. The students were not to tell him the answer to the sum, or to try and guess at an answer. Instead, they were to tell him how they would go about *working out* the answer.

The sum then flashed up on the screen: $86 \times 12 + 18$.

There followed a moment's silence while his students took it in. He then asked them to talk in pairs and try to decide how they would work out the answer. After a minute or two, he stopped the class and asked them for their methods. As each method was presented, the teacher displayed it on the screen at the front so everyone could see.

Initiate: $86 \times 12 + 18$. How would you do it?

Respond: We would do 86×10, then 86×2 and add them together, then add 18.

Explore: Thank you. Would anyone do it differently to that?

Respond: We thought 80×10 and 6×10 and add them together; then 86×2 and add that on; then add the 18 at the end.

Explore: Anyone have another way to do it? Michael?

Respond: We'd use a calculator!

Explore: OK! Thanks for that, Michael—I'll write it down too! Did anyone have another way?

Respond: We did $12 + 18$, then times it by 80, then times it by 6, then add it together.

Explore: Thank you. There's four different ways. Did anyone do it differently to those?

Respond: We did. We tried it by doing 100×12 first. Then we did 10×12 and 4×12 and added those together. Then we would take [away] that answer from the first one [100×12]. Then add 18.

Teacher: So now we have five different ways to do the same sum. Shall we see if we get the same answer each time? In your pairs, work out the answer to the sum using three different ways, then use Michael's suggestion and check it with a calculator. We're trying to work out whether each method gets us to the same answer.

Having tried this out for a few minutes, the students were then able to share their results. Working through the sums together on the screen, the students were able to see how the process was done. The teacher modelled the thinking by using brackets to show what he did first and second and talked through all the methods. One of the methods the students used (the fourth one) didn't bring the same result as the rest. Rather than suggest that this was a bad thing, he simply asked the class to explore again:

Teacher: Look at this example in your pairs. Why do you think it didn't get us to the same answer as the other methods? Can you work out what needs to be changed to get to the right answer?

All of the students were then engaged in exploring the mistake at the same time. There was no intention to return to the student who gave that suggestion in the first place; everyone was focussed on learning from the mistake. There is value in knowing why something doesn't work as much as there is in what does work.

The teacher then extended the students' thinking even further by adding an extra part to the sum, asking, 'If the sum was now $86 \times 12 + 18 - 9$, how would you do it? Not the answer, but the method you would use'.

Again, the students worked in pairs to work out a method and explain their thinking to the class. The teacher then put up another sum that looked similar but with different numbers and asked the students to use two different methods to work out the answer and then test it with a calculator.

At the end of the lesson, the students were able to talk about the methods they could use to work out more complex sums. This understanding of how the process of arithmetic works is transferable, and the students in this group were more likely to retain it for longer (and apply it in other situations) because they had actively experienced the thinking for themselves.

2.4 • USING THE EXPLORE STEP TO FOCUS ON PROCESS

Consider the same dialogue if it had appeared in the I-R-Evaluate sequence we saw in 2.0, without focussing on the process of learning *how*:

Initiate: What is $86 \times 12 + 18$?

Respond: 1,050.

Evaluate: Well done.

Look at all the missed opportunities there would be!

There is no intention to explore other possibilities or engage more students in the thinking or learning, and as the intention for many students would not be clear, the integrity of the questioning sequence would be in doubt. This is likely to mean that many students would disengage if they hadn't explicitly been instructed to take a note of the method for themselves.

Compare that Evaluate example with the Explore example experienced earlier. In that example, the students explored and tested a variety of methods and therefore developed the skills they needed to do it for themselves. The emphasis on exploring process meant that when faced with another, similar, calculation, students were more likely to be able to transfer their learning.

It is clear both what the teacher intended with the questioning sequence, and what he values highly in his classroom.

2.5 • CHALLENGE AND THE I-R-EXPLORE PATTERN

In this chapter, we have seen that the same starter question can lead to a number of different questioning sequences and therefore outcomes. The *question* is not as important as *how* you question.

The I-R-Explore pattern promotes a more rigorous and challenging path to learning as a way to reach a deeper understanding of concepts. The approach is based on the belief that challenge is an addition to learning that makes a situation more demanding or stimulating and therefore encourages students to learn more than they otherwise would.

To illustrate this idea, compare the two paths shown in Figure 3. As you will see, the path on the left is straightforward and is likely to get you to your destination quickly and with little effort. The path to the right, however, is filled with obstacles and will require greater effort to reach your goal.

If you were in a rush or if you just wanted a relaxing stroll without any hard work, then the obvious path to take would be the one on the left.

But if you wanted to choose the path most *interesting*, then the path on the right would appear to be more engaging, thought-provoking, and maybe even a little exciting! The right-hand path is more likely to lead you into discussion with other people about the best strategies to use to go forward, and it is more likely that you will feel a sense of satisfaction when you eventually reach your goal and review your journey with enthusiasm. It is possible too that you will remember the journey weeks, months, or even years afterwards, because of the effort you put in to get through it.

In *Challenging Mindset*, Nottingham and Larsson (2019) use the metaphor of the Learning Challenge Paths to demonstrate the active, cognitive processing needed for deeper learning.

This imagery is one way to describe what cognitive conflict might feel like. Whereas the left-hand path represents answering questions that are easy and straightforward in which there is no cognitive conflict, the right-hand path represents more challenging questioning that requires more active, cognitive function.

The intention of the Explore step, then, is to take the 'right path'. You can see one way to view the connection between deeper learning and the I-R-Explore sequence in Figure 3.

▶ **Figure 3:** I-R-Explore version of the Learning Challenge Paths.

Source: Nottingham & Larsson, 2019.

Compare the path metaphor with the I-R-Explore sequence. What do you notice? How are the two connected? Can you apply the Explore steps in the example dialogues from 2.3 to the Learning Challenge Paths?

The first two steps of the basic questioning sequence often follow the easy path. It is the Initiate phase, which is often based on recall and where responses can often be concise (though they don't need to be), that gets the sequence started. The Initiate phase here is often something accessible and closely connected to the current instruction or text. It checks for knowledge.

The Initiate step draws your students in and sets them off on the easy path (always a nice way to start a journey!), but the questioning step after your students' first response should then encourage the dialogue into the Explore path.

This Explore step can encourage challenge, longer answers, variations, reasons, opinions, or just getting more participants to engage. Explore focusses on process, so the questioning is likely to involve *how* and *why*, as well as *what*.

If the path is intended to be more challenging, then the Explore step can of course include cognitive conflict and increase the cognitive demands on the respondents.

This means that your students are more likely to make mistakes. Your response to mistakes is feedback to your students about your expectations—whether you value them as an inevitable part of the learning process, to be examined and learnt from, or as a catastrophe to be avoided so we head back to the easy path as quickly as possible.

2.6 • QUESTIONING AS FEEDBACK

In the example in 2.3, the teacher was accepting of mistakes. When one of his students' responses didn't lead to the correct answer, he didn't shy away from it, hide it, or correct it; the intention to test methods and focus on process still applied, so rather than just give the students the correct answer, he used it to explore what can be learnt from the mistake.

Using mistakes in this way validates error and normalises failure. This adds to the integrity of the questioning sequence and builds trust in the culture of high expectations you are aiming to establish through your questioning. In *Challenging Mindset* (Nottingham & Larsson, 2019), we talk about the importance of valuing mistakes and failure as learning experiences; making mistakes is not a good thing, but learning from them is.

Using the Explore step consistently in your questioning sequences allows you to demonstrate that you value the process of learning, that there might be more than one way to reach—or express—an answer, and that you always intend to follow up and take first responses further. Initiate-Respond-Explore therefore represents an intention to process learning so that students retain it for longer.

This intention is a significant aspect of your questioning as feedback. How you respond to your students' answers is feedback to them—feedback about your expectations, about what you value, and about how you want them to think and behave next time you question. It shows that you value learning and challenge, rather than 'those who know the answer', and therefore encourages a 'challenging mindset'.

In the Evaluate pattern (2.1), most of the sequences closed with praise. The praise was aimed at stating how good it was that the student already knew the answer. This kind of 'fixed mindset' praise reinforces other students' views that 'some of us have it, and some of us don't'.

In the Explore pattern, however, each question from you demonstrates that you value thinking, challenge, and effort, and the opportunity is created for students to engage in these actions. The Explore step therefore might never reach the 'well done' stage. Rather, it should aim to create a bridge to the next action or activity in the lesson.

Questioning should enhance the learning activity and accelerate progress toward the learning goal.

2.7 • REVIEW

In this chapter, we considered how we might improve a commonly used (though unconscious) pattern of questioning, to focus more on the process of learning than on getting the right answer.

The IRE pattern that ended with an Evaluate step demonstrated how we can often unwittingly close down a dialogue. It is this step in the sequence, and not the Initiate question, that showed the questioning was closed; there are no such things as good (open) and bad (closed) questions, only questions. It was when we changed the Evaluate step to an Explore step that we saw how the sequence opened up to further possibilities for more students.

This chapter has covered the following main points:

i. Questioning often follows the pattern of IRE: Initiate-Respond-Evaluate.

ii. The Evaluate step closes down the sequence and places emphasis on getting the right answer. When we use the Evaluate step too frequently, students come to think we value those who already know the right answer more highly than those who don't.

iii. Some students may disengage from questioning because they are not able to contribute or because they don't value the praise they get as a reward for knowing the answer.

iv. This is why 'Plan Your Reponses' is so important. The more questions you have prepared and ready at hand to follow up your students' responses, the less likely you are to miss opportunities to engage your students in effective questioning.

v. Changing the Evaluate step to an Explore step creates an intention to open up the questioning sequence for more thinking, more possibilities, and more talk from more students.

vi. The Explore step focusses on process as much as on the answer.

vii. Using the Explore step gives feedback to your students about your values and expectations.

viii. It is OK for a student to give the wrong answer if you then take the Explore step. You can continue with your intended questioning, as mistakes are to be embraced and learnt from as part of the learning process.

ix. Making a mistake is not a good thing; learning from it is.

2.8 • REFLECTION

Following this chapter, you might like to try these exercises:

- **Reflect on your own questioning sequences, without planning them in advance or identifying your intent. How often do they end up in the typical IRE pattern and end by closing down the sequence when a right answer appears?**

- **Try planning an IRE sequence with the intention of using the Explore step. Plan a few questions you could ask after you get the first student response. Use the five frames from 1.2 to help identify your intent first, then plan some questions to help your students work toward that goal.**

- **Start with a question you know you will ask tomorrow. Picture how the students might respond. What are they likely to say? If they respond, what can you ask next?**

- **Think about missed opportunities. How often do they happen in your lesson? If you have the chance to observe a colleague, look for missed opportunities. Where could your colleague have asked a question that would extend the dialogue and thinking?**

A good way to reflect on your questioning is to video or audio record your questioning in the classroom. Terrifying, I know, but well worth it!

- Try recording a sequence where you use I-R-Evaluate and one using I-R-Explore. Compare the two; what do you notice (about yourself, the students, the language used, the expectations, and so on)?

- When trying an I-R-Explore sequence, focus on the feedback it gives your students about your expectations. What do you think they picked up from that episode? When you do it again (and again), what are you starting to notice about the impact of your questioning as feedback on expectations and values?

- Try using the following table to observe how students respond to your questioning or to the questioning of a colleague you observe (with permission, of course!). Record how the students respond, whether they engage, how long they talk for, and what happens when they make a mistake; try it during an Evaluate and an Explore sequence and compare the two.

Questioning Sequence	I-R-Evaluate	I-R-Explore
Describe the sort of answers given by students.		
What form of feedback did the students get from you?		
Count the number of students choosing to engage. How do you know?		
Note the effect of the questioning on student behaviours. (Include those who are *not* answering, not just those who are.)		
Respond to mistakes.		

'Most teachers have been given snippets of information . . . but few teachers have been taught a practical pedagogy of questioning'.

—Ivan Hannel (quoted in Marzano & Simms, 2014, p. 12)

QUESTIONING TOOLS: PLANNING EFFECTIVE SEQUENCES

3

In the previous chapter, we looked at the IRE pattern (Initiate-Respond-Explore). Once you are familiar with this pattern, you can use it as the basis for all effective questioning, adapting and extending what happens at the Explore step. The key to making IRE work brilliantly is to know your intent when asking the Initiate question so that when the first question is asked, whatever response comes next from the students, you are open to exploring the idea further.

Throughout the rest of this book, we will look at how you can adapt and extend the basic IRE sequence and look at ways of preparing your questioning in advance to make the Explore step more meaningful, engaging, and thought-provoking for your students.

While the Evaluate sequences are useful in some situations, planning for the Explore step means you can introduce more variety into your lessons and create more meaningful sequences of dialogue, which will raise the expectations in your classroom. It is this focus on an *intent to explore* that will ultimately make the biggest difference for your students.

3.0 • THE STARTING POINT: INITIATE—WHERE QUESTIONS ARE BORN

As Dylan Thomas (1954/2004) aptly wrote, 'To begin at the beginning . . .'

So, let us begin with our starting point for questioning: the Initiate question. You will be familiar with this already, as the Initiate step is one we all do regularly! Initiate questions are the ones you ask to get the students to respond and share their current knowledge.

Remember that the questions are not closed or open—they are just 'questions'—at the Initiate stage; you can't judge whether the intent is open or closed until you see what happens at the *E* step.

For many of us, the Initiate and Respond steps are easy. We can think of Initiate questions at the drop of a hat and at any moment in any lesson, often because we throw questions into our instruction and delivery or because they flow easily from a text we are reading. In reality, thinking of an Initiate question is really just thinking of *any question* you might ask your students!

Here's an example of how questioning is often sparked in a classroom:

> Teacher [reading to the class from *Jane Eyre* (Brontë, 1847/2006, p. 249)]: 'Do you like this sunrise, Jane? That sky with its high and light clouds, which are sure to melt away as the day waxes warm—this placid and balmy atmosphere?'
>
> 'I do, very much.'
>
> Initiate: What time of day do you think it is?

In this example, the teacher is reading the words from a text. All of the language used and the context of the dialogue in the text set the scene and suggest at what time of day the narrative takes place. So the Initiate question, 'What time of day is it?', emerges as an obvious one to ask.

In the following example, the teacher is explaining magnetism through direct delivery:

> Teacher [quoting Wagner, 2001–2002]: Scientists' thinking about magnetic sources has changed over the centuries. The only form of magnetism known until the 19th century was ferromagnetism. Certain materials, when 'magnetized', would attract certain other materials. Since only certain materials exhibited magnetic properties, scientists thought that magnetism was an inherent property of materials.
>
> Then, in the 19th century, scientists studying the relatively new field of electrical currents discovered that moving charges produce magnetic effects. They discovered that 'electromagnetism' occurred when current travelling through a loop of wire created a magnetic field along the axis of the loop.
>
> Initiate: What are the two types of magnetism?

Here, the teacher has outlined the discovery of two different types of magnetism, and so the Initiate question is sparked by the key themes of what was just said, and the key subject language being taught. Having defined two types of magnetism, it is natural to ask, 'What are the two types of magnetism?'

Now consider this example from a music lesson:

> Teacher: The rhythm in this piece goes 'stamp, stamp, clap . . . stamp, stamp, clap . . .' People in this group [over here] will keep that rhythm going for us while the rest of us are singing.
>
> Initiate: How does the rhythm go?

The explanation from the teacher here is very brief, but the Initiate question emerged from the skill she just demonstrated.

Each of these examples shows us how Initiate questions often emerge. They tend to be based on what was just said, read, or done. The reason they are so easy to think of, and therefore easy to ask, is that we have just rehearsed the language for asking them (it's now in our own heads and on the tip of our tongues) and have just demonstrated the focus for learning and reinforced the subject language—or indeed subject skill— being taught.

But this does not make these questions 'closed'! It simply makes them Initiate questions; each is the first question in a sequence. Letting questions emerge from the lesson like this is perfectly fine, and absolutely natural. In each of these examples, the context of the lesson is like the fertile earth out of which a question sprouts. Questions emerge from circumstance.

It is not really worth spending any effort reframing your Initiate questions so that they look more open. This is where many teachers have become confused, and therefore put off questioning, by the notion of 'closed as bad' and 'open as good'. Teachers who have wrestled with how to phrase a question so that it looks 'open' have found it not to be that worthwhile when the next thing they do is close the dialogue down by evaluating the first response!

Initiate questions are a springboard for the rest of the dialogue and should never be thought of as closed or open questions—no matter how they are phrased.

Of course, that doesn't stop you from planning ahead by predicting the questions you might ask when you are teaching your lessons. Predicting the Initiate questions makes it more likely that you will ask them and, more importantly, that you will then follow them up with your planned questioning at the *E* step in the IRE sequence.

When you can predict your Initiate question and plan your follow-up questions, you are more likely to achieve your intent to explore, and therefore have more impact on your students' learning, than if you don't predict your Initiate question and don't plan ahead to the next question in the sequence.

In the second step of the IRE structure, the students will respond. They may give you a short, factual answer, or a yes or no; they may give you a lengthy, thoughtful reflection; or they may demonstrate an action. In our examples, the responses from the students are likely to be, respectively:

Respond: Morning.

Respond: Ferromagnetism and electromagnetism.

Respond: Stamp, stamp, clap . . . stamp, stamp, clap . . .

At this point, the Initiate question does not reflect the intent of the questioner, and we are unable to say whether the intention is to evaluate or to explore—to extend the thinking, invite others to speak, demonstrate understanding, or challenge the concept. We will have to wait until the *E* step to find out what the questioner intended!

So, tune in next week, same time, same channel, to find out. (Or, see Section 3.2 if you can't wait!)

3.1 • A REFLECTION SECTION

It is always worth looking at your current practice as you embark on any professional learning, so asking yourself, 'Where am I now?' means you can build on your current reality and make the right call for your next steps.

The more you spend time on the Explore path, the more you aim to challenge your students and expect them to think. Perhaps unsurprisingly, then, this is likely to place increasing demands on both the respondent *and* the questioner.

In the following box, write down examples of Initiate questions (that is, any question at all!) you have used in a recent lesson or could use tomorrow. (What could be simpler?)

_____

_____

_____

_____

_____

_____

_____

_____

Now, we are working one step at a time, so let's try to analyse your questions at this stage and just consider these in relation to the Respond step. When you asked each question,

- What answers did you expect your students to give?

- What responses did you get from your students?

- After asking each of your questions, how long did you give your students to consider their response before you took the first answer? (Caution: one second is a lot longer than you think, and a minute is excruciatingly long!)

- How many students wanted to answer?

- For how long did each of the students talk when they gave you their answers?

Let us consider one of the important messages in this book: Know Your Intent.

Ask yourself now, 'What was your intention when you asked your Initiate questions? Were you hoping that the dialogue would continue? Did you have a follow-up question to ask? Were you checking knowledge? Were you hoping to engage lots of students in answering?' And so on.

Try to be clear on whether you knew the intent before asking the question, or whether it is only apparent now that you're thinking about it after the event.

Write your questioning intent in the following box. What impact did you hope to have on the students?

Now try this:

Reflecting on action is much easier and far more powerful if you have some data or evidence to work from. Try taking a video of your lesson and recording your questioning sequences (a smartphone or iPad will do it well enough). You don't need to watch the whole video; just focus on the questioning sequences. A handy tip, if (like me) you hate watching yourself on screen, is to just point the camera at your students. You will still hear your questioning, but find it far easier to see the impact of your questions on *them*.

Consider the questions we asked you to reflect on in the previous two boxes, but this time answer them while watching your video.

Box 1. What responses did you *expect*, and what responses did you actually *get*?

Box 2. What was your intention in asking your Initiate question? Did you succeed in working toward your intent? Were you aware of your intent before asking the question? Were your students aware of your intent? How do you know?

From your list, I imagine that you have identified many different reasons for asking Initiate questions (quite probably including some that were simply to check knowledge recall and therefore *evaluate*).

One purpose you might have identified is 'to check understanding'. As I wrote in 1.2.2, understanding is not the same as knowledge. Checking understanding would mean that you want the students to go deeper, give you explanations, and connect to prior learning or other concepts. Knowing whether you are checking *knowledge* or checking *understanding* has profound significance for what you do in the *E* step. So, try to use those words carefully if you have put them in your intentions box!

Now that we know the starting point (any question will do!), you've identified your intention in asking the first question, and you've considered possible student responses, then you are in good shape to start planning for the next step in the sequence.

3.2 • YOUR OPTIONS AFTER THE FIRST RESPONSE: PLANNING WITH A FLOW CHART

Generating deliberate steps to extend your students' thinking means predicting the Initiate questions you are likely to ask in your lesson and then planning the questions you could ask next to follow up on first responses.

Consider the following flow diagram to demonstrate one way of imagining your questioning sequences ahead of time. This is the example from the English lesson we saw in 3.0 again, based on the text from *Jane Eyre*:

'Do you like this sunrise, Jane? That sky with its high and light clouds, which are sure to melt away as the day waxes warm—this placid and balmy atmosphere?'

'I do, very much.'

The teacher's intention is given at the top of the flow chart so you can see how each possible response connects back to what the teacher wants the questioning sequence to achieve: for students to be able to infer from text.

Know Your Intent: to be able to infer from text

Initiate — *What time of day is it?*

Respond — *Morning*

| *It is, yes. well done.* | *How do you know that?* | *Can you give me some evidence from the text?* | *What time of year is it?* |
| Evaluate | Explore (Option 1) | Explore (Option 2) | Explore (Option 3) |

Using a flow diagram in this way introduces a useful structure for planning. In this example, you can predict the Initiate question based on the text you will read, imagine how the students will respond (here we predicted the correct answer would be given!), and then imagine some options for a possible next step.

It is, of course, possible to *evaluate* and end the dialogue sequence there, if your intent is to check that a particular student was listening, or if it is vital that the students know the scene takes place in the morning—as long as your *evaluation* doesn't happen just because you haven't given any thought to an Explore option!

Here, we have planned three possible Explore options. If the intention is to explore the skill of 'inference from text', then Option 1 seems like a purposeful step; what did the students read or hear that made them think it was the morning? In comparison to the Evaluate option, this step would build on the first response by looking for reasoning.

Option 2 gets directly to the idea that the students need to justify their thinking. This could be asked of the same student who gave the first response or bring different students into the dialogue.

Option 3 is looking to extend the inference beyond just the day and use the evidence in the text to decide what season it is. This is taking inference to the next level and increasing the demands on the students' cognitive function.

In actual fact, the teacher in this example used all three options. Here's the dialogue in full:

Initiate: What time of day is it?

Respond: I think it's probably the morning.

Explore: *How do you know that* it's probably the morning?

Respond: It mentions the sunrise.

Explore: Can anyone else *give me some* more *evidence from the text* that it's probably the morning?

Respond: It says the clouds will melt away as the day gets warmer. I think that's what it means.

Explore: What means . . . ?

Respond: The 'waxes warm' bit. Like it's going to get warmer later.

Explore: So *what time of year* do you think it is?

Respond: I think it's . . . spring.

Respond: Or summer. Maybe.

Explore: *Can you give me some evidence from the text* to support either of those?

Respond: The warmth. Sunshine.

Respond: There's clear blue skies.

Respond: Placid and balmy atmosphere.

Respond: It says in an earlier paragraph about April showers as well, so it must be spring.

Explore: OK. So Charlotte Brontë doesn't directly say 'it was morning and it was spring'. What do we have to do to *infer it from the text*?

Respond: Look for evidence.

Explore: Anything else? What kind of evidence?

Respond: Clues. You have to pick out key words that give you an idea of what it might be like there. Like she talks about roses just before, so you know they're outside . . .

Respond: And you have to imagine it from the words she gives you. Like *balmy* and *blue sky*.

Evaluate: So, if you have to infer from a text in a book you're reading yourself, or in an exam question, then you'd be able to use evidence, or clues from the text, and imagine what it's like from the key words you have.

I have included this example dialogue because the teacher had recorded the lesson and afterwards she and I talked about the recording. She said after listening to it that she would never have thought to ask some of those questions and continue to push the students for further reasons and answers, if it wasn't for the fact that she had planned them all ahead of time. It was only because she knew her intent and knew what she *could* ask to explore their thinking more that she continued the dialogue.

You can't see it on the written example, but there is a sizeable gap where nothing was said between 'it must be spring' and 'OK. So Charlotte Brontë . . .' In this gap, the teacher and I had a quick conversation during the lesson and suggested that she try to get the students to verbalise their learning about inference from text. This reflective gap is quite useful as teacher *processing-time* (see Chapter 5).

Using the flow diagram is a useful way to think ahead to a few different options for a dialogue in your classroom. You don't have to write it as a flow chart; it can be just as useful as a mental frame. Either way, it helps to identify opportunities to expand your questioning sequences so that students explore the first response further.

Let's look at a few other tips and structures to move your questioning sequences from *Initiate* to *Explore* and build on first responses.

3.3 • PLANNING TO EXPLORE: STICK WITH IT!

Taking the Explore path can be quite demanding. In fact, if it is going well, it probably should be demanding, both for you as the questioner and for your students as the thinkers. I-R-Evaluate is easy to do. I-R-Explore isn't always.

The Explore phase involves longer exchanges than you would expect to see in an I-R-*Evaluate* sequence. This does not mean that the students necessarily talk for longer in every answer; they may do, but equally they may not. The key is that each question deliberately seeks an answer indicative of thought or creates an opportunity for thought *before* an answer is given.

This takes time and practice to do well, and to do purposefully, without missing opportunities. Sometimes things take a turn you didn't expect, or you can't think of a question quickly enough. But don't panic; stick with it. Here are a few tips to help you keep going on the challenging path!

A key is to keep the dialogue active so that questioning sequences are not closed down, whatever answer you get from your students! In this example, the teacher is aiming for I-R-*Explore*. He tries the same question in two classes.

His intention is for his students to share opinions, give reasons for those opinions, and then agree or disagree with each other. With that intent in mind, he begins his questioning sequence:

Initiate: Do you think that testing medicine on animals is fair?

In the first class, one student offers this first response:

Respond: Not really. I don't like animals being used for tests because they don't have a voice to say, 'No, I don't want this'. Especially if it's just for perfumes and things. I guess with medicine that's a better reason, but I still don't like it.

In this example, the student has done what the teacher hoped—given an opinion and done so with reasons. The teacher could then go on with his planned next step and ask the rest of the class if anyone agrees, or disagrees, with this response and build an open dialogue from there. The Explore step he has planned would work nicely.

But in the next class, he asks the same question, 'Do you think that testing medicine on animals is fair?', and this time the first student says a single word . . .

Respond: Yes.

. . . and does not elaborate any further!

Now, this does not mean that the teacher's questioning has failed! We are not suddenly going to start calling it a closed question, and say it was *bad*! His intention is still to encourage opinion and reasoning and get the students to open up a dialogue on whether they agree or disagree. The success of that rests not on that first question and answer, but on how he responds to the student's 'Yes'.

So he sticks with it, and follows up:

Explore: Why do you think it is OK?

But the response he gets is another single word:

Respond: Dunno.

It is still an open questioning sequence because the teacher has not allowed it to close down after the initial response. The intention is to encourage the respondents to think and give reasons to justify their answers. So he sticks with it, and encourages reasons from others in the class:

Explore: OK. Does anyone else think it's fair?

He then encourages reasons from still more students in the class:

Explore: Does anyone think it's *un*fair?

And finally he comes back to the original student with a direct question:

Explore: Earlier you said you thought it was fair to test medicines on animals. What have you heard that you think is a good reason to support your view?

This encourages such students to take part, but also gives them an opportunity to verbalise their ideas (even if those ideas are borrowing language from others at this stage) or to agree or disagree with the points that have been made. This reinforces the expectations in the classroom that all students can, and should, think for themselves whilst also contributing to the collaborative learning in the room.

To plan your options for Explore questions, it is useful to think again about the purpose of your questioning. If it is understanding or skills, then it is likely to involve thinking in some form or another. From the examples we have seen so far, you might notice that the Explore step uses questions that are often constructed with thinking commands in the stem:

- Can you explain why . . . ?
- What do you think . . . ?
- How is this different from . . . ?
- Why is . . . important?
- Do you agree that . . . ?

When your students are responding to such questions, look for key indicators of cognitive processing in words or phrases from your students, like these:

- I think . . .
- . . . because . . .
- I agree/disagree with . . .
- It could be that . . .
- I feel that . . .

So when you plan for Explore questions, use stems like these to begin with so that you get a sense of the purpose of the question when you ask it. A word of caution, though: Don't fall into the trap of believing that thinking stems automatically lead to thinking!

They can contribute and make it more likely, but *only if* you have the intention to allow the dialogue to develop that way.

The key purpose of Explore questioning sequences is to:

1. **Encourage your students to think and reflect.**

2. **Ask your students to voice reasons, give opinions, and make connections.**

3. **Share participation in the conversation more equally with and among your students.**

In the next section, we provide a scaffold for planning a deliberate sequence of questioning steps. This is a really simple but effective way of planning for the Explore phase and ensuring that even when the challenging path gets tough, you can stick with it!

3.4 • PLANNING QUESTIONING SEQUENCES: THE FUNNELLING TECHNIQUE

We have already seen that it is often necessary, and possible, to open up an apparently closed question for exploration. To do this smoothly and effectively in the classroom requires some forethought, so plan your responses!

The funnelling technique is based on the I-R-Explore pattern. It uses the same idea of an Initiate question to get a first response from your students, only this time the Explore step is divided into two parts: *Explain* and *Extend*. This is to provide a scaffold to thinking and ensure that your questioning sequence has considered progress.

Explain places emphasis on process and reasoning, while *Extend* aims to personalise the learning to create meaning—usually an opinion, connection, or perception. These two steps together should demonstrate and frame your students' understanding (as opposed to just knowledge).

Figure 4 illustrates this sequence graphically, using the funnel metaphor to suggest that with each step of the sequence the intention is to 'open out' and encourage a wider spectrum of thinking, and encourage longer exchanges between more students.

▶ **Figure 4: Funnelling. Planning a questioning sequence that breaks down the Explore step into a deliberate, progressive sequence. Planning your questioning in this way helps you be more explicit about what you want to gain from your questioning.**

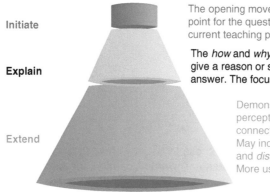

Initiate — The opening move, which establishes the starting point for the questioning. Should relate to your current teaching point, and therefore intent.

Explain — The *how* and *why* question; the students could give a reason or say how they arrived at an answer. The focus is on process or clarification.

Extend — Demonstrates understanding and perception, so is usually opinion, connection, challenge, or comparison. May include cognitive conflict, *agree* and *disagree*, or *similar* and *different*. More use of subject-specific language.

The technique can be used as a planning tool to help structure the questioning pattern you want to use in your lesson, thus ensuring that your sequence has purpose and demonstrates progress in learning.

In many ways, funnelling can be viewed as creating a writing frame for oral exchanges. The key to the funnelling technique is to plan a series of questions which each focus on a point given in the last answer so they assume at least one student response in between each step.

A good tip in planning questioning sequences, therefore, is to try to predict what your students might say in response to your questioning. If this sounds difficult, it isn't. You know your students well, and you will know the likely answers they will give you when you ask certain questions. Use that knowledge to help prepare your questions in advance. And if the students give you a different answer to what you expected, don't worry; your question will probably work just as well with that response. To be prepared is to be more effective!

▶ **Figure 5:** Funnelling. Planning a questioning sequence in maths.

Initiate — What is 42 × 4?

Explain — How did you work it out?

Extend — Could you have done it any other way?

In the example shown in Figure 5, the teacher has asked a mathematics question ('What is 42 × 4?'). This might seem an odd way to initiate an exploration, in that there is only one correct answer. However, the intention in the next step is to deliberately ask your students to 'explain'. So, once the students have responded with their first answer, the teacher has planned to ask, '*How* did you work it out?' This places emphasis on the process and the intention of being able to find different ways of doing mental arithmetic. It ensures that the dialogue continues and is open for the students to continue talking.

In planning the sequence of questions, the teacher has predicted what the students are likely to say back after each question. From this, the teacher plans the next step, which might look like this:

Teacher: What is 42 × 4?

Student A: 168.

Teacher: How did you work it out?

Student A: I multiplied 4 by 4 [16]. Then I multiplied that by 10 [160], multiplied 2 by 4 [8], and added the two together [160 + 8].

Teacher: Could you have done it any other way?

Student A: I could have done 42 × 2 (84) then doubled it (84 × 2).

Having planned the questioning sequence, however, we can't always rely on students to do what we think they will! So what if the teacher has prepared the questioning sequence, and then this happens?

Teacher: What is 42 × 4?

Student A: 186.

Can the teacher still ask the question she planned to ask next ('How did you work it out?')?

The answer is yes, of course, she can. The student will hopefully then realise for himself where his calculation went wrong or be able to compare the calculation with the way others in the class have done it. The intention is to focus on process to find different ways of doing mental arithmetic. Learning from mistakes is a powerful tool.

The important idea to remember here is that funnelling has to do with planning. Because the teacher has planned her questions, she is so well prepared for the next question that even when a wrong answer comes up, she stays on the Explore path. Without that preparation, she would be far more likely to revert to I-R-*Evaluate* and shut the dialogue down by saying, 'No, that's not right', or explaining the correct method *herself*. But because she has prepared her questioning sequence in advance, she is able to continue with the exploratory dialogue and get the student doing the active cognitive processing.

Of course, funnelling isn't always a dialogue between the teacher and a single student; it can be opened up to the rest of the class at any point in the sequence. Look at Figure 6 and the accompanying example from a history lesson.

▶ **Figure 6: Funnelling. Planning a questioning sequence in history.**

Initiate — Who became king in 1485?

Explain — How did he become king?

Extend — Do you think this was fair?

Teacher: Who became king in 1485?

Student A: Henry VII.

Student B: Henry Tudor.

Teacher: How did he become king?

Student C: He won the Wars of the Roses.

Student D: He defeated Richard of York.

Student E: And he had a bloodline to the throne.

Teacher: Do you think this was fair?

Student F: Yes, he won the war and had a right to be king because of his family connection.

Student G: No, it's not fair because nobody chose him to be king; he just took it.

Here, the questions have all been posed to the whole class, and a different student has answered each time. Of course, it doesn't usually work in as regimented a fashion as that in real life, and the same student may answer two or three times. However, the example script serves to show that funnelling can be used to target individuals, pairs, groups, or the whole class. And, of course, a combination can be used deliberately:

Teacher [to Student A]:	Who became king in 1485?
Student A:	Henry Tudor.
Teacher [to the whole class]:	How did he become king?
Student B:	He won the Wars of the Roses.
Student C:	He defeated Richard of York.
Student D:	He had a bloodline to the throne.
Teacher [to Student B]:	Do you think this was fair, Student B?

Although funnelling is ostensibly a way to practise the move from Initiate to Explore by planning sequences of questions in advance, as with any scaffold it becomes a more natural way to ask questions the more you use it, and the need for a scaffold becomes less necessary as the questioning moves become more intuitive.

It can also be an effective way of drawing usually reticent students into a dialogue. Getting the first response helps them build confidence, and then you can build their trust by showing that you value their thinking in the next two steps. And if you have any students who are really struggling with confidence, then you can ask two or three Initiate questions to engage them in the dialogue before taking the next two steps.

Use the blank funnelling template in Figure 7 to plan your own questioning sequences.

▶ **Figure 7: A blank funnelling template. Have a go at planning out a sequence of questioning you could use tomorrow!**

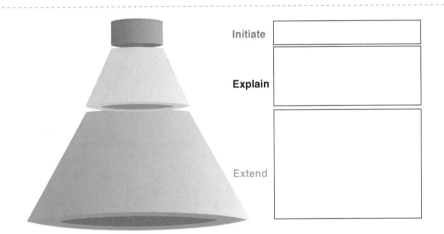

3.5 • USING THE FUNNELLING TECHNIQUE TO PLAN LONGER SEQUENCES

In Section 2.1, we saw how some patterns of questioning in classrooms can close dialogue down by reaching an Evaluate step after the first response. These very short sequences—sometimes accidentally, sometimes intentionally—focus on checking the recall of knowledge.

When using the funnelling technique to transform *Evaluate* to *Explore*, you will notice that the exchange can become much longer as you intend to encourage more thoughtful dialogue. Longer exchanges can mean longer answers (individual students talking for longer), more possible answers (more students contributing different answers), building answers (different students contributing to the same answer), or a longer sequence of questions and answers (more time spent on the full dialogue). Typically, longer exchanges are a combination of all of these.

By using the I-R-Explore pattern and the funnelling technique to complement each other, you can begin to plan longer, more meaningful dialogue exchanges. Consider Figure 8 and notice how the first two steps (Initiate and Respond) are the same in both exchanges. At the third step, the *E* has been used to create a knowledge focus on the left (Evaluate) and an Explore sequence on the right using the structure of the funnelling technique. Look at how each example on the right deliberately seeks to create a longer exchange using the steps of Explain and Extend to explore the theme.

In this example, the teacher is planning a questioning sequence for her Grade 1 students. She has planned the sequence in different ways so she can see exactly how the expectations on her students are different. Let us look at the first two sequences she has planned: an I-R-Evaluate sequence and an I-R-Explore sequence.

In the lesson, her students will be reading a story about Peter, a boy who is waiting outside for his friends in cold weather. Her intention is to get her students to learn about the weather from a story. She has predicted how the students might respond to her questioning, considering a few options that they are likely to say. Her predicted responses appear in parentheses next to the Respond steps in the sequences shown in Figure 8.

▶ **Figure 8: Planning a sequence of questioning using IRE.**

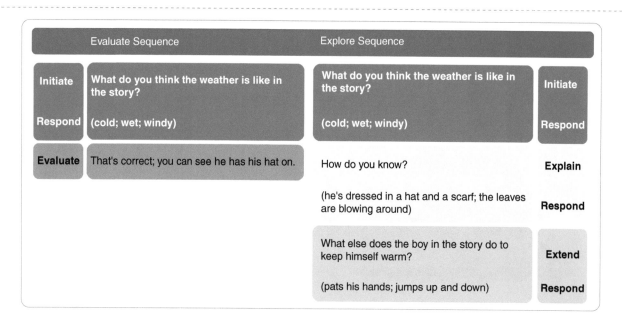

It was obvious to the teacher when she planned these sequences which one she would prefer to use with her students to encourage them to think more carefully about the story. She had worked with questioning for a while, and so was ready to consider how to take the funnelling technique further. Figure 9 shows how she developed Initiate-Respond-Explore to plan for a longer exchange and include a deliberate conclusion to the dialogue, using a prepared Evaluate step to bring the dialogue to a close.

► Figure 9: Planning a sequence of questioning, extending beyond IRE.

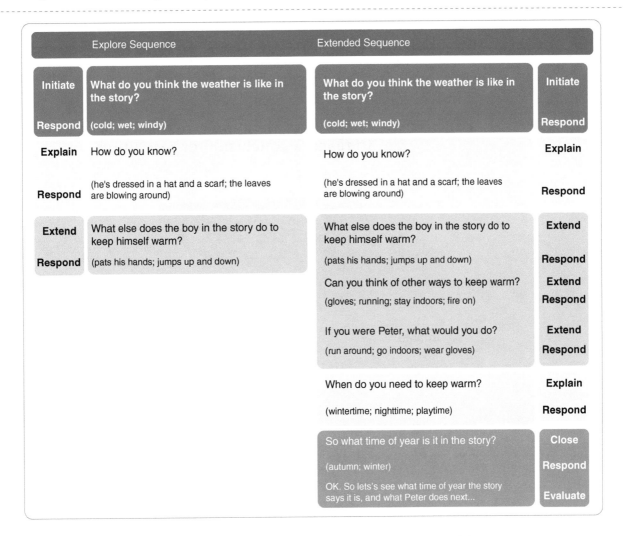

After the lesson, the teacher reported back that the shorter sequence (on the left in Figure 8) was easy to do and had become well-practised. The extended dialogue was much harder, and without the preparation in advance, she would not have considered asking many of the Extend questions 'in the moment', as they would be too hard to think of while the dialogue was taking place.

And there was an additional benefit in having prepared questions in advance; when the dialogue got to the Extend section of the sequence, some of the students struggled for an answer, gave some unconnected thoughts, or said things she hadn't expected. She reported back that without knowing the next question in the sequence, she would have given up the questioning and stopped the dialogue. It was her planning of the sequence beforehand that gave her the resilience to continue, despite the setback, and the confidence to persevere.

Although it can be challenging to prepare questions in advance and intend longer, extended dialogues, it can also be challenging to end exploration in a meaningful way that elicits a conclusion from your students or, at least, an expression of their current standpoint during an exploration. What this example shows is how the teacher deliberately opened up the possibilities, and then closed them down toward the end of the dialogue to reach a specific conclusion at that point in time and return to the story.

Figure 10 shows how the funnelling technique can be reversed to draw open dialogue in the Explore phase back to a conclusion (Evaluate) step. Notice in this example, though, that the Evaluate step has become an expectation for the students to create, rather than one for the teacher to give. Having done the exploring, it is much more indicative of progress and more natural to round off the effort of thinking that your students can reach an endpoint in their own understanding.

Of course, it is useful—and sometimes necessary—to add your own evaluation to that of your students and confirm what they have understood or not, but it makes this step more valuable in terms of high expectations when you are affirming the collaborative conclusion, rather than directing it.

▶ **Figure 10: Funnelling. Planning a sequence of questioning to reach a conclusion or resolution.**

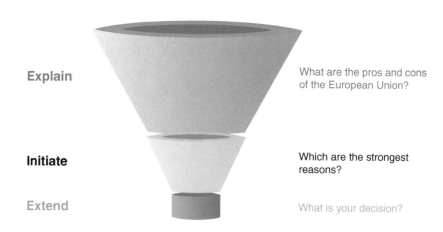

Explain — What are the pros and cons of the European Union?

Initiate — Which are the strongest reasons?

Extend — What is your decision?

As with any good lesson or classroom activity, moving questioning sequences from Evaluate to Explore and from Explore to Evaluate requires careful planning to be effective. Broadening the funnel challenges your students to explain their reasoning and to speculate further; narrowing the funnel helps clarify current standpoints (that may require opening up again later).

3.6 • SO WHY DON'T WE EXPLORE MORE?

Although teachers recognise questions are one of their most familiar—and maybe even one of their most powerful—tools, observational research evidence suggests that most classroom inquiry is short, based on recall, often exclusive, and sometimes even harsh. Moreover, these qualities turn out to be remarkably resistant to change. Extended sequences of questioning in which the information builds from facts toward insight or complex ideas rarely take place (Goodlad, 1984, and Sadker & Sadker, 1985, cited in Wolf, 1987).

So we need to consider what the barriers to success might be so that we can address them, and create more conducive environments for questioning.

We have addressed a few already, but here are some other key barriers that prevent the move from I-R-Evaluate to I-R-Explore:

1. Old habits die hard (for both you and your students—remember, questioning sequences that have the intention of developing thinking and reasoning may not just be new to the teacher; this could also be a new way of thinking for the students, and to begin with, they may be unsure of the expectations).

2. Sequences of questions are not easy to think of 'on the spot', whereas Initiate questions are. If I am teaching about full stops, it is very easy to ask, 'Where does

a full stop come in a sentence?' and then say, 'Well done' to the response. It is much less natural to follow that response with a question that will prompt, probe, and extend understanding. So, we are more likely to evaluate an answer than ask more questions because we can do it spontaneously, whereas sequences require planning and deliberate forethought.

3. It takes practice, time, and skill to create a climate for inquiry. There are few places where teachers can be supported in developing—or being rewarded for—their endeavour. Schools as a whole rarely have a climate in which teacher trial and error are rewarded. In fact, teachers more commonly cite their school ethos, rather than their students, as a barrier to trying new questioning techniques (Stahl, 1994).

All three barriers are connected to the idea that questioning might require time and practice to get right. So if you want to improve your questioning techniques (and we assume that you do if you have made it this far through the book), then it is absolutely essential that you:

- Are willing to make mistakes and learn from them

- Try things in practice and reflect on their success before trying again

- Put in the time, effort, and planning to give it the opportunity to succeed

- Are supported in taking risks by your school leadership team or department

- Have access to resources, ideas, and support to develop your expertise, ideally through in-school coaching

3.7 • PROMPTED TO EXPLORE!

When I started out to develop my questioning techniques, the first barrier I encountered was uncertainty about the actual questions I should be asking; as you enter the Explore phase and need to plan questions that will encourage thinking and challenge, what is it possible to ask?

At that time, I didn't have the language of question*ing*; I was primarily concerned with trying to find a bank of questions that would do the job for me! Before I had access to a planning tool like the funnelling technique, I found lots of questions that I could ask but which didn't seem to elicit the sorts of responses I was expecting.

Once I realised that it was how I follow up the first response that mattered, and that I needed to identify my intention in questioning first, I began by compiling a list of questions that I thought would be useful to explore first responses further, and which might deliberately encourage longer exchanges with my students.

That list became a 'prompt sheet': a list of questions—from other teachers, from books, and from videos—that I thought would work very well for the purpose. My first list actually only had four questions on it, one of which was simply the word *why*!

Over time as I practised, and as other people contributed to my list when they knew I was interested in questioning, I added and removed questions so that it was constantly changed, updated, and rearranged.

Figure 11 is an example questioning prompt sheet, just like the one I used, that can help get you started in the same way. The idea is not to ask all the questions in one lesson, but to use it to help plan a sequence in the Explore stage. The purpose of the prompt sheet, then, is twofold: to support you in planning your responses for the Explore phase, and to practise those responses so that they become a more natural part of your everyday practice. The idea of a prompt sheet (and, indeed, any of the scaffolding tools in this book) is that you shouldn't need it forever!

Questioning Prompt Sheet

Use this guide to help prompt your questioning and explore beyond students' first responses.

The questioning stems should help you consider your questioning sequences ahead of time, as well as act as a reminder during the lesson.

Questioning Stems	Intention
• What did you decide/create? • Why do you think that? • Can you give me an example/evidence? • Are there any other reasons?	To encourage reasoning
• How did you reach that conclusion? • Are you happy with your final answer? • Could it have been anything else?	To encourage reflection
• What similarities/differences did you notice? • What assumptions did you make, and why? • Is there another way you could look at it? • How does [this] affect [that]?	To create cognitive conflict
• Tell me more about . . . • What do you mean by . . . ? • So, are you saying . . . ?	To extend and clarify language
• What if . . . ? • Is that the same as . . . ? • Does that fit with this [example/idea]?	To encourage speculation
• Does that fit with this [example/idea]? • What do you think now? • How did your understanding change? • Where else could you use this [thinking/skill/strategy]? • What did you find difficult? • How did you overcome that? • What do you still need to find out/do?	To identify progress and promote transfer

As well as in my planning, I also used this prompt sheet while teaching by placing a copy of it on my desk and referring to it through all my lessons to practise some of the questions that I wouldn't normally ask. This is particularly useful during the Explore phase, as these questions are much less natural to ask. After all, if you were in a pub with your friends, every time they ordered a drink, you wouldn't ask them, 'Why did you choose that drink?' or 'Tell me more about your choice' or 'Could you have chosen something else?'

You would soon find yourself drinking alone!

Similarly, in the classroom it does feel a little clunky asking questions by referring to a sheet for prompts! But the more you use the prompt sheet to aid your preparation, or use it in the classroom itself, the more it becomes natural to ask these types of question, and you soon drop the scaffold of the prompt sheet as you develop questioning regularly in your practice.

I remember using the prompt sheet in one Grade 7 class, and having just had a very detailed and impressive answer from one student about a character in the text we were reading, my mind went blank; all that planning of questioning, and I couldn't remember where to go next in the sequence! So after a slightly uncomfortable pause, I went to my desk, looked at the prompt sheet, returned to the front of the class, and asked, 'So what assumptions did you make there?'

There were a few bewildered looks on the students' faces, but the boy duly answered in a faltering way before I went back to my desk and asked him another question. This time the students looked at me like I was a madman, and asked, 'What are you doing, sir?'

'What do you mean?' I asked innocently.

'Well, why do you keep walking backwards and forwards and asking us weird questions?' was the reply!

And so I told them. I told them I was practising questioning and was hoping to give them the chance to think more and talk for longer about their answers than they usually would. But I also told them, 'I'm not very good at it yet, so I need to practise, and this sheet on my desk is helping me'. The students seemed quite happy with this and accepted that I was learning along with them.

A few days later, I was teaching the same group of students and still referring to my prompt sheet when one of them asked, 'Wouldn't it be easier to just give us the prompt sheet?'

Admittedly he was joking, but in fact we ended up doing just that. I put a copy of the prompt sheet on the students' tables, so they had a copy in each group. And that worked really well for a number of reasons:

1. It encouraged me to use questioning more efficiently.

2. The students were working on their responses to the questions before I asked them (for example, looking at a text and thinking about inference, because they were anticipating being asked about it later in the lesson).

3. The students started to ask each other the same questions.

In terms of modelling thinking, that last point is crucial. Because the students knew the questions, they prepared for them, asked each other the same questions, and then came to expect me to ask them. Our classroom very quickly developed a culture of collaborative inquiry, in which the students *expected* to be challenged.

I have been lucky enough to work with elementary, middle, and high schools over the last 12 months as they look to embed a culture of challenge and exploratory talk in classrooms. They have developed a number of strategies to encourage their students to think collaboratively and explore concepts through dialogue. One of the aims has been to develop questioning that encourages a deeper level of cognitive processing. Figure 12 shows a classroom with a prompt sheet on a student's desk to support the development of extended questioning sequences.

▶ **Figure 12: A questioning prompt sheet in use in West Aurora District 129.**

Having looked at the questioning prompt sheet in Figure 11, which questions might you want to try asking with your students? If you used those questions with your students:

- **What answers did you *expect* your students to give?**

- **What responses did you *get* from your students?**

- **For how long did each of the students talk when they gave you their answers?**

Just remember, these are not magic questions—by themselves they will not make the students 'think': they are prompts to help build a sequence of questions that will keep your students exploring their understanding and skills, so the prompt sheet certainly shouldn't be used as a replacement for good preparation.

Take another few moments to look at the prompt sheet (Figure 11). You have probably spotted some questions on there that you already use a lot. There will also be some that you don't use very often, or perhaps a few that you haven't thought to use at all. Whichever way, the prompt sheet is simply to aid your planning and ensure that when you are in the heat of the lesson, you don't forget some of the questions that you might not normally ask.

3.8 • REVIEW

Whatever your starting point, you can develop questioning sequences that engage your students in thinking more deeply and thus help them develop better language to express their learning and understanding. Creating more effective questioning sequences requires deliberate preparation to do well, and sometimes, because encouraging others to explore their thinking is not natural conversation, we need prompts to support our practice.

In this chapter, we have covered the following main points:

i. Questions will often emerge naturally out of what you have said, read, or done. Ask these questions (no matter how they are phrased) as they can *initiate* longer sequences of questioning.

ii. We can plan more successfully for our questioning sequences if we anticipate what the students are likely to say in response to our questioning.

iii. The key purpose of the Explore step is typically to:

   a. Ask the students to think and reflect.

   b. Encourage the students to voice *reasons*, *opinions*, and *perceptions*.

   c. Share participation in the conversation more equally between and among your students.

iv. The funnelling technique is a planning tool to carefully consider the questioning sequence in advance of the lesson.

v. The funnelling sequence complements the I-R-Explore sequence and uses an Initiate, Explain, and Extend structure to build from your students' first response.

vi. Planning questioning sequences improves students' thinking, learning, and engagement.

vii. Funnelling can be used to open up a dialogue to explore understanding and then be inverted to narrow down to a conclusion or establish a current standpoint.

viii. The Explore step, including Explain and Extend, is not a 'natural' way to communicate: it needs to be learnt, developed, and planned for. Planning your questioning and using a prompt sheet ensures that questioning with the intent to explore is more likely to happen.

ix. Improving questioning takes practice, patience, and skill in a school environment that welcomes risk, mistakes, and professional reflection on practice.

3.9 • REFLECTION

i. Try planning a sequence of questioning from Initiate to Extend using the funnelling technique.

ii. Reflect on the success of your questioning by asking yourself:

   a. Did I get the response I was expecting from the students?

   b. Did my second and third questions build on the students' last responses?

   c. Would I have asked those questions naturally if I hadn't planned them in advance?

iii. Use the prompt sheet provided in Figure 11 to scaffold your own development in questioning.

iv. Reflect on:

   a. Which questions are new to you?

   b. What impact did each question have on your students' thinking and learning?

   c. Which questions would you remove from or add to the prompt sheet to make it your own?

v. Offer the students the same questioning prompt sheet as a scaffold to create a collaborative culture of inquiry.

> Advances are made by answering questions.
> Discoveries are made by questioning answers.
>
> —Bernard Haisch

QUESTIONING FLOW

In this chapter, we will explore the idea of questioning flow—that is, making your questioning sequences more natural and more incisive, from initiating first responses to drawing in more voices, challenging thinking, and moving toward the learning goal.

So far, we have focussed on planning questioning sequences that scaffold into the Explore step and create a culture of high expectations. The purpose of the questioning has been to initiate the dialogue and then encourage your students to go beyond their first response, to develop a language for thinking and for the subject.

As we begin to challenge your students' thinking further, your questioning sequences will need to extend, both in time (how long your questioning sequences run for in a meaningful way) and in breadth (how many students you draw in to the thinking).

Thinking ahead to the dialogue is still essential good practice, and you should always consider the dialogue beforehand, even after years of practice, because the more you plan for questioning and think about your questioning moves, the more natural it becomes and the less you need to prepare the early questions, leaving you free to consider the more challenging elements of the dialogue to follow.

When your questioning leads from the students' first response, draws out their thinking, and generates challenge in a smooth and natural way, I call that being 'in flow'. Questioning in flow looks smooth and effortless, bouncing between students with purpose and energetic focus, creating a sense of mental drama and engagement.

Questioning sequences in flow are a joy to observe and even more exciting to be an active part of.

Perhaps counterintuitively, the best way to increase flow is to slow down! If you want to feel confident in guiding your students through your questioning—and you want your students to have confidence in your guidance—then the key is to be urgent but unhurried.

If you have a lot to say, take your time. If you don't have a lot of time, say less.

When questioning, I like to think of the double meaning of *philosophical*. It can describe a study of the fundamental nature of knowledge and reality, or it can mean having a calm attitude toward difficulty.

To get your message across in questioning, it is better if both you and your students feel like you aren't rushing through your sequence: you should be calm in order to create space for thinking and for talking so you can explore the nature of the students' knowledge and understanding. Give yourself permission to be unhurried, but with the urgency of challenge and engagement.

I find that Pause and Paraphrase are two useful ways to keep my questioning 'sharp but unhurried' and effectively refine the Initiate-Respond-Explore sequence to create a more considered culture of inquiry.

Pause and Paraphrase are very well known in cognitive coaching terms as ways of questioning to clarify understanding and help the respondents think through their own ideas. They are often referred to as the 3 *P*s, as the sequence contains a Probe step (Costa & Garmston, 1994). For the purposes of this book, I am using a variation that integrates Pause and Paraphrase into our IRE sequence, replacing the Probe step with our more familiar Explore move as follows:

> Initiate
>
> (Pause)
>
> Respond
>
> (Paraphrase)
>
> Explore

The key for us in refining our questioning, and improving flow, is the addition of the Pause and Paraphrase steps into our IRE sequence before Explore.

Adding Pause and Paraphrase into IRE, then, works as follows:

(Intent: To get students to consider how history is passed down from generation to generation)

Initiate:	When you are old, what do you think your children will ask you to tell stories about?
Pause:	[Wait 3 to 5 seconds.]
Respond:	I think my children will want to hear about what we did as a family, with my parents—their grandparents—where we lived and what we did together when we were growing up.
Paraphrase:	They'll want to hear about your life at home with your parents.
Explore:	Why do you think that will be interesting for them?

Notice that the Pause step gives the students thinking time, and the teacher stays silent. This is one of our essential skills: Stay Silent (and Listen). As a result of the 3- to 5-second

silence, notice how long the student's response is. He had time to consider his answer before verbalising it to the teacher.

To add to that opportunity to rehearse language, depending on the situation, your Pause step could include an opportunity to turn and talk to a Thinking Partner for a few seconds.

You will find a lot more on the use of think-time in Chapter 5. If you want to explore the skill of staying silent (it's not as easy as you think it is!), then jump to that chapter now, and return here afterwards.

Of course, Pause-Paraphrase-Explore (PPE) doesn't only work at the Initiate and first response stage. You can continue it through the dialogue to get into your questioning flow and create a sequence that is urgent but unhurried. Let's use the same example as earlier, but this time I have included the full exchange, taking into account Thinking Partners and extending the questioning as the dialogue develops:

(Intent: To get students to consider how history is passed down from generation to generation)

Initiate:	When you are old, what do you think your children will ask you to tell stories about?
Pause:	Talk to another person and share your ideas [for 20 seconds].
Initiate:	So, what do you think your children will ask you to tell stories about?
Respond:	I think my children will want to hear about what we did as a family, with my parents—their grandparents—where we lived and what we did together when we were growing up.
Paraphrase:	They'll want to hear about your life at home with your parents.
Explore:	Why do you think that will be interesting for them?
Pause:	[Wait 3 to 5 seconds.]
Respond:	I think they'll be interested to know what it was like and how it was different to now. And because they know my parents, they'll want to know what we did that was the same and different. Like how we acted, traditions . . . like Christmas.
Paraphrase:	They'll be interested to know about the traditions you had.
Explore:	Is that something you are interested in knowing about your parents' childhood?
Pause:	[Wait 3 seconds.]
Response:	Yes, I guess. But then I suppose I know some of the traditions because we still do them now.
Explain:	Can you give me an example?
Respond:	Like, at Christmas, you know, when we all go downstairs together, and you're not allowed in the room until we're all there. Then you open your presents from under the tree and then have breakfast, and then come back and open the bigger presents. That's what we do now, and that's 'cause that's what my dad did when he was little.
Paraphrase:	So, Christmas is something that stayed the same. You said before that some things might be different.
Explore:	What might be different? What might change that your children would want to ask about?
Pause:	Talk to the person next to you [for 20 seconds].

4.1 • A REFLECTION SECTION

Take a moment to think about this questioning sequence. Read it aloud with a colleague or friend, to get a better sense of how it happened in the lesson.

- What do you notice about the flow of the dialogue in this example?

- What is the purpose of the think-time in this example? How is it used, and how does it impact on the students' responses?

- How do you think the Paraphrase step contributes to the flow of the questioning?

- What benefits might paraphrasing have for the students? And what benefits might it have for the teacher?

To carry on the example, here's the next response from a student:

Respond: We thought television would be quite different. The programs would be all new and have different people on. Maybe we wouldn't be watching the same things anymore.

Or it might be completely different and be completely interactive or something. So, kids might want to know what we watched or what our telly was like.

- Continue the questioning sequence: plan a Paraphrase step and an Explore step in the following table based on the student's response:

Paraphrase (what the students have just said)	
Explore (what question emerges from your paraphrase to keep exploring the idea)	

Don't forget—there might be more than one way to paraphrase the same response! And the way you paraphrase might well lead you to a different questioning step.

4.2 • PARAPHRASING

The benefit of paraphrasing is to make a link between what the students have just said and your next question. It forms the bridge between their existing knowledge and what you'd like them to consider next.

Paraphrasing also gives you some thinking time to work out your question. While you paraphrase, you are often unconsciously processing the next step. In 3.0, we looked at how we naturally initiate questioning, by letting questions emerge from the things we have just said, read, or done. Paraphrasing works in the same way: a question can emerge from what you say.

A paraphrase will undoubtedly contain a key principle within it. So use this principle to construct your next questioning move. For example:

Paraphrase: You said that a pet is something that *lives in your house.*

Explore: Can something that doesn't *live in your house* still be a pet? Like a rabbit in a hutch?

The key principle of what your student said is repeated in the question. It is the fact that you said what the student said that helps the question emerge!

Of course, there are always lots of possibilities for questions that you could ask using the same principle, and as you work with questioning sequences, questions will begin to emerge more naturally and smoothly. If you are not yet at that point, and are still practising your questioning sequences, then make sure you plan your questions in advance.

Take the previous example. If you considered the dialogue (about pets) beforehand, you might expect the idea that a pet lives in your home to come up. Based on that principle, design a few questions you could ask to explore the idea of a pet being something that lives in a house. That way, you are more likely to ask those questions when you get to the dialogue in the lesson.

Here are some options that might emerge from the same principle when planning:

Paraphrase:	You're saying that a pet is something that lives in a house.
Explore [options]:	Do all pets live in a house?
	What made you say that pets live in a house?
	Can it be a pet and not live in a house? [like a dog in a kennel]
	Can you think of an example of a pet that lives in a house?
	Can you think of an example of a pet that doesn't live in a house?
	Who else lives in a house? Does that make them pets?
	What other animals/insects live in a house? Are they pets?
	Why might people want an animal to live in their house?
	We have a pet that lives in school, not a house. Is it still a pet?

Paraphrasing a student's answer helps you create the next question in the sequence and ensure that it builds on the last thing that was said. As long as your intent is to explore, then your question should keep the dialogue going and form a natural bridge between what was just said and where you want to go next, adding to the flow of the questioning.

In this example, my colleague Steve Williams had been working on the qualities of good teamwork with a class of Grade 6 students in relation to Captain Robert Falcon Scott's ill-fated expedition to the Antarctic. Steve had the class agree on nine qualities that they would look for in a team, knowing the hardships faced by Scott's team. They wrote the words on cards and ranked them in terms of importance.

A PPE questioning sequence might run as follows:

Initiate:	Which quality do you think is the most important, and why?
Pause:	[Wait 3 seconds.]
Respond:	We have chosen the communication card as the most important skill in teamwork because we think that a good team talks to each other, so they can ask each other for help and tell each other what to do.
Paraphrase:	So, communication is important because good teams talk to each other . . .
Explore:	Does anyone else have communication as an important element of teamwork for any other reason?

In this example, the teacher's Explore step is aiming to get more reasons from more students in the class; the intent is to widen the viewpoint. You will see some parallels here with the funnelling technique, both in the way the questioning sequence is structured and in the way the questions have been planned.

Here are some other possible questions that you could plan to ask in the Explore step.

All of the examples follow on from the same student response as used earlier, and the words in brackets represent the questioning intent:

> Respond: We have chosen the communication card as the most important skill in teamwork because we think that a good team talks to each other, so they can ask each other for help and tell each other what to do.

Version 1 [further explanation]:

> Paraphrase: So you thought communication was important because good teams talk to each other.
>
> Explore: Did you have any other reasons for choosing communication?

Version 2 [clarification]:

> Paraphrase: You said that communication is about telling each other what to do.
>
> Explore: What do you mean when you say 'telling each other what to do'?

Version 3 [specific example]:

> Paraphrase: You're saying that communication in a good team is about helping each other.
>
> Explore: Can you give me an example of when a team might need to help each other?

Version 4 [presenting a different perspective]:

> Paraphrase: So you went for communication at the top.
>
> Explore: Did anybody have it lower down? [To the new group] Why did you see it that way?

Version 5 [challenging the response]:

> Paraphrase: You said good teamwork means telling each other what to do.
>
> Explore: So, if I tell you to clean up the classroom, is that an example of good teamwork?

Version 6 [the Scooby-Doo ending]:

> Teacher: I thought I knew what communication meant . . . and I'd have gotten away with it, too, if it wasn't for you meddling kids.

As well as creating flow in your questioning, paraphrasing has other benefits too. It is a powerful way to build rapport with your students: it shows that you have given what they say full attention, that you want to understand what they say, and that you value their ideas. This allows you to connect in a way that makes your students feel safe, which is important in an environment of high expectations and when you have the intention to challenge.

Paraphrasing is also useful to check understanding. By paraphrasing, you are modelling that you are trying to understand your students' ideas. But your students are also checking that you have understood them. This search for clarity creates active cognitive processing as the questioner and the respondent test each other's statements for accuracy. For example, if your student says, 'I don't think it is right to test perfumes on animals', and you paraphrase that as 'You're suggesting that animal testing is not right', then the respondent has to test the paraphrase and consider how well it represents his view.

'The paraphrase is possibly the most powerful of all non-judgmental verbal responses because it communicates that "I am attempting to understand you" and that says "I value you"' (Costa & Garmston, 1994, p. 49).

Paraphrasing doesn't always mean talking. It can also mean writing ideas down and capturing what your students say on a flip chart, screen, or shared document. As your students share their ideas, record what they say as bullet points (paraphrases) where everyone can see it. This again shows that you value their responses, and it gives you a very deliberate list of key principles that you can explore—giving you a good basis from which to develop your questioning sequence. As you write, keep checking for accuracy and make sure you are capturing their ideas as your students want them to be.

4.3 • GETTING IN FLOW

In classrooms where questioning is in flow, you will notice:

Fewer . . .	More . . .
• Short, single questions	• Thoughtful questioning sequences that are linked together to push student thinking
• Accepted first responses	• Challenging and extending of all responses
• Questions directed to the whole class, with few students responding	• Questioning directed to Thinking Partners or small groups before being shared with the whole class
• Questions that ask students to state small pieces of knowledge unrelated to the larger context	• Questioning that helps students to make connections between knowledge and ideas, to better understand concepts
• Questions that ask *what* students know	
• Questions with quick answers	• Questions that ask *how* students know
• Questions asked in a rush because 'there's not much time'	• Questions with extended answers
	• Thinking time, because the lesson is unhurried
• Questions limited to current knowledge	• Questions that extend understanding and language
• Activities to keep the students busy and in their Comfort Zones	• Planned questioning sequences that enhance the learning activity and guide students toward the Learning Intention for the lesson
• Easy work tasks	• Struggle
• Questions with no purpose	• Questioning with the intent to explore, think, develop language, and make progress

In this example, the teacher has been working with Initiate-Respond-Explore, funnelling, and Pause-Paraphrase. She has planned her questioning sequence to support progress toward the learning goal. Her Learning Intention is to help the students understand how different substances affect the boiling point of water. The Grade 5 students (9- and 10-year-olds) have a Bunsen burner, a thermometer, a beaker of water on a tripod, and a tray of different substances, including salt, sugar, and sand.

The intention of her questioning is to model scientific inquiry and encourage her students to think for themselves.

To prepare for the experiment, the students have boiled a beaker of water, and on the board, they have written down the temperature that it boiled at, and how long it took to reach the boiling point. It is unclear from the audio recording how many students were in the class, though it is useful to know that there appear to be around eight different student voices responding at different times through the sequence.

Teacher: What is the boiling point of water?

Response: One hundred degrees.

Teacher: How long did your water take to reach a hundred degrees?

Response: [Various voices shout answers out.]

Teacher: OK. A few slightly different ideas there. Let's have a think. What do you think might happen if we add one of these substances to the water and we boil the water again?

Response: I don't know.

Response: It will take longer to boil.

Teacher: Why do you think it will take longer to boil?

Response: Sand is heavy. So the flame won't get to the water.

Teacher: Won't get to the water? What do you mean?

Response: The sand will stop it getting hot because it's there [on the bottom of the beaker] so the water is on top of it and the flame hits this bit [the underneath of the beaker] where the sand is.

Response: The sand will get hot, but the water won't.

Teacher: So what if I put sugar in? Will sugar do the same as sand—will it make the water take longer to boil for the same reason?

Response: No.

Teacher: No? Why not?

Response: It's lighter.

Response: The sugar will disappear.

Response: It dissolves, doesn't it?

Teacher: It disappears or dissolves, you said? How do you know that?

Response: It happens in a cup of tea. When you drop a sugar cube in, it dissolves into nothing.

Teacher: Why does it do that?

Response: Because the tea is hot. And liquid? Maybe.

Teacher: So will it change anything in your experiment, do you think? Will the water take longer to boil with sugar in it?

Response: No, because it will just disappear in the cup.

Teacher: OK, so if it dissolves, it won't change anything. Is that right?

Response: [A few shout out, 'Yes!']

Teacher: Lots of nods. And what about the salt? Will that change anything? Will it dissolve?

Response: Hmmm . . .

Response: Yes. It'll be like sugar, I think.

Response: Looks like sugar.

Teacher: OK. Why don't you try it out? Set up your experiments again, but this time add a new substance. Write down the boiling point and the time it takes to boil each time.

In this example, the teacher used a range of approaches to questioning. Take a moment to think about it. Then read it through with a colleague or friend, or even with a few friends, and put on a show! Then reflect:

- **How would you describe the questioning sequence overall?**

- **Did you notice where she paraphrased?** *You could put a P on the script next to where she did so.*

- **How did she encourage the students to keep talking and thinking?** *Write an E next to the Explore moves she made.*

- **What do you notice about the different questions she asked? How did she flow between them?**

- **When were the students in their Comfort Zone and in their Learning Zone?**

- **What types of thinking are the students being asked to do, and when?**

After the experiments with the three substances, the teacher gathered the students again and began a second, planned sequence:

Teacher: What is the boiling point of water with no substances added?

Response: One hundred degrees Celsius.

Teacher: How long did it take to boil?

Response: [Various answers are shouted out, referencing those on the board.]

Teacher: So what happened when you added the sand?

Response: It took longer.

Teacher: Longer. And at what temperature did the water boil?

Response: A hundred [degrees Celsius].

Teacher: So it took longer to boil, but the temperature was the same. What about the salt? Did that take longer to boil?

Response: Yes.

Teacher: But what temperature did it boil at then?

Response: 105 degrees on ours.

Teacher: And the sugar?

Response: That was longer, and it boiled higher than a hundred . . .

Response: 103.

Teacher: OK, so what difference do these substances make to the boiling point of water? In your books, write down how each substance affected the length of time it took [to boil the water], and if it changed the boiling point.

Again, consider the approach to questioning that the teacher used here.

Is it the same or different from the questioning *before* the experiment?

You will notice that the questioning starts in the same way in each example but continues very differently.

What do you think the teacher intended with the questioning approach she took in the second dialogue?

Remember that the Learning Intention in the lesson was to help the students understand how different substances change the way water boils. With that in mind:

Did the two questioning episodes successfully support the students making progress toward that intention?

Why do you think the teacher employed two different approaches to the questioning process during that lesson?

Coming back to the idea that all questions are valid, and that it is the flow of questions that makes a difference, notice how the teacher initiates each of these episodes. The first question could easily have led to an Evaluate step after the first response, but she clearly had other ideas and wanted her students to explore their thinking and develop language to describe the process.

Once the students had completed the final written task that she set them, what questions might she have planned to ask next: to debrief the learning, highlight struggle, and cement the key language?

What questioning sequence would *you* plan?

You can see from the example sequences in this chapter how the teachers are moving from whole-class to small-group and individual levels. Questioning isn't best done in any one way: there are many different ways to question, and so a balance of these is always going to be better than any one way used too often. And as with all dialogues, questioning at the individual, Thinking Partner, small-group, or whole-class level still comes down to your intention in asking your questions in the first place. What do you want your students to get out of the sequence, and what questioning steps will you plan to get there?

4.4 • IT'S NOT ABOUT GIVING UP CONTROL!

Some teachers worry about whole-class questioning. There are two common reasons for this. The first is a concern that their students won't engage with the thinking needed in the Explore step. And the second is a perception that in extended whole-class dialogues, they are giving up control of the conversation, so it could go *anywhere*.

In terms of the first concern, we have already seen how questioning sequences are more likely to engage more students, because they have the opportunity to actively process information for themselves. When we ask for their views, stay silent and listen, and then paraphrase their responses, they feel understood and valued. Using Thinking Partners to rehearse the language needed for the responses also creates a safe environment for thinking for all.

The challenging path often looks more interesting for students than the easy path, so they learn to engage in a safe environment with high expectations.

In terms of the second concern, the Explore step is based more on the development of critical thinking than on the recall of information (though, of course, knowledge is essential to it), but this doesn't mean that you are giving up control of the conversation. The intention is still to develop 'understanding', or 'be able to', so exploring is not just a free-for-all; it is a well-planned, focussed dialogue that aims to improve understanding and subject terminology in context.

The perception of putting the students in control is reinforced in much of the literature around closed and open questions (closed questions are teacher-focussed and open questions are student-led) but is categorically *not true*. Control of the conversation is still in your hands: you have the ability to guide or steer the dialogue and open up (or close down) any line of questioning you desire.

Of course, you can offer more opportunities for your students to question each other and respond to one another's ideas *if you think it will have more impact on their learning*.

The more you develop and practise your questioning, the more skilfully you can guide the dialogue and keep it focussed on the intention, without undermining your students' ownership of the process. Your aim is to become a community of inquiry (searching for understanding together) in which you play the key role, rather than becoming a bystander to your students' musings.

4.5 • MANAGING QUESTIONING SEQUENCES IN WHOLE-CLASS DIALOGUES: GET THE IDEAR!

To help support the development of a community of inquiry in the classroom and create the sort of flow that makes whole-class questioning smooth and purposeful, it is necessary to think in a bigger frame than the short steps of funnelling and I-R-Explore.

Once we start to break down the Explore step into Explain and Extend, and once we add the Pause and Paraphrase steps, our sequences become more expansive, and a little harder to predict. No longer can the whole dialogue take place between you and one student, or a small group of students; you will want to start thinking about how you manage extended dialogues with larger groups, and successfully making your sequences inclusive of more students.

The IDEAR Framework is one I developed to help teachers manage whole-class questioning and create a smooth purposeful 'flow' to their sequences. This is the 'Big Picture' in which funnelling, IRE, and Pause-Paraphrase can work to support extended dialogues with larger groups.

The basic concept of IDEAR is to *initiate* the sequence (often this results in one or two keen students contributing!) before deliberately *drawing in* more students, expecting a higher number of participants in the dialogue, to encourage *everyone* to begin to think! Once you have pulled more students into the dialogue and the thinking, you can *extend* the idea, exploring reasons and opinions, to engage everyone in active, cognitive processing. Once everyone is engaging in thinking, you can then move your students into the Learning Zone by *abstracting* the concept, and challenging their assumptions, reasons, and first responses. At this stage, your students may even feel a little uncertain of their thinking, and will be looking to construct new understanding, using more refined language, so *reflection* on progress—and process—is key.

IDEAR, then, is five steps:

Initiate

Draw In

Extend

Abstract

Reflect

IDEAR is a way of trying to impact on as many learners as possible and create a community that is thinking and inquiring, so each stage of the framework is not intended to be one question long—you can spend as much time and ask as many questions as you like at each stage. Use the name of each stage as a cue for intent; how many students have I *drawn in* to the dialogue; is everyone *extending* their thinking beyond where we started?

Figure 13 shows how the steps work to create flow in relation to your questioning moves.

▶ **Figure 13: Showing the purpose of each stage in the IDEAR Framework.**

	IDEAR Stage	Purpose of stage
Step 1	Initiate	Get the dialogue started with the intent to *explore*. All questions have value, so ask anything you like, in any way—usually connected to what you have just read, said, or done. Take the first student response(s) and be sure not to *evaluate*!
Step 2	Draw In	Imagine you are waving your students to come closer to you, gathering them together as a 'community of inquirers' with all brains starting to think. Your work here is to welcome as many students as possible into your sequence. Make eye contact, encourage, and ask questions that are an open invite for *all* your students to engage with.
Step 3	Extend	Promote further thinking and go beyond first responses. Look for reasons, opinions, and new ideas. This is where you want active, cognitive processing as students share, and develop, language and understanding. Thinking words are key here: *describe*, *explain*, *compare*, *connect*. Encourage your students to keep talking and clarify thinking. Push your students to interact with each other, instead of always through you: *I agree with . . . because . . .*
Step 4	Abstract	Challenge your students and take them out of their Comfort Zones. Cause them to think and rethink ideas. Highlight misconceptions, point out assumptions, and create cognitive conflict. Imagine their ideas are being put to someone who knows nothing at all: Do they make sense? What doesn't fit? Give examples that create positive struggle. Put them in the Learning Pit (Nottingham, 2007) and exercise the brain muscle!
Step 5	Reflect	Define the current standpoint. This can include how far the students have come since their first response, how far they still have to go, and what they need to do or learn next to improve. It could be the presentation of final ideas or decisions—a consideration of the process and learning in it, including the knowledge, understanding, skills, and attitudes that can be transferred.

4.6 • QUESTIONING MOVES IN THE IDEAR FRAMEWORK

After your Initiate question, you can ask as many questions as you like in each step, and take as many responses as you like, so you are not rushing through to the end: remember—urgent but unhurried. Stay focussed on your intent and spend time where the potential is greatest to help your students learn.

Figure 14 provides some possible questions that you might ask at each step. As with the prompt sheet in Figure 11, these are an aid to plan your sequences, or can be used as a reminder during the lesson if things go further than you anticipated, or if you get different responses than you predicted. I have not included example questions at the Initiate step because, as discussed in previous chapters, all Initiate questions have value if the intention is to *explore* after the first response.

Compare the example questions in Figure 14 to the purpose of each step as outlined in Figure 13. How might each question contribute to the purpose of each step, and what other questions could you add into each box?

▶ **Figure 14:** Example questions at each step of the
IDEAR Framework.

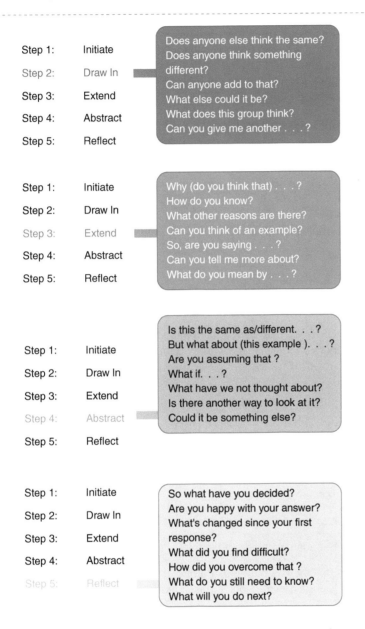

Step 1:   Initiate
Step 2:   Draw In
Step 3:   Extend
Step 4:   Abstract
Step 5:   Reflect

> Does anyone else think the same?
> Does anyone think something different?
> Can anyone add to that?
> What else could it be?
> What does this group think?
> Can you give me another . . . ?

Step 1:   Initiate
Step 2:   Draw In
Step 3:   Extend
Step 4:   Abstract
Step 5:   Reflect

> Why (do you think that) . . . ?
> How do you know?
> What other reasons are there?
> Can you think of an example?
> So, are you saying . . . ?
> Can you tell me more about?
> What do you mean by . . . ?

Step 1:   Initiate
Step 2:   Draw In
Step 3:   Extend
Step 4:   Abstract
Step 5:   Reflect

> Is this the same as/different. . . ?
> But what about (this example). . . ?
> Are you assuming that ?
> What if. . . ?
> What have we not thought about?
> Is there another way to look at it?
> Could it be something else?

Step 1:   Initiate
Step 2:   Draw In
Step 3:   Extend
Step 4:   Abstract
Step 5:   Reflect

> So what have you decided?
> Are you happy with your answer?
> What's changed since your first response?
> What did you find difficult?
> How did you overcome that ?
> What do you still need to know?
> What will you do next?

▶ **Figure 15:** An example questioning sequence using only one
question at each step of the IDEAR Framework.

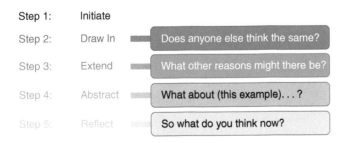

Step 1:   Initiate
Step 2:   Draw In   Does anyone else think the same?
Step 3:   Extend   What other reasons might there be?
Step 4:   Abstract   What about (this example). . . ?
Step 5:   Reflect   So what do you think now?

Using the IDEAR Framework helps to create an environment in which both you and your students understand the structure and expectations of questioning, which means that your students will not only engage in extended reasoning and challenge, but come to *expect* to be engaged in reasoning and challenge.

4.7 • A QUESTIONING EXAMPLE IN THE IDEAR FRAMEWORK

The example questions in Figure 14 and the single-question example in Figure 15 give you an idea of how the IDEAR Framework creates opportunity for more effective dialogue. Here's an example from a classroom with 5- and 6-year-olds, working on the subject of 'toys'. I have labelled the people speaking this time (using names beginning with A, B, C, etc, for the children) and labelled the script to show the step from the IDEAR Framework.

Intent: To explore the characteristics of toys; to be able to sort ideas and information

IDEAR Stage	Speaker	Script
Initiate	Teacher	What is a toy?
	Alfie	A car.
	Teacher	OK. Anything else?
	Bina	My doll. And this [Lego].
Draw In	Teacher	OK. Well, I have brought in three toys of my own to show you. First, here's Frank. He's my teddy bear.
	Children	Aw!
	Teacher	I have also brought Thomas [a plastic train]. And I've brought this drinking glass . . .
	Children	[Simultaneously] What? A glass? No!
	Teacher	What's wrong?
	Conrad	That's not a toy [laughs].
Extend	Teacher	It's not a toy, Conrad? Why not?
	Conrad	Because it's made of glass!
	Teacher	So, can toys not be made of glass? What about this toy, everyone [brings a marble out]? This is made of glass; is it a toy?
	Dara	It is, but the glass isn't.
	Teacher	Why not?
	Dara	Because it can break!
	Teacher	What do you mean, Dara?
	Dara	It could fall and smash.
	Teacher	So, if it can break, is it not a toy? What about Thomas the train? One of his wheels has come off. He's broken, so is he not a toy?
	Alfie	But he won't hurt you. The glass would hurt you.
	Teacher	But what about this bit of metal here where the wheel came off. If I touch it . . . ouch! It hurts. So is something broken not a toy? Talk to your Thinking Partner and decide [in 20 seconds].

IDEAR Stage	Speaker	Script
	Teacher	So, what do you think—is it a toy if it's broken?
	Evelyn	I have a doll made of glass . . .
	Teacher	OK . . . [nods for her to continue]
	Evelyn	Well. It's a glass doll [really meaning china]. My mum puts it up on a high shelf . . . so I can't touch it. I'm not allowed to play with it, in case I break it.
	Frodi	That's what we said!
	Teacher	You have a glass doll too, Frodi?
	Frodi	No! We said you play with it. If it's a toy, you play with it.
Abstract	Teacher	Did anyone else say that? Is a toy something you play with?
	Children	*Yes!* [said with lots of nods and smiles].
	Teacher	OK. But I'm looking at Ganya here. I've been watching Ganya play with her hair, see? Is hair a toy if it's something you play with?
	Children	[Slightly uncomfortably] *No!*
	Teacher	Why not?
	Hye	Because it's soft.
	Teacher	What is?
	Hye	Her hair! It's soft!
	Teacher	So is Frank [the teddy bear]. He's soft. So is he a toy?
	Children	*Yes!*
	Teacher	So toys can be soft. What else makes something a toy? Talk to your Thinking Partner and decide [in 20 seconds].
Reflect	Teacher	OK, what did you decide a toy is? I'm going to write your ideas on the board as you shout them out.
	Children [various]:	Something you play with
		Something for children
		It won't hurt you
		You have to look after them and tidy them away
		They can be soft and cuddly
		Your favourite things
		They're for fun
		You keep them at home
		They're special
		You get them for Christmas

Compare these responses to the students' first thoughts (a car, a doll). There is more language, more nuance, and more understanding, albeit a little uncertain understanding at this point.

To build understanding, the teacher then set up an activity for the children and asked them to go and find things in the classroom that they thought were toys, and things in the classroom that they thought were not toys. The children were asked to find one thing each and then, with their Thinking Partner, place them into one of two hoops on the floor, labelled Toys and Not Toys.

This added to the reflection and created an interesting moment when one pair brought a spatula across and couldn't place it in a hoop.

Reflect

Teacher	What's the trouble, Ismay?
Ismay	We found this in the play kitchen over there, but I don't know where it goes.
Teacher	Why not?
Ismay	Because it's a toy in the kitchen. But my mum has one at home and it's proper, to cook with. It's not a toy.
Teacher	So what could you do with it? I'll leave you two for a moment to decide and see what you come up with [steps to one side, leaving the two girls to talk].
Teacher [seeing movement]	What have you decided to do with it?
Kendra	We've made a new hoop that's both. It's a toy *and* it's not a toy!

Following this, the rest of the students were called over to have a look at the new hoop. They went on to reflect further, moving any 'toys' and 'not toys' they thought might be in the wrong place, and going searching for other examples of items that could go in the middle hoop.

If you were to find yourself in a similar situation, it can also be useful to clarify understanding by asking the children to come up with a new name for the middle hoop that they think will describe the items in it more accurately than Toys and Not Toys—for example, Tools You Can Also Play With.

4.8 • IMPACT OF THE IDEAR FRAMEWORK

With extended questioning sequences like these, you can see how they take time to establish and to work through in the lesson. As you extend your questioning sequences in this way, it is worth considering the impact on your students. You can look for clues in the change of language used, changing attitudes to challenge, and more clear reasoning; and ask your students, too: What do they find helpful about your questioning? How does the act of processing information and ideas work for them? What is it like to have to work it out for yourself?

In teaching and learning terms, we sometimes refer to this kind of questioning as 'the students working harder than the teacher!' It's not quite true to say that, as making the right questioning moves and staying focussed is a demanding task. But the idea is a good one that we shouldn't do all the work for the students; we should encourage them to think more for themselves: learn it, rather than be taught it.

Here are some thoughts on the IDEAR Framework and its possible impact on your students:

	IDEAR	Intent	Impact
Step 1	Initiate	Get the dialogue started with the intent to *explore*.	Now know the theme; a few contributors; many students will wait to see what happens after the first response, before committing to the dialogue.
Step 2	Draw In	Invite all your students into a 'community of inquiry' with all contributions welcome.	Students realise that you want many possible answers; early thoughts; simple responses; possible lack of clarity; uncertainty about why this is important; feeling valued; learning the expectation.
Step 3	Extend	Promote further thinking and go beyond first responses. Look for reasons, opinions, and new ideas.	Opportunity to think together with others and rehearse language; recognise that the theme has meaning for them; opportunity to agree/disagree; accessing knowledge in their own way, on their own terms, and in their own language.
Step 4	Abstract	Challenge your students and take them out of their Comfort Zones to create positive struggle.	Thinking more urgently and with more care; trying to connect understanding and examples together; needing the support of others; engaged for their own sake; start to think more about how to learn it as well as what to learn; need a new language to express nuances.
Step 5	Reflect	How far have they come since their first response, final ideas, or decisions and transfer?	Value the progress they have made; know where they are now (current standpoint); can identify next steps to continue making progress; feeling of self-efficacy.

As with any process that is presented on a page, the IDEAR Framework can look linear, as if you have to follow the steps in a certain order. Of course, you can do that if you wish, and it will work well, because fundamentally the five steps in increasing numerical order will create a smooth flow that will have a powerful impact on your students' thinking. You only need to look at the example transcript earlier in the chapter to see that. But if you want to extend your questioning sequences even further, then you can jump back and forth at any time between any of the steps (perhaps with the exception of Initiate!).

You could, for example:

Initiate

Draw In

Abstract

Extend

Abstract

Reflect

Draw In

Extend

Reflect

There is no one rule. But, starting out, it is worth planning your questioning sequences to follow the five steps of IDEAR first, and then play with the order as you get used to it.

In the Explore phase, your questioning will largely focus on the Draw In and Extend steps as you apply strategies like funnelling and PPE. In the next chapter, we are going to focus in detail on the Abstract step and share some advanced questioning techniques that have the intention to challenge!

4.9 • REVIEW

In this chapter, we have used the IDEAR Framework to manage whole-class dialogues and improve our questioning flow. When you have a clear structure and purpose for extended dialogues, it is much easier to create incisive challenge and ask the sorts of question that elicit the best thinking from your students.

i. The IDEAR Framework breaks down the questioning sequence into five steps. These steps give you a smaller chunk to focus on at one time in terms of your intent and your planning.

ii. The five steps of the framework are:

- Initiate
- Draw In
- Extend
- Abstract
- Reflect

iii. Using Pause and Paraphrase is a good way to build flow. These steps link each response to the last question so that your students can follow easily as the dialogue builds, and they create a good rapport with your students. Paraphrasing is particularly strong for this and has the added benefit of framing your next question for you.

iv. Pause allows thinking time for your students, and for you, to rehearse language, process ideas, and therefore contribute more readily to the dialogue.

4.10 • REFLECTION

Go back to the script from the science lesson we saw in Section 4.2. Compare it with the steps of the IDEAR Framework.

What do you notice?

How does the teacher draw other students into the dialogue, or leave openings for others to take part?

How does she extend their thinking?

In what ways did she abstract the concept: How did she search for same and different, for example?

She uses her questioning sequence to reflect. How does she get the students to reflect? What progress do you think her students might have made based on the questioning sequence you can see?

i. Now that you are well versed in the funnelling technique, try adding Pause and Paraphrase to your repertoire: Initiate-Pause-Respond-Paraphrase-Explore.

Video record yourself using Pause and Paraphrase and refine how you use it.

How long do you typically pause for? Can you try extending to 5 seconds?

What is the impact of that pause?

How does it benefit your students, how does it benefit you?

ii. How often do you paraphrase?

Try deliberately paraphrasing in a lesson.

What is difficult to do, and why?

How does it help contribute to the construction of your next question?

What is the impact on your students when you paraphrase?

iiii. Plan a sequence of questions using the IDEAR Framework.

Start by using each step separately and plan a few questions you could use in each one. Then link them together until you have a full sequence.

Try your sequence out, not forgetting to pause and paraphrase.

iv. Once you've tried your sequence out, consider the flow.

How smooth was it?

How well did you draw in your students to engage in the inquiry?

How well did you use your Explain and Extend questions during the Explore step?

How well did you challenge the students during the Abstract phase? Did you manage to provide examples that didn't fit with their current thinking, or make connections they hadn't seen before?

Silence in itself is rich. It is exclusive and luxurious. A key to unlock new ways of thinking. I don't regard it as a renunciation or something spiritual, but rather as a practical resource for living a richer life.

—Erling Kagge (2017, p. 35)

STAY SILENT (AND LISTEN)

5

In the last chapter, we looked at the importance of questioning in encouraging students to expect to be challenged, and to have opportunity to inquire. We have also shown how questioning is an effective way to engage students in active, cognitive processing.

5.0 • LESS TIME TO PROCESS MEANS LESS IMPACT

Not all questioning is effective, despite being used a lot. Or, I should probably correct myself there and say that '*questions* are used a lot'. In fact, questions are perhaps overused!

According to the research of Mary Budd Rowe (1972), a teacher will ask on average more than 400 questions per day. Four hundred! That's a *lot* of questions. If you were invited to complete a questionnaire that included more than 400 questions, how eager would you be to get started?

And yet, Rowe's research has been repeated many times over since 1972, and results remain consistent: those 400+ questions, spaced evenly throughout the school day, would mean that students are typically asked a question every 43 seconds!

But even with this quantity of questions being asked, they are not having the impact on students' thinking that we might expect: reports of increased achievement from so-called higher-order questions is at best inconsistent, and at worst sometimes less than the use of so-called lower-order questions (Marzano & Simms, 2014)! *More questions* do not improve student learning or thinking.

A key reason for this is that, after asking a question, the typical amount of 'thinking time' a student gets before the teacher takes the first response is around 0.8 seconds. Yes, you read that correctly: 0.8 seconds of thinking time! Less than one second for a student to work out a response before someone else shouts out an answer or the teacher gives a hint, asks a supplementary question, or even gives the answer himself!

And with only 0.8 seconds to think of an answer, it is perhaps to be expected that students don't talk for very long when giving answers either; the average length of a student response is only 1.3 seconds! In effect, from the time a teacher has finished asking the Initiate question, it is just 2.1 seconds before the student's involvement is over.

So questioning, like feedback and dialogue, is not simply about doing more of it. Our real focus should not be on whether we are asking questions, or how many questions we ask, or even what type of questions we ask; rather, we should be focussing on what the *impact* of our question*ing* is on student learning, and ensure that it is effective not only in eliciting responses, but in giving time for thinking too.

This is a timely reminder of the importance of our core elements of effective questioning:

1. Know Your Intent
2. Plan Your Questioning
3. Stay Silent (and Listen)

In this chapter, we want to focus on the third of these essential skills: Stay Silent (and Listen). This might sound like an odd thing to suggest as a skill to improve questioning, but I would actually go as far as to say that it might actually be the most important one of the three to master! Simply because, if you learn how to wait, you provide time and opportunity for thinking and talking to take place, and this will have huge impact on your students' thinking, learning, language, and engagement.

When anyone asks me, 'What should I do to improve my questioning?', my first reply is often 'Get comfortable with silence'.

So, although it may seem odd to devote a chapter to the deliberate act of doing nothing, this is a crucial element of the questioning process, so often missed out on even by teachers experienced in questioning and dialogue. You do not have to talk all the time, and if the students are not talking either, it is not a bad thing! Trust in the fact that good things are happening in the students' heads. For questioning to succeed, you need to have the intention to involve as many students as possible in dialogue and thinking. That is much harder for students to achieve if you are always talking!

In this chapter, we encourage you to get comfortable with gaps in conversation, resist your natural urge to fill silences with answers or rephrasing questions, and not be afraid to wait.

You are modelling a vital skill in that quiet time, encouraging reflection, and requesting that the students give your (and their own) questions serious consideration. There are actually many different ways of waiting, and many things you—and the students—will be doing, modelling, or signalling during the waiting period. Doing 'nothing', then, is surprisingly active!

5.1 • WAIT-TIME

Waiting has measurable effects on the quality of classroom inquiry (Tobin, 1987) as the time is used to develop ideas and language and encourage thoughtful participation.

The research of Mary Budd Rowe (1986) suggests a very simple way to improve questioning, which is to introduce 'wait-time' of around 3 seconds *before* taking an answer from the students, and then wait another 3 seconds *after* taking an answer from the students. The resultant effects in the classroom are staggering:

- The length of explanations increases fivefold amongst advantaged groups, and sevenfold amongst disadvantaged groups.

- The number of volunteered appropriate answers by students greatly increases.

- Failures to respond and 'I don't know' responses decrease from 30% to less than 5%.

- The number of questions asked by students rises.

- The scores of students on academic achievement tests show a tendency to increase.

And wait-time has benefits for teachers' practices too:

- Their questioning strategies tend to be more varied and flexible.

- Teachers decrease the quantity and increase the quality of their questions.

- They ask additional questions that require more complex information processing and higher-level thinking on the part of students.

Rowe's research has been repeated many times over in many different countries, and the results are consistent: in the typical classroom, students get very little time to process information, language, and ideas, in order to be able to contribute to a meaningful dialogue (Stahl, 1990). Thus many students disengage, and classroom questioning can quickly become the private preserve of a privileged few—the bright, the confident, the male, the native-speaking (Wolf, 1987).

Cotton (1988) was one such researcher who built on Rowe's original work, and she further discovered that students whom teachers perceived as slow or poor learners were given even less wait-time than those students whom teachers viewed as more capable. Observational research of teachers' practice suggests that one of the reasons for this is that teachers feel they need to manage the class and spoon-feed more in lower-ability groups but may feel less pressured in higher-ability groups.

The simple fact is that if you give students perceived as less able more time and opportunity to think, then the gains are higher than for those of higher ability; Rowe (1986) reports an increase in length of answers seven times the norm for lower-ability students.

For that reason, Stahl's (1994) update of the research coined the term 'think-time' to replace the idea of 'wait-time' to demonstrate that students are actively processing in that period, rather than waiting passively.

5.2 • THINK-TIME

This seemingly small alteration from wait-time to think-time is a powerful one in changing pedagogical practice in questioning, as it makes explicit the instruction to students that they are expected to contribute even when not speaking, by being involved in active, internal dialogue. Sharing this expectation explicitly can make the act of remaining silent much easier for you to stick to too!

Stahl (1994) explains the importance of think-time in this way:

Information processing involves multiple cognitive tasks that take time. Students must have uninterrupted periods of time to process information; reflect on what has been said, observed, or done; and consider what their personal responses will be.

It is worth bearing in mind that the length of think-time need only be 3 seconds. That doesn't sound like a long time reading it on paper, but it can feel like a lifetime in the classroom, especially when you ask a question and the room remains motionless! It can feel like a tumbleweed is blowing through the classroom; saloon doors creak in the background as the piano player in the corner stops playing and everyone turns to look at you . . .

However, the 3-second rule is simply there because this length of time represents a breakthrough point: it is after *at least* 3 seconds that a significant number of very positive things happen to students and teachers:

- Improvements in student retention

- Increases in the number of higher cognitive responses generated by students

- Increases in the amount and quality of evidence students offer to support their inferences

- Increases in contributions by students who do not participate much when think time is under 3 seconds

Having said that, it is not the case that 2.9 seconds of silence is bad, while 3 seconds is good, and 4.8 seconds is great! The key is to provide the period of time that will most effectively assist every student to complete the cognitive processing needed in that particular situation. It is about varying an appropriate length of time, not getting the egg timer out!

During Initiate-Respond-Explore, Pause-Paraphrase-Explore, and Socratic questioning sequences, there seems to be no threshold for think-time, and students appear to become more and more engaged, and perform better and better, the longer the teacher is willing to wait for responses. Cotton (1988) presents these improved teacher expectations from the adoption of think-time:

- Teachers listening more and engaging students in more discussions

- Increases in teacher expectations regarding students usually thought of as slow

- More flexibility of teacher responses

5.3 • THINK-PAIR-SHARE

To explicitly create think-time in the classroom, we regularly use the strategy Think-Pair-Share as a very simple reminder that students need time to think and to process their ideas and, most importantly, to practise the language needed to contribute to a dialogue.

After asking a question, give your students think-time (at least 3 seconds) so they can begin constructing a response independently. Ask your students to pair up with a Thinking Partner and talk to one another about their possible answers. After 30 seconds or so, invite them to 'share' their answer with the class.

- Ask a question.

- *Think* on your own for a minimum of 3 seconds.

- In a *Pair*, discuss your possible answers.

- *Share* your ideas with the class.

The advantage of this approach is that your students get ample opportunity to prepare and practise the language they need to answer your questions. By preparing internally first, then verbalising their response, then comparing their idea with another student's, they have time to rehearse the language and refine their answers. Your students will be more willing to contribute their ideas, more able to use the target subject language, and more willing to take the risk of being wrong.

You can use Think-Pair-Share alongside the funnelling technique. Here are the same open questioning sequences we tried in Chapter 3, this time with the Think-Pair-Share structure applied:

Teacher: What is 42 × 4?

(*Wait at least 3 seconds* while students use their think-time to work it out individually.)

Teacher: Tell the person next to you the answer you each got.

(*Wait 10 seconds* while students talk in pairs.)

Teacher: What are your answers?

(The teacher can choose a pair to share their answers or wait for a pair to put their hands up, or students can hold up their answers on paper.)

Alternatively, to stick with the planned questioning sequence in Figure 5:

Teacher: What is 42 × 4?   [*Think*]

Teacher: How did you work it out? Tell the person next to you [*Pair*]

(In pairs, students share their answers and how they calculated them, comparing their approaches and outcomes.)

Teacher: How did you reach an answer? [*Share*]

(Students explain around the class the different calculation methods used.)

The deliberate act of waiting during the Think-Pair-Share structure allows you to model good thinking behaviour.

5.4 • DON'T FORGET *THINK-TIME 2!*

In Rowe's original (1972) research, the findings pointed to two kinds of think-time: *think-time 1* is the amount of time between a teacher asking the question and taking the first response from a student, while *think-time 2* is the amount of time the teacher waits *after* the student has given a response and before the same student, or another student, reacts.

Most of the research and subsequent questioning guides have focussed on think-time 1. And so it is fairly common to hear teachers asking a question and waiting for a response, or using a strategy like Think-Pair-Share to ensure that processing-time occurs after asking a question.

It is much less common to see teachers pausing *after* a student has stopped talking; we instead see them jump in with their next question or an evaluation, sometimes even before the student has finished expressing an idea. Typically, the length of think-time 2 is also around 1 second (Stahl, 1990), so the same principles apply as in think-time 1: students don't have any time to process the answer they heard to the question, so they don't ask further questions or extend the answers given, but come to expect that any first response is sufficient to satisfy the teacher.

Extending this gap between student answer and teacher reaction creates:

- A wider variety of responses offered by students
- Decreases in student interruptions
- Increases in student-to-student interactions (Cotton, 1988)

Your students are more likely to elaborate on what they say if you encourage them with gentle prompts such as nods or phrases like 'go on', or by signifying they have your full attention through sustained eye contact. These gentle (often nonverbal) prompts for students to keep talking are referred to as minimal encouragers (Geldard, Geldard, & Yin Foo, 2016) and are a useful way to approach think-time 2.

Try to ensure that your encouragers do just that: encourage. Sometimes students can take too many nods or 'uh-huh' to mean 'hurry up, we need to move along'. Try to balance active engagement with being nonjudgemental (Geldard et al., 2016), to ensure that your students will not only have the opportunity to, but develop the expectation that they *will*, talk for longer.

If you can use think-time 2 to wait calmly and encourage your students to elaborate, many positive benefits are established:

- Trust in the relationship between teachers and pupils
- Time for pupils to look at the question from several angles
- Freedom to provide answers of substance
- Encouragement to speak their minds
- Shared responsibility for learning
- Increased student-to-student interaction and student-to-teacher responses

In the most effective questioning, questions can be used sparingly.

Reducing the number of questions, and planning those questions that you do ask more carefully, means that your questioning is likely to become more focussed, have more impact on learning, place higher demands on the students and the questioner, and increase cognitive and verbal function.

A Reflection Section

Video record yourself and see how often you are silent during questioning. If possible, watch your video with a colleague or friend and discuss the impact of your think-time.

- **Do you leave think-time 1 *and* think-time 2?**
- **How long do you give your students to think *before* and *after* asking a question?**
- **How often do you use Think-Pair-Share?**
- **How often do you use minimal encouragers (don't be tempted just to say 'a lot'!)? Look for evidence of the minimal encouragers you use. What do they signal to your students?**
- **What is the impact of these on your students?**

5.5 • A TAXONOMY OF CLASSROOM SILENCES

Think-time 1 and think-time 2 are both very powerful ways to encourage cognitive processing and active participation in students in the group. But there are many other times when silence is more appropriate than talk in the classroom.

Stahl (1994) identified eight categories of pause time—that is, times and places where silences are likely to occur in dialogue—and describes some of the characteristics, benefits, and functions of each for teachers and students.

These are adapted in Figure 16 to show how they can be applied in questioning sequences in Renton's Taxonomy of Classroom Silences. The taxonomy is designed to be a collection of types of silence—and their functions—to help perfect the approaches we have discussed so far, such as the funnelling technique. A clearer understanding of the types of silence you can use, and their purpose, means you plan for deliberate periods of think-time, and do not just leave it to chance during a lesson.

Figure 16: Renton's Taxonomy of Classroom Silences.

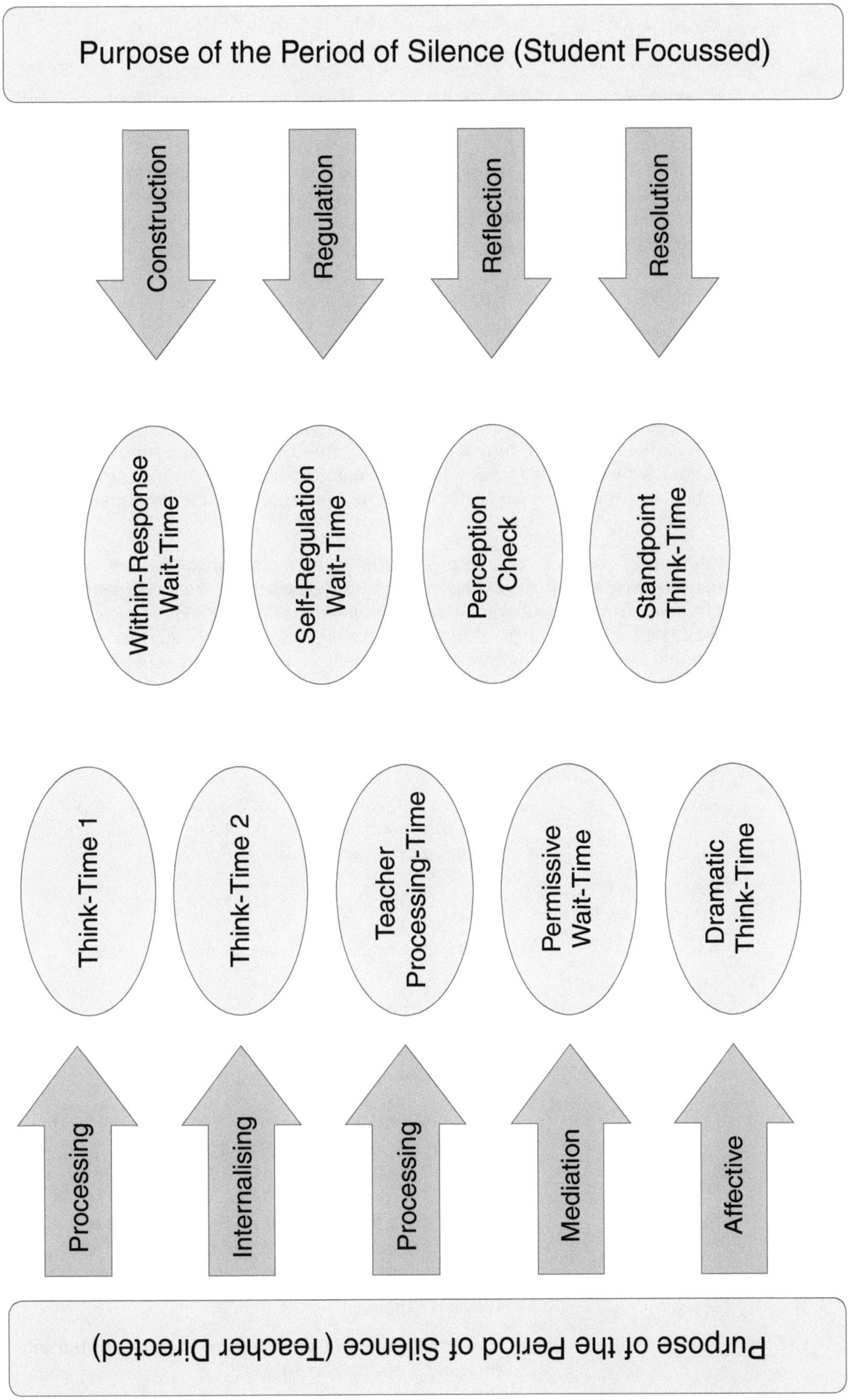

Purpose of the Period of Silence (Student Focussed)

Construction — Within-Response Wait-Time

Regulation — Self-Regulation Wait-Time

Reflection — Perception Check

Resolution — Standpoint Think-Time

Think-Time 1 — Processing

Think-Time 2 — Internalising

Teacher Processing-Time — Processing

Permissive Wait-Time — Mediation

Dramatic Think-Time — Affective

Purpose of the Period of Silence (Teacher Directed)

In Renton's Taxonomy of Classroom Silences, there are nine classifications, all of which aim to improve the outcomes of questioning. Sections 5.5.1–5.5.9 give a description of each of the types of silence, including some examples of how to use them in practice.

5.5.1 • Think-Time 1

We discussed think-time 1 earlier in this chapter, and in *Challenging Learning Through Dialogue* (Nottingham, Nottingham, & Renton, 2017), so it may now be very familiar to you. After you have asked a question, leave at least 3 seconds of silence during questioning to allow students time to prepare an answer and rehearse the language needed to respond. Think-time 1 is most effective during well-planned Pause-Paraphrase questioning sequences which contain sufficient cues to help the students construct a response.

5.5.2 • Within-Response Wait-Time

When questioning sequences deliberately seek longer answers, your students are expected to talk for longer than the 1.3 seconds reported by Rowe (1972). No matter how well prepared they are after think-time 1, students are likely to have to do at least some processing *while* they are speaking—clarifying, correcting, or extending their thinking—as their response may not be fully formed yet. This can lead to hesitation or repetition. *Within-response wait-time* is to ensure that there is no interruption from the teacher, or from other students, while the responding students pause to gather their thoughts.

It is common for teachers to interrupt students and prevent them from completing their answers, especially when the pauses are beyond 0.5 seconds (Stahl, 1994). When left uninterrupted, students often follow these periods of silence by volunteering information that is relevant or pertinent to the line of questioning. This silence has the additional benefit of setting the tone of trust, as the students feel they are being actively listened to.

Here's an example:

Teacher:	What makes it unique, Aaron?
Aaron:	Well, it's not just the fact that it was the first symphony to have the choral section in, but it's more about, kind of . . . the people? . . . erm . . .
Teacher [nodding and raising an eyebrow]:	OK . . . ?
Aaron:	So like their reaction to it was completely different.
Teacher [quietly]:	Right . . . ?
Aaron:	Well, the text says that the symphony created 'thunderous applause that Beethoven couldn't hear . . .'
Teacher:	Aha . . . ?
Aaron:	So in a way it's unique because it is so popular, and because it's . . . everyone likes it . . .
Teacher:	[Nods.]
Aaron:	And he wrote this thing that was new at the time, but then he couldn't even hear the applause, so . . . he wrote, like, one of the best pieces of music ever, but couldn't hear it.
Teacher:	[Waits 4 seconds.]
Aaron:	I think that's what makes it unique—that it's so amazing and yet he couldn't hear it at all.

Notice how Aaron's language changed through the questioning sequence. He clarified his thinking and then articulated a much clearer point at the end. The teacher used *within-response wait-time* to allow Aaron to clarify his thinking: she didn't interrupt or finish his sentences for him.

Notice too that she is still questioning. She used minimal encouragers to prompt him to continue. This is why we say that there is no such thing as a 'good' or 'bad' question: in the context of the questioning sequence, 'Aha . . . ?' is the ideal question to prompt Aaron to extend his thinking, yet you would never find it in a 'little book of great thinking questions'!

5.5.3 • Think-Time 2

We have also considered think-time 2 in more detail, so it will suffice to add a reminder of the importance of the 3-second pause *after* the response is given from the student. This allows the responding students to consider their response and if they have anything further to add, while also allowing other students to contribute with responses or additional thoughts. This period of silence is crucial for modelling the expectation that students can respond to students.

5.5.4 • Self-Regulation Wait-Time

This silence is to ensure that students are not interrupted during pauses or hesitations when they are making unsolicited, self-initiated comments, responses, or questions. As in *within-response wait-time*, this silence is to encourage the students to 'regulate' their ideas and clarify their language before continuing, and so lack of interruption from the teacher or another student is crucial.

Students who initiate a statement should be able to decide how long they need to regulate their response before they begin talking again. Typically, this is within 3 seconds, though of course it can sometimes be longer.

Waiting for students to self-regulate their unsolicited, relevant comments demonstrates a commitment to collaborative inquiry and models the behaviour we would expect to see from a community of inquiry. You can read more about community of inquiry in Chapters 11 and 12 of *Challenging Learning Through Dialogue* (Nottingham et al., 2017).

Teacher:	[Reads from a text.]
Ji-Min [interrupting]:	But I don't understand. Can I just ask . . . ?
Teacher:	Of course . . .
Ji-Min:	It says that the punishments they used back then were cruel and they weren't tolerant of crime or criminals, but then . . .
Cassie:	They're just saying that the . . .
Teacher:	Just a moment, Cassie. Let Ji-Min finish her thought.
Ji-Min:	Well, no, I was just thinking that if they're saying that they weren't tolerant, then . . .
Teacher:	Go on . . . [*Pause*]
Ji-Min:	Well, if they're not tolerant, but aren't they still criminals, so that . . . if you've done a crime, then you should expect to be punished, but . . .
Teacher:	[Waits 3 seconds.]

Ji-Min:	Right. So. Well, they make it sound like intolerance is a bad thing, but maybe when it comes to crime, it's not, even if the way they dealt with it is harsh . . .
Teacher:	[Waits 2 seconds.]
Ji-Min:	Harsher than now anyway.
Teacher:	So, you're wondering whether they were right not to tolerate crime, though the methods were harsher than today? [*Paraphrase*]
Ji-Min:	Yes, exactly.
Teacher:	What do you think, Cassie? Were they right not to tolerate crime, or are the punishments *too* harsh?

Here, Ji-Min raised an unsolicited, though not yet fully formed, question. By accepting the question and not allowing the thought to be interrupted by Cassie, the teacher demonstrated the expectation of inquiry: it's good to ask questions. This short exchange sparked a whole-class dialogue that ran for a further 3 minutes on tolerance of crime and the harshness of punishment in medieval England, referencing the text they were reading. As this was the Learning Intention of the lesson, the space to think and inquire added to the students' development of understanding and language.

5.5.5 • Teacher Processing-Time

This 3–5 seconds of silence follows a student answer, question, or challenge and is designed to give the teacher some thinking time before responding or taking action. You don't have to answer everything straight away; take a few seconds to compose your response or next question, and you will find that you are far more satisfied with your interactions than if you blurt out the first thing that comes into your head.

You could use teacher processing-time to refer to your questioning prompt sheet (Figure 11) before taking the next step. In any dialogue, students may well state an opinion, ask you a question, or seek clarification. They may ask for an example from you. Remaining silent before responding gives you some thinking time, and:

- Increases the variety of responses they receive from you
- Increases the likelihood of you throwing back another question, or counter-challenge
- Models the process of think-time 1 and think-time 2

5.5.6 • Perception Check

The perception check is a way to encourage students to think about what they have heard so far and create meaning from it. This period of silence is most commonly used during direct instruction or lengthy episodes of teacher talk in information-heavy sessions, but it is equally important during questioning sequences.

It involves pausing the flow of the dialogue and remaining silent while the students have uninterrupted time to reflect on the ideas and information they have heard from you (during direct instruction) or from their peers (during a questioning sequence). It is an opportunity to consolidate or assimilate learning so far in their own words.

During direct instruction: information transfer is often broken up only by I-R-Evaluate questioning sequences, and therefore creates little opportunity for processing the target subject language. The perception check replaces the I-R-Evaluate sequence and provides the students with opportunity to make sense of the information in smaller chunks, rather than all at once.

As a guide, for every 1 minute you talk, add 10 seconds to the next perception check. The 'Rule of 12' suggests that 12 minutes is the longest anyone can process information presented through talk without a break. So if you talk for 12 minutes, give the students a 2-minute perception check and Think-Pair-Share their current understanding. Ideally, talk for 3 or 4 minutes and give them a 30-second perception check so they can process more regularly.

This models the value that 'what the student learns' matters more than 'what the teacher teaches'.

During questioning sequences: we recommend that if the dialogue has lasted for 1–2 minutes, create a perception check for 20 seconds so that students can consider the range of ideas from you and their peers. This period of uninterrupted thinking will often encourage unsolicited questions from your students.

5.5.7 • Permissive Wait-Time

Permissive wait-time is literally to 'give permission' for your students to continue a dialogue. This latitudinarian approach means stepping back from direct involvement and allowing your students time to explore their own questions and perspectives in open dialogue. In this silence, it is not thinking time for individual respondents that you are encouraging but talk time between two or more students.

This means that your students might well add ideas to what the last person said, disagree with what was last said, or challenge an idea that was said.

Your role in this silence is active listening. You are not opting out of the dialogue to be a passive bystander, but listening for patterns, cues, clues, and examples as the dialogue builds so that you can rejoin the dialogue at the right moment to extend it further.

Try to rejoin with a paraphrase of something the students said that is on track and ask another question from there. This ensures that you don't undermine the inquiry and allows for the dialogue to continue productively.

Wherever possible, try to let the dialogue build, and use nonverbal cues to encourage other students in the room to contribute to the dialogue if it looks like they can: a point, a nod, a wink. You may need to intervene in the dialogue to reinforce the rules of exploratory talk, for example if one student is telling others that they are 'right', 'wrong', or 'stupid'. To ensure that you remain 'permissive' and do not shift roles from mediating to policing, correct the behaviour by using dialogue stems—'Remember, Mark, we say, "I agree or disagree with that idea because . . ." rather than "I disagree with *you* . . ."'—and step back to allow the dialogue to continue. Most students then just repeat the same sentence but with your stem in front.

Being permissive in a dialogue works more effectively when conventions for talk behaviour are established and shared as a class. This can include the following:

Convention	Example of the Convention
Dialogue Stems	I agree/disagree with their idea because . . .
Student Question Prompt Sheet	Why do you think that . . . ?
Rules for Talk	Don't interrupt while someone is in mid-flow!
Thinking/Command Words	Explain . . .

As your students become more skilled at managing their own dialogues with you in the role of active listener, they will begin to use some of the other silences during their conversations too—in particular, within-response wait-time and think-time 2.

Here's an example of permissive wait-time in action in an excerpt from a questioning sequence in an English literature lesson:

Teacher:	So is that what led [Macbeth] to kill the king?
Mackenzie:	I don't think so. I think that was more to do with his wife . . . she made him kill the king.
Shannon:	But don't you think he wouldn't have done it if it weren't for him already wanting power? Do you think he would've listened to her if he weren't desperate to be king?
Mackenzie:	No, she convinced him. He didn't seem that convinced before she went on at him.
Shannon:	He wasn't happy about it, right, but he knew what he would get . . . become king . . . if he went through with it. He wouldn't have thought of it by himself.
Quinn:	I think you're both wrong. I don't think . . .
Teacher:	Quinn . . . "I don't agree with this idea because . . ."
Quinn:	Oh. Yeah. Sorry. Right, I don't agree with this thing about it being his wife, because I think it was more to do with what the Witches told him.
Hakim:	The Witches? How did they make him do it? They weren't even there.
Quinn:	Well, they got him thinking about it. And that seemed to set him off thinking he could be king.
Teacher [quietly]:	Pru . . . ?
Prudence:	I agree with that. It *did* affect him, because he thought he was immortal then.
Shannon:	How d'you mean?
Prudence:	Well, that stuff about nobody woman-born can kill him and the forest moving . . .
Rainer:	Is he not just mad?
All:	[Laugh.]
Quinn:	He is a bit of a psycho. Do you reckon he was losing the plot?
Mackenzie:	Definitely. And his wife was a psycho as well.
Teacher:	That's interesting that you're getting into this idea of his mental state. Duncan isn't the first person he's killed, is he? How is killing Duncan to become king *different* to killing Macdonwald to become Thane of Cawdor?

If the student-to-student dialogue has been extensive, it can be useful to round off the dialogue with a perception check, rather than an extension, so that all of your students can debrief what they learned from taking part, or from listening.

5.5.8 • Standpoint Think-Time

In this step, you create explicit silent time for your students to summarise where they are now in their thinking or understanding: to commit to a current standpoint. It is an opportunity to reach resolution following a questioning sequence, even if only temporarily.

The students are asked to write, record, or verbalise to another student what their current thinking is on the topic discussed. By doing this after a questioning sequence (rather

than at the end of a lesson), there is the expectation that you will return to the discussion, learning, or questioning later and add to their current standpoint. Standpoint time often raises questions, misconceptions, or cognitive conflicts and so should be seen as a step on the journey, rather than the destination.

Writing, or in some way recording, their current standpoint is a way of demonstrating with students the cognitive progress they are making. Your questioning sequences should help your students move forward, and standpoint time provides the uninterrupted gap they need to recognise that progress. So asking them to consider what they thought at the start of the dialogue and what they think now, for example, is a simple way of reflecting on progress made.

The silence in this category always applies to the teacher but may also apply to other students if they are asked to record their thinking in writing. The length of silence can vary according to the time the students need to commit to a standpoint, but *at least* 1–2 minutes is ideal.

5.5.9 • Dramatic Think-Time

The 'drama' in dramatic think-time is created by varying the lengths of silence in a questioning sequence: sometimes cutting short the silence and sometimes leaving longer spells. The idea is to create suspense, uncertainty, anticipation, or wonder, all for the purpose of engaging the students further in the questioning process.

Varying the periods of silence is quite tricky and requires careful handling to get right, so as not to leave any students feeling bewildered. Think of your questioning as a foxtrot: slow-slow, quick-quick-slow! The shorter gaps of two or three rapid-fire questions can have the students engaged but struggling, then slow it down to give time for thinking and processing before moving the conversation quickly again into other avenues.

For dramatic think-time to work, it is essential that after every two or three quick questions there is at least one slow question with opportunity to think and talk. Without the gaps of silence in the slow questions, you run the risk of falling into rapid-fire questions that can disengage some students.

This method of chopping, then extending silences, works extremely well with the Socratic method described in Chapter 8, especially when using counter-examples. Because of the way that dramatic think-time creates positive uncertainty, it aims to explicitly develop resilience and challenge. This means that reflection after the questioning sequence can be as much in the affective domain as the cognitive.

5.6 • THE SKILFUL USE OF SILENCES IN EFFECTIVE QUESTIONING SEQUENCES

Figure 17 demonstrates when each of the types of silence described in 5.5.1–5.5.9 might occur in the classroom and how long the silence should last to maximise impact on students' cognitive function. There are also some tips on what to avoid doing in order to maintain the silence—even if that proves difficult to do. The 'Try to Avoid . . .' column should help you resist every natural urge to break the silence!

Figure 17 can act as a prompt, in much the same way as the questioning prompt sheet (Figure 11). We suggest that you use it as a guide to help plan your think-time and try to develop silence as a key element of your questioning. Before you start, ask yourself:

- Which types of silence are familiar?

- Which do you do a lot?

- Are there any under 'try to avoid' that you find yourself doing in the classroom?

Type of Silence	Points When the Silence Occurs	Try to Avoid . . .	Duration of Silence
Think-Time 1	After you have asked a question	Taking a first response too quickly; don't answer your own question	3–5 seconds
Within-Response Wait-Time	As the students are giving their response, they hesitate or pause while trying to find the words or phrases they need	Interrupting students when they hesitate; don't be too hasty to judge them 'finished'	2 or more seconds
Think-Time 2	After a student has responded to a question	Jumping in with an 'evaluation' (e.g., 'Good answer', 'Well done'); don't rush to ask another question	3–5 seconds
Self-Regulation Wait-Time	When students begin an unsolicited, self-initiated comment or question, and hesitate in order to clarify their own thinking, or find the words they need	Interrupting students when they hesitate; finishing their thought for them	3 or more seconds
Teacher Processing-Time	After students have raised an unexpected, unsolicited question or comment, directed at the teacher	Feeling that you have to answer quickly; don't say the first thing that enters your head; consider options	3–5 seconds
Perception Check	During extended instructional delivery; when you have talked for more than 5 minutes, or when an open questioning sequence has lasted more than 2 minutes	'Constantly moving on'; thinking that because it's been taught, it's been learned	10 seconds of reflection per 1 minute of dialogue
Permissive Wait-Time	Applies when two or more students enter into a dialogue, questioning and challenging each other; this wait-time is active listening, allowing the students space to develop their own ideas further	Jumping in too quickly to bring 'all eyes back to you'; acting as police; letting the dialogue go too far off-intent; being a passive bystander	As long as the students can sustain focussed dialogue
Standpoint Think-Time	During or after an extended questioning sequence; students identify where they are now, and progress made: 'This is where I started, and this is where I am now'; could be verbal or written	Summing up a discussion *for* the students; telling them what they have learnt; assuming they will all have the same concrete resolution	At least 1 minute
Dramatic Think-Time	When you need a change of pace in the dialogue; to create further engagement; when you want to change the mood of the room; when building up to a question that will challenge the students	Asking the same questions with the same lengths of silence; using the same 'pace' all the time; avoid using only one questioning approach	Vary between less than 3 seconds and up to 1 minute!

As you look at your own practice in questioning and develop silences that encourage better thinking, look also for examples of the progress students are making in thinking and learning as a result. You will probably notice that there is a link between the types of questions you ask and the amount of time you wait in silence. The more complex the demands you place on your learners through questioning, the more you can utilise silences in your classroom.

You will also notice a direct link to higher cognitive function as, when you ask questions, you are modelling a process that students can—and should—use themselves; so encourage your students to use the same silences, questioning strategies, and think-time to assess what they have learned and to develop their thinking and study skills further.

> There are few instructionally sound reasons for not allowing at least 3 seconds of silence. The teacher should deliberately and consistently wait in silence for 3–5 seconds or longer . . . [and] . . . should ensure that all students also preserve the disturbance-free silence so that both the students and teacher can consider and process relevant information and then act accordingly. This skilful use of think-time contributes significantly to improved teaching and learning in the classroom. (Stahl, 1994)

So, by the time you have practised using the prompts in Figure 17, you should certainly feel able to *get comfortable with silence*!

5.7 • REVIEW

In this chapter, we have covered the following key points.

   i. Get comfortable with silence!

   ii. Waiting just 3 seconds before and after asking questions has a significant impact on student outcomes and learning behaviours.

   iii. Waiting 3 seconds has an impact on teacher behaviours, too, encouraging more variety and more complexity in the questioning sequences.

   iv. Think-time is active waiting, ensuring that the students are focussed on learning during the silences.

   v. Use Think-Pair-Share as a structure to guide student reflection and to promote thinking about the questions asked.

   vi. There are nine types of silences to use through your questioning sequences, which are collected together into Renton's Taxonomy of Classroom Silences.

5.8 • REFLECTION

   i. Focus on the use of silence in your classroom just now. What is the ratio of teacher talk to student talk?

   ii. Try using think-time 1 and think-time 2 and record any noticeable differences it made to your practice and to student outcomes.

   iii. Try using Think-Pair-Share to encourage reflection and language rehearsal.

   iv. Use Renton's Taxonomy of Classroom Silences to plan the gaps in your questioning so that you encourage students to think and talk. Use the following table to record your experiences with think-time: which ones you used, how it went, and what impact you think you had!

Period of Silence	What You Learned From Doing It	Impact on Your Students

PART II
QUESTIONING AND CHALLENGE

I have divided the book into three parts. So far, we have looked at the foundations of improving questioning. In this, Part II, we will look at what we mean by challenge—its importance in learning and how we can develop our questioning with the intention of challenge.

Developing your questioning techniques can take a lot of practice. All of the tools, tips, and techniques we have tried so far can be used together or separately. As you practise with them, keep returning to each approach so that your questioning has time to mature, becoming more fluid and incisive.

Trying each technique once will not change your questioning habits or encourage the students to think more; you need to keep trying these techniques again and again until they become second nature and you feel like 'I've never done my questioning any other way'.

The more you work with each of the tools and techniques in this book, the more you will drop 'the rules' and each tool, strategy, or approach will start to blend together with others to form your individual questioning style.

In Part II of the book, we are going to build on those questioning essentials you have developed so far and encourage further challenge. Before we dive straight in and add more tools and techniques on top of those you are already practising, it is useful to consider the concept of challenge itself, and why it is so crucial to learning. As we develop our understanding of challenge, you can then refine your questioning sequences to increase the cognitive demands on your students.

So, here, we will focus on what challenge looks like and then return to questioning that promotes it.

Desirable difficulties enhance learning.

—Elizabeth Bjork and Robert Bjork (1994)

THINKING ABOUT CHALLENGE

This book has the title *Challenging Learning Through Questioning*. It is about using questioning to facilitate a process of more effective learning, which means both *making learning more challenging* and *challenging the way that learning takes place*. It is based on the belief that questioning encourages desirable difficulties.

Arguably the very best way to create this positive struggle is by using deliberate and incisive questioning sequences. Questioning can draw your students out of their Comfort Zones. This will help them to find their own ways past difficulties, solve their own problems, and express their understanding in new and more complex ways.

In effect, questioning is guided induction into the process of thinking. This makes it a powerful way to facilitate new learning.

6.0 • THE BENEFIT OF STRUGGLE

Thinking back to my very first year of teaching, what seems like many moons ago now, in a middle school (which is sadly now gone), I thought I had a very clear idea about what teaching was. I knew my role: to make sure that the students found out everything they needed to know. I would teach them history (facts, information, and dates); I would teach them geography (places, features, and map skills); I would teach them English (reading, writing, and spelling); and I would teach them mathematics (number, function, and formula). I focussed on everything I knew, and how I would pass that on to my students.

That first year was difficult (as it is for most new teachers), but by the second year, I had become more confident and more comfortable in my role. My teaching was more consistently effective. I was creating well-planned 'fun' lessons with exciting activities. And I thought I was dynamic, inspiring, and enthusiastic in my approach. By the end of that year, I felt like an old pro: well established and quite at home in the school.

As a new teacher, I was assigned a mentor—though I often thought of him as a 'tor-mentor'!—called Jim. Jim was 'old school'. He had been there for years. Some even suggested he had a hand in building the place. He had done everything and seen everything and knew everyone. He had taught the grandparents of the students we were now teaching; he was a 'community institution'.

In his role as my mentor, Jim would often come in to observe my lessons during my first year. He would watch the lesson, take some notes, and then give me some positive comments, a few top tips, and a pat on the back.

So when Jim asked if he could come to observe one of my lessons during my second year of teaching, I was perfectly happy for him to do so; why not—it would be just like all the observations he'd done the year before, wouldn't it?

But it wasn't.

The feedback he gave me at the end of that lesson changed the way I taught. Forever.

At the end of the session, Jim said:

> *How much did your teaching get in the way of your students' learning?*

At first, I wasn't sure what he meant. So I asked him to repeat it. And he said:

> *How much did your teaching get in the way of your students' learning?*

I couldn't answer. I felt very uncomfortable! This wasn't the usual easy feedback and laid-back, supportive comment; this felt like criticism! I asked him to explain.

As a reply, he simply described a short example of something he'd observed during my lesson:

Two students were sitting at the front of the classroom, working away on the activity I had set (a problem-solving activity using measurement). Most of the class were working quietly, but these two students had become quite animated. They were talking heatedly, scratching their heads, frowning, rubbing things out, scribbling again, and getting quite exasperated.

Then, I appeared! Swooping in (with Superman cape flowing), I came to the students' rescue! 'What seems to be the trouble here?' I asked in true superhero fashion. One of the students explained that 'they were stuck' on one of the activities. So I knelt down at their desk, picked up one of their pencils, and said, 'First, do this [scribbled a short calculation], then you can add this [scribbled a bit more], then just add these . . . and what do you get?' (the students shouted out the answer with big grins). With their shouts of 'Thank you, Mr Renton' ringing in my ears, I took to the skies once more in search of more struggling students to rescue, proud of my work in helping them get to the correct answer.

With this example clear in my mind, Jim repeated:

> *How much did your teaching get in the way of their learning?*

And the penny dropped.

I had come in with all best intentions of helping my students. I saw them struggling, so I went to rescue them so they didn't feel uncomfortable. To help them, I fed them the answer. In my desire to teach them, I had stopped them from doing the learning for themselves.

Before my intervention, the students were trying to solve their own problem. They had a go one way, and when that didn't work, they tried another. They were talking to each other—talking about maths, about solutions, about strategies. They were using their language to express their thinking, asking the questions that they needed the answers to, speculating, using trial and error, compromising, negotiating, trying and failing, and trying again.

And when I stepped in, they stopped doing all of that.

Of course, I'm not the only person ever to have done that, and I won't be the last. Many of us do the exact same thing: we all want to be helpful, and we don't like to see students struggling. But struggle is essential to learning. Without struggle, we are just repeating things we can already do.

It is good to struggle.

Struggle means we can't do it yet, but we aren't far away. Struggle means it's just out of reach but getting closer. Struggle is 'Once more and we'll nail it, this time!' Struggle is your first attempt at Level 2, immediately after you've cracked Level 1 . . .

Positive struggle is the gap between what you can do and what you want to be able to do; the tools are there—they just need to be sharpened and applied. With the right support and the right prompting, desirable difficulties enhance learning (Bjork & Bjork, 2014).

But, of course, we don't want too much struggle. If your students are so frustrated by the challenge and the goal is so unattainable with the tools they have that they give up, then we don't want to put them in that situation every day. So the trick is to time your intervention correctly so that it allows your students to struggle and learn for themselves, but provides the support and the prompting they need to improve.

So I asked Jim, 'What should I have done instead?'

A Reflection Section

- **Can you identify times when you have come to your students' aid too quickly or led your students to the answer to save them from struggling?**

- **If you had left your students to struggle for longer, what might the outcomes have been?**

- **What could you have done instead?**

- **What is the learning you could reflect on with your students after they have struggled?**

6.1 • HOW TO THINK ABOUT CHALLENGE IN LEARNING

To understand why positive struggle is so vital, we can look at Vygotsky's (1978) idea of a Zone of Proximal Development, or 'Learning Zone', which explains in a simple adapted model the process of learning that was happening in the example in 6.0.

▶ **Figure 18:** The Zone of Proximal Development; adapted from the Comfort Zone Model, after the work of Lev Vygotsky (Luckner & Nadler, 1997).

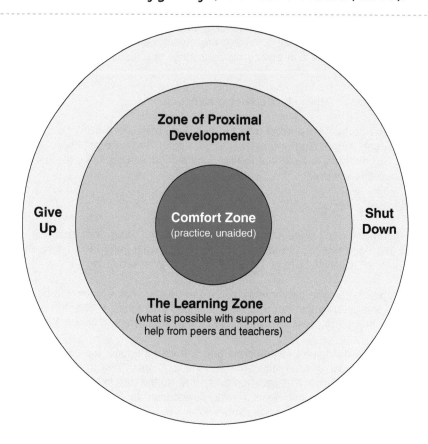

As shown in Figure 18, Vygotsky's model suggests that students need to come out of their Comfort Zone to take their next developmental step, but without being pushed too far, to a point where they don't feel that the goal is attainable, even with support.

The Comfort Zone represents a place of repetition and lack of struggle. It is what we are capable of now. In their Comfort Zone, your students can complete tasks unaided—that is, without the help of teachers, parents, or peers.

Being out of your Comfort Zone encourages new learning to take place. The Learning Zone is the next step of development beyond your current level. Here, there is positive struggle as you wrestle with things that are just outside of what you can currently do, make sense of, or complete unaided.

Being out of your Comfort Zone is like two sides of a coin. On the one side, being out of your Comfort Zone can make you feel uncertain, uncomfortable, even anxious or frustrated. But on the other side of the coin, being in your Learning Zone can be motivating, exciting, liberating, and engaging.

So to help your students develop the courage to work outside their Comfort Zone, you should provide them not with the answers, but with strategies, ways of thinking, and a language for learning. The better prepared they are to face difficulties, the more likely your students will be to choose to leave their Comfort Zone of their own accord. This is your role as mediator: to question your students so they feel pushed—but supported to be—outside of their Comfort Zone. Learning strategies is just one of the important inputs needed to help the students grow their Comfort Zones, allowing them to become more confident with increasingly complex thinking, as shown in Figure 19.

Beyond the Learning Zone is often where your students want to give up. This is because they are trying to engage with something that is beyond their next accessible step (it is not proximal development), so, even with support, they still feel ill equipped to learn.

If we consider the way that apps and electronic games work, they allow you to develop your skills and collect (often literal) tools to use during one level. When you complete that level, you can be said to be in your Comfort Zone: what is now possible without support. When you move to the next level, it becomes just a bit too difficult to do straight away. You can see how your skills from the last level helped, so you practise them, refine them, and try new things that allow you to complete the new level. When you complete that level, you have developed the skills for a slightly harder next level, and so on. Each subsequent level is just out of reach.

If you were to jump from Level 1 straight to Level 5, you would probably find the increase in difficulty too much, and therefore give up.

But on the other side of the coin, having completed Levels 2 and 3, if you then go back to Level 1, you can complete it without any effort at all. The higher-level skills and understanding you learned in Levels 2 and 3 will have equipped you to deal with the earlier challenges much more competently.

In this way, by moving into the Learning Zone, your Comfort Zone expands with you so that as your understanding and skills improve, you become more comfortable with greater complexity and sophistication in knowledge, understanding, and skills.

In Figure 19, you can see how learning through challenge helps to create the skills, understanding, and strategies that expand your Comfort Zone so that you become more comfortable with ever-more complex concepts, problems, and language. As your students' Comfort Zone expands, you will notice that anxiety diminishes and resilience increases over time as the students become better equipped to deal with complex thinking.

Effective questioning should facilitate the move from Comfort Zone to Learning Zone, providing a framework and a prompt to explore challenge, which moves your students

▶ Figure 19: The Expanded Comfort Zone Model shows the purpose and outcomes of working in the Learning Zone.

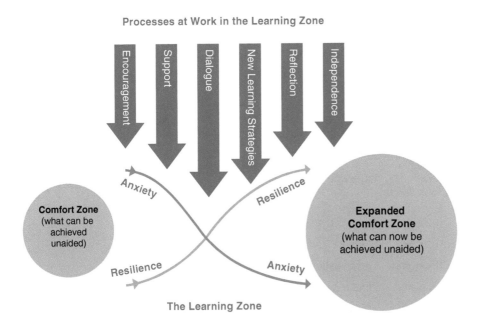

out of their Comfort Zone, but then also offers the reflective support needed to develop in the Learning Zone.

As we have seen already, questioning is a key vehicle to use to explore the right-hand path, which effectively encourages new learning through positive struggle.

> From a Vygotskian perspective, the teacher's role is mediating the child's learning activity as they share knowledge through social interaction. (Dixon-Krauss, 1996, p. 18)

6.2 • QUESTIONING TO ENCOURAGE AND SUPPORT STRUGGLE

So, thinking about this idea of being in the Learning Zone, let's return to my conversation with my mentor Jim in 6.0: 'What should I have done instead?'

This is what he told me:

> Next time, go to the students. It's important to go to them and let them know you're there; 'having a go and trying again' can quickly become 'failing and giving up', so go to the students and let them know you are there. But don't step in. Don't take over. Don't try to rescue them.

A simple question will suffice, like 'What are you struggling with?'

This is the opener. The students know you understand they are struggling, and now they know you are interested in them and they are not alone with their struggle. But, as with all questioning sequences in this book, it is not about that question (that won't make any difference by itself); it is what you do with the response you get. So listen to what the students say, and then follow up their answer, not with a solution; don't evaluate, but ask another question and explore their struggles:

- Why are you finding this one difficult?
- Have you done anything like this before?
- What did you do then?
- What have you already tried?
- Did you feel like anything you tried then was on the right lines?
- What have you not tried yet?
- What might you do differently?
- If you were to ask someone else, what might they tell you?
- Who else might be able to help?

As with the structures we have looked at throughout this book, it is about planning a sequence of questioning moves beforehand so that when your students are struggling, you go to them with a mindset of helping them learn for themselves, rather than going in with the answer (which is much easier and arguably more 'natural').

So a questioning sequence using the funnelling technique and Initiate-Respond-Explore might look like this:

(Intent: To allow the students to work it out for themselves)

Initiate: What are you struggling with?

Respond: This question here. We can't get the answer.

Explain: What have you tried so far?

Respond: We tried [this].

Extend:	What is it that you think doesn't work?
Respond:	This bit because [of this].
Explore:	So what are the possible things you might do? Have a think and I'll come back in a minute and see what ideas you've come up with . . .

With the intention I have—to support them but get them to do it for themselves—I have a sequence of questions planned that will encourage my students to keep thinking and continue with the struggle. The message I want those students to take away is that 'struggle is good', rather than 'I'm stuck, so I'll get the teacher to do it for me'.

I can plan my questioning in advance. OK, so I don't know what each student might get stuck on, but I can think ahead to the lesson and work out that if any of my students get stuck, there are questioning moves I can make to help them work it out for themselves. Having a series of questions planned means I am more likely to ask them in the lesson than if I try to make them up on the spot.

Notice, too, that the sequence ended with a prompt to action: 'Have a think and I'll come back in a minute . . .' That prompt lets the students know your intent (to work it out for themselves) and lets them know you are there for them. Once you've said that to the students, though, don't forget to go back to them!

If you go back and they are still struggling, have another question or two that will keep them thinking. On a second visit to a struggling group or individual, I usually try to make one of the steps in the sequence: 'Who else can help you?' This suggests a positive resolution to their struggle but also creates the expectation that it won't always be you who helps them. Getting help from other students is a positive strategy for developing independent learning.

Notice, too, that Jim's advice to get them to think independently doesn't say, 'Just leave them to it' or 'Abandon them', or suggest that 'If you do nothing, they'll work it out'. Because invariably that's not true. Learning requires focussed intervention. Jim's suggestion is that learning is best facilitated by questioning that prompts thinking, encouraging students to develop the learning strategies that they need to solve problems for themselves.

6.3 • KNOW YOUR INTENT: GET INTO THE LEARNING ZONE!

To get the best from your questioning sequences, your intention should reflect the outcomes you want to see from the students. You could phrase your intention as simply as 'to get my students out of their Comfort Zone and into the Learning Zone'.

This intention is like taking the Explore path, so you will want to plan deliberate questioning moves that prompt the use of subject-specific language, demonstration of knowledge applied in context and connected to other knowledge, skills applied, and understanding clarified or perspectives shared.

When you plan your questioning sequences, you can improve the flow of the dialogue by trying to predict the students' responses. Try to think about not just the answer, but how easy you think the answer was for the students to arrive at. If you think their responses are well within their Comfort Zones, then consider what you could ask instead to make them think differently or require more effort.

Have a look at this sequence. Picture your students and the responses they might give.

Initiate:	What do we mean by 'an excuse'?
Explain:	Can you give me an example of an excuse?
Extend:	How do you know something is an excuse?
Explore:	Can anyone add to that idea?

Explore:	So what makes it different from 'a reason'?
Explore:	If I say, 'I'm late because I missed the bus', is that a reason or an excuse?
Extend:	Can you give me an example of a reason that is not an excuse?
Extend:	Can you give me an example of an excuse that is not a reason?
Explain:	So what is the difference between a reason and an excuse?
Reflect:	What do you mean by 'an excuse'?

Depending on the age of your students, you might be able to predict their responses to these questioning moves. Or if your students are not the appropriate guinea pig, then how would *you* respond to each of these steps?

At what point do you think the questioning takes the students from their Comfort Zones into their Learning Zones? At what point might they begin to feel positive struggle?

Of course, I have assumed that the example sequence here is appropriate to the level of the imagined students so that the questioning doesn't make them want to 'shut down'. But it is worth considering the following intervals in your questioning as a means of supporting your students' thinking time so that they are less likely to give up when they feel struggle.

| Extend: | How do you know something is an excuse? |
| Interval: | Tell the person next to you how you know when something is an excuse, then we'll hear from three or four pairs. |

[Hear from the pairs.]

Explore:	Can anyone add to that idea?
Explore:	So what makes it different from 'a reason'?
Interval:	Talk to the person next to you for one minute and see if you can decide together.

[Hear from two or three pairs.]

Explain:	What is the difference between a reason and an excuse?
Reflect:	So, what do you mean by 'an excuse'?
Interval:	Talk to the person next to you again and write down your definition now.

We refer to these intervals where you talk to someone else as 'Thinking Partners', which is a useful name to use with your students, too. It emphasises your focus on thinking and demonstrates the value you place on talk and collaboration.

The purpose of these intervals is to provide a strategy for your students to feel supported in the Learning Zone. This allows your students time to think and engage in processing. Sometimes it's hard to verbalise your thinking when asked a question, so taking time to talk to a Thinking Partner is a good way to rehearse the language needed.

Of course, when your students talk to a Thinking Partner, it may not help to clarify their first thought. Getting someone else's perspective can often conflict with your own emerging ideas, so collaborating on active thinking tasks like questioning can also be a benefit by helping to extend struggle in a meaningful way.

Vygotsky's notion of the Zone of Proximal Development had much of its root in collaborative learning. The intent to share language and to share with others how we understand things is also key to explaining, extending, and exploring. So, as you plan your questioning moves, consider how it takes your students into the Learning Zone—practising and extending their use of language in context and developing and refining understanding.

One of the most helpful models for getting students into the Zone of Proximal Development to expand their Comfort Zones is the Learning Challenge framework (Nottingham, 2017).

The Learning Challenge promotes questioning, dialogue, and a growth mindset. It offers participants the opportunity to think and talk about their own learning and encourages a depth of inquiry that moves learners from surface-level knowledge to deep understanding. It encourages an exploration of causation and impact, an interpretation and comparison of meaning, a classification and sequencing of detail, and a recognition and analysis of pattern. It builds learners' resilience, determination, and curiosity. And it nurtures a love of learning.

Sections 6.4–6.6 have been written by James Nottingham.

6.4 • THE LEARNING PIT

I created The Learning Challenge (2017) to build on my earlier metaphor of the Learning Pit (2007, 2010). My intention was to give my students a way to describe being out of their Comfort Zone without feeling bad about it. Even though I had talked a lot with them about 'wobbling' being good because it means you're improving, and that mistakes are not something to be ashamed of because they are actually opportunities to learn, still many of my students felt bashful about admitting that they were struggling. So, I had to find a metaphor to describe this situation in such a way that there would be no feelings of guilt or failure. I have written about it in depth in *The Learning Challenge: How to Guide Your Students Through the Learning Pit to Achieve Deeper Understanding* (Nottingham, 2017).

The Learning Challenge is designed to *encourage* (literally: give courage to) your students so that they might better understand themselves and each other, so that they develop a sense of clarity and discernment in their thinking, and ultimately so that they become more aware of who they are and what they stand for. As one of my students once said: 'How do you know what you think until you've thought it?'

People can be said to be 'in the pit' (Figure 20) when they are in a state of cognitive conflict—that is, when they have two or more ideas that make sense to them but when compared side by side appear to be in conflict with each other.

▶ **Figure 20: The Learning Challenge: A Quick Guide.**

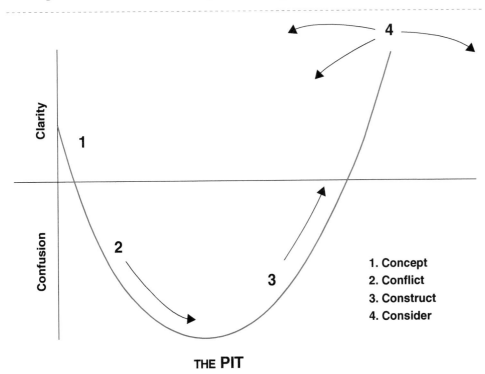

1. Concept
2. Conflict
3. Construct
4. Consider

THE **PIT**

Examples of cognitive conflicts that commonly arise in Learning Challenge episodes include:

- I believe that stealing is wrong, but I also believe that Robin Hood did the right thing.

- Children are taught that an odd number cannot be divided into two but three cakes can be shared equally between two friends.

- A liquid is thought of as a substance that flows freely, but sand flows freely and is not a liquid.

- Telling a lie is viewed as negative, but writing fictional stories is viewed as positive—so what is the difference?

- A hero is someone who takes risks on behalf of others, but then so do terrorists.

Wrestling with cognitive challenges, making new connections, and developing strategies to cope with difficulty mean we come out of the pit stronger, better learners; more reasonable; and with a better understanding of complexity. And that is the intention: to make learning more challenging and thought-provoking.

In other words: to take deliberate and strategic questioning steps that get people out of their Comfort Zone! Though this might seem perverse—particularly given the ever-increasing pressures of the curriculum—the justification is that through challenge, your learners will develop more resilience and greater self-efficacy, and will build many of the strategies they will need for learning in—and beyond—school. Being in the pit is where your students will think more deeply, more critically, and more strategically.

6.5 • THE LEARNING CHALLENGE STAGES

There are four stages involved in a journey through The Learning Challenge. They begin with a concept.

6.5.1 • Stage 1: Concept

It is important, at this first stage of the model, that you have identified your concept clearly (that you know your intent) so that when you plan your questioning, it guides your students toward the twin goals of first challenging, and then understanding, the concept better.

If lessons focus on concepts, then there is more opportunity for your students to wonder, question, challenge, and think. Facts are necessary, of course, but concepts more readily allow thinkers to go on a journey of exploration.

The concept can come from the curriculum, the media, conversation, or observations. So as long as some of your students have at least some understanding of the concept(s) you wish them to explore, then the challenge can work.

It is important to note that learners are not in the pit when they have *no* idea. The pit represents moving beyond a single basic idea to having multiple ideas that are as yet unsorted. This happens when learners purposefully explore inconsistencies, exceptions, and contradictions in their own or others' thinking so as to discover a richer, more complex understanding.

6.5.2 • Stage 2: Conflict

The key to The Learning Challenge is to get your students 'into the pit' by creating cognitive conflict in their minds. This deliberate creation of a dilemma is what makes The Learning Challenge such a good model for challenge and inquiry, reasoning and reasonableness. Focussed questioning with the deliberate intention of disrupting students' thinking is the key here. We will look more closely at techniques for this in Chapter 8.

Cognitive conflict prompts people to seek solutions or alternative answers, to try to identify the cause and effects, to ask for advice, to think about the relative merits of one approach compared with another, and so on. In other words, the point of cognitive conflict is to get people to think.

There is also a moral purpose to cognitive conflict in that it helps people to become more judicious and deliberate. It does this by using deliberate questioning sequences that prompt people to reflect more compellingly on their assumptions and inconsistencies. For example:

> Teacher: Is it wrong to steal?
>
> Student: Yes.
>
> Teacher: But what about Robin Hood? He stole. Was that OK?

Of course, sometimes it is easier just to leave these assumptions and inconsistencies as they are. Yet there are a great many benefits to be gained from examining conflicts one by one. For a start, it can be interesting and often quite funny to think about the many contradictions we live with. Second, it can offer your students an enjoyable way to learn how to resolve conflicts and make decisions.

It is also worth bearing in mind that the etymology of 'critical thinking' is *kritikos*, the Greek word for 'making judgments' (Harper, 2020). So, if your questioning encourages your students to analyse different sides of an argument with a view to making reasoned judgments, then you will also be familiarising your students with one of the central procedures of critical thinking.

6.5.3 • Stage 3: Construct

After being 'in the pit' for some time (and that 'time' might be minutes, hours, or sometimes even days or weeks, depending on the context), some of your students will begin to climb out of the pit. They will do this by making sense of their learning, making links, constructing meaning, performing the skill more adroitly, examining options, connecting ideas together, and explaining cause and effect.

Your usual classroom activities can support this construction of new understanding, and your questioning will enhance those learning activities by prompting and promoting language and thinking that will help your students emerge from the pit with a more sophisticated comprehension of the concept than they started with.

The purpose of climbing out of the pit is not necessarily about reaching *the* answer because depending on context, there might be many possible answers. Instead, it is about your students creating a more complex and thorough understanding of the concept.

Often (though not always) this leads them to a sense of 'eureka' in which they find new clarity. This sense of revelation is one of the reasons why the effort of going through the pit is so worthwhile.

6.5.4 • Stage 4: Consider

Students who have reached Stage 4 should reflect on their learning journey. They can do this by considering how they progressed from simplistic ideas (Stage 1), to the identification of more complex and conflicting ideas (Stage 2), to a deeper understanding of how all these ideas interrelate (Stage 3). At Stage 4, they are able to think about the best ways to relate and apply their new understanding to different contexts and to challenge others.

Reflecting on struggle can be a somewhat abstract concept, so it can be useful to consider The Learning Challenge journey as a scaffold for reflection and metacognition. As an accessible metaphor for learning for all, you can create a shared language with your students around the Learning Pit, to express both what, and the way, they have learned through a lesson or questioning episode. They can chart their journey, explore one aspect of their development, highlight a strategy they have used, or demonstrate progress in understanding from Stage 1 to Stage 4 (see Figure 21).

Questioning sequences for reflection on learning can use the four stages as a scaffold. As with many of our examples in this book, assume that your students will respond in between each question, and predict likely responses to build on:

Concept:	What were your first thoughts when we started talking about [this]?
Conflict:	What made you struggle?
	Why was that a conflict for you?
Construct:	What did you discover that helped you?
	How did that help?
Consider:	What would you do differently next time?
	What would that look like?

As you will notice, the questioning process looks forward as well as back. Reflection is not just something to be done at the end; you can reflect all the time you are learning and use your reflection to help shape your next response. So encourage your students to look ahead when reflecting as well as looking back, so that reflection, supported by your deliberate questioning, is purposeful and essential to next steps.

In *Visible Learning for Teachers* (2009), John Hattie identified students who are able to talk about their learning as one of the most powerful factors in improving achievement. He refers to three key questions that your students should become adept at answering—and asking—themselves:

- Where am I going?
- Where am I now?
- What are my next learning steps?

Used with these three questions, The Learning Challenge can become central to the way your students think about their learning. It allows them to explain when they have had difficulty and to support each other in identifying strategies that work, or that don't. These three questions, as a sequence, encourage students to verbalise the goal, consider their progress toward it, and identify what they should do next to get there.

Figure 21:

Review the learning journey with your students. Questioning them about each stage allows you to create a shared language for—and about—learning.

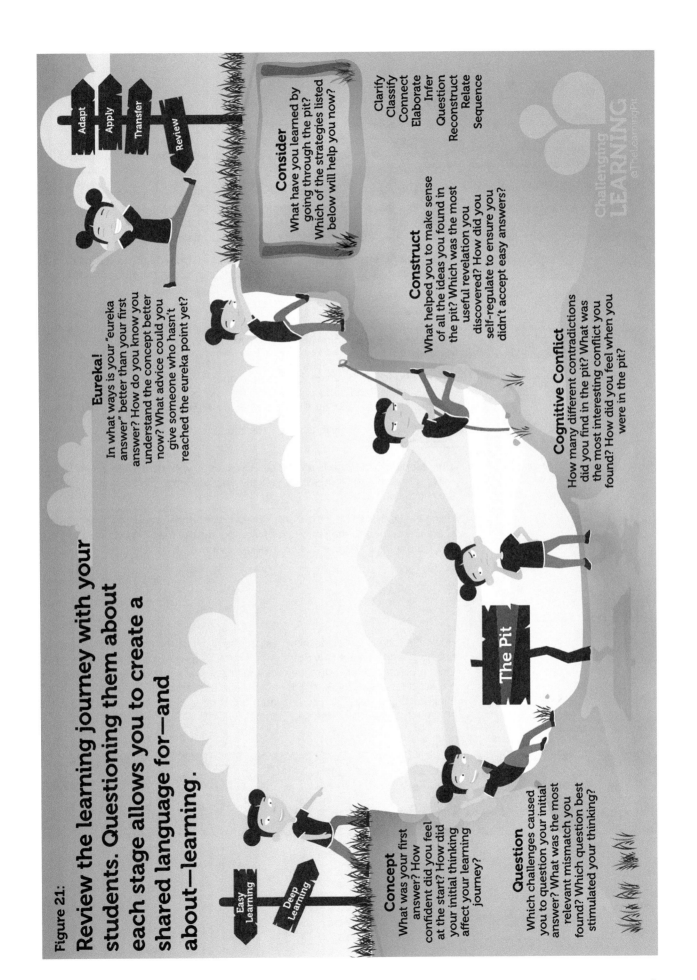

Eureka!
In what ways is your "eureka" answer better than your first answer? How do you know you understand the concept better now? What advice could you give someone who hasn't reached the eureka point yet?

Consider
What have you learned by going through the pit? Which of the strategies listed below will help you now?

Clarify
Classify
Connect
Elaborate
Infer
Question
Reconstruct
Relate
Sequence

Construct
What helped you to make sense of all the ideas you found in the pit? Which was the most useful revelation you discovered? How did you self-regulate to ensure you didn't accept easy answers?

Cognitive Conflict
How many different contradictions did you find in the pit? What was the most interesting conflict you found? How did you feel when you were in the pit?

The Pit

Concept
What was your first answer? How confident did you feel at the start? How did your initial thinking affect your learning journey?

Question
Which challenges caused you to question your initial answer? What was the most relevant mismatch you found? Which question best stimulated your thinking?

Easy Learning

Deep Learning

Adapt
Apply
Transfer
Review

Challenging LEARNING
@TheLearningPit

This chapter has covered the following main points:

i. Consider how much you are teaching, and how much the students are learning. Sometimes our teaching gets in the way of learning, and we can—often unwittingly—step in and stop our students' thinking, instead of helping them work it out for themselves.

ii. It is often helpful to struggle; it is a natural part of the learning process and requires effort. It is the role of the teacher to promote struggle and effort, rather than to 'feed the student the answer'. The teacher as mediator will draw the students out of their Comfort Zone and into the Zone of Proximal Development.

iii. Challenge is what we meet when we leave our Comfort Zone. Outside of the Comfort Zone it can feel uncertain and frustrating, and at the same time engaging and exciting. Get the students comfortable with discomfort!

iv. The Zone of Proximal Development (or Learning Zone) is what the students can do with prompting, support, and encouragement from peers, parents, and teachers. That support should come in the form of mediation, and never in the form of doing the work for them.

v. By working in the Learning Zone, your Comfort Zone expands with you so that as your understanding and skills improve, you become more comfortable with greater complexity and sophistication in knowledge, understanding, and skills.

vi. Use a 'Thinking Partner' to give your students time to process and practise vocabulary.

vii. The Learning Challenge is a useful tool to support reflection on learning. Using it will create a shared language for you and your students to explore what and how they have learned.

viii. Using the Learning Pit as a metaphor for cognitive conflict encourages students to share the strategies they are developing and identify their next steps in learning. It has the additional benefit of normalising struggle.

6.7 • REFLECTION

i. How often does your teaching get in the way of learning? Record yourself teaching, and make a tally mark each time you give students an answer or tell them a piece of information they want to know. Make a tally mark each time you answer a request for help or information with a question or encouraging them to think for themselves. Aim to get more tally marks in the Independent Learning column than the Spoon-feeding column!

	Spoon-feeding Tally marks showing the number of instances where I did it for the students or gave them the answer.	Independent Learning Tally marks showing the number of instances where I encouraged them to do it for themselves.
Week 1		
Week 2		
Week 3		
Week 4		

ii. Using the data you collect in the table, talk to a colleague about your examples. Ask them to observe you, or show them a video of a typical lesson. What do they notice about when and how you help the students?

iii. Choose one instance from the video where the students are struggling. What do they do? How do they react to difficulty? Are they finding it a positive struggle?

iv. Plan a questioning sequence you could ask that might help those students continue the struggle for themselves.

v. Try encouraging a student or group of students to struggle on. Tell them you'll come back in a minute to see how they are getting on. Come back in one minute. What do you notice? How did they respond?

vi. Try using Thinking Partners. Create a gap in your questioning to give time for your students to talk to the person next to them and share their thoughts and current understanding. What did that do to your dialogue? How did it help the students? What sort of responses did you get when your students had time to prepare their thinking?

vii. Once your students have experienced being in the pit, encourage them to design their own Learning Challenge models. Use some of their images, or a Learning Challenge poster (available from www.corwin.com), to get them talking about their learning and reflecting on progress. Try asking:

What did you struggle with today?

What did that feel like?

How did you overcome the struggle?

What do you still need to work on, or what might you do differently next time?

viii. Make a note of questions that worked well with your students to help them reflect. Add these to your questioning prompt sheet (see Figure 11) so that deliberate time for reflection becomes a core part of your learning culture.

The Learning Challenge is 'an inspirational guide to creating lessons that are thought-provoking and meaningful, and at the same time theoretically sound'.

—Carol Dweck (2010)

QUESTIONING ACTIVITIES TO CHALLENGE THINKING

7

We have looked at ways of structuring your questioning sequences so that the moves you make take you toward your intention. In each case, we have considered the Initiate question to arise from your delivery: what you said, read, or did immediately prior to initiating your questioning sequence.

In this chapter, we will look at specific tools that create fertile opportunities for questioning: they are learning activities in their own right, but enhanced by incisive and focussed questioning. The key to the success of these activities is to engage the students in active cognitive processing and exploratory dialogue, so they are the perfect opportunity for you to use your funnelling technique, Initiate-Respond-Explore, and Thinking Partners.

The aim of any thinking skills activity is to encourage your students out of their Comfort Zone and into the Learning Zone. But while there should be struggle in the activity itself, it is the questioning that enhances the struggle and makes the learning both challenging and explicit.

Questioning should enhance the learning activity and accelerate progress toward the learning goal.

All of the tools are excellent ways to engage your students in dialogue. You can learn more about the value of exploratory talk in our companion book, *Challenging Learning Through Dialogue* (Nottingham, Nottingham, & Renton, 2017), where you will also find a number of tools and strategies that will be greatly enhanced by your use of focussed questioning, like Opinion Corners, Odd One Out, and Mysteries.

In this chapter, we will use ranking exercises to apply our exploratory questioning to.

Your role in these activities is to *mediate* learning. This means drawing on the questioning skills you are practising in order to facilitate and activate the students' thinking. It is also worth referring to the questioning prompt sheet (Figure 11) alongside the activities, to plan the questions you want to ask to encourage your students into their Learning Zones and elicit more thoughtful responses from them.

The tools create the opportunity for students to engage in exploratory dialogue; and if you use the questioning approaches discussed in this book so far, then they provide a means for you to probe students' thinking further.

7.0 • RANKING EXERCISES

Ranking exercises are a simple way to encourage students to reason through choices they have made, by questioning them about the relative importance of key concepts.

Ranking exercises ask students to place statements, objects, or images into a set shape—for example, a diamond, triangle, or column. In so doing, the students make decisions about how to rank each idea and give reasons for the choices they have made in placing one above another. The students are being asked to engage in thinking critically, literally meaning 'being able to make judgements'.

Thinking critically is a broad term and encompasses a vast number of thinking skills within it. The specific intent of a ranking exercise is to teach your students these critical thinking skills:

- Prioritising
- Decision making
- Reasoning

Along with these thinking skills, a range of attitudes are also needed to be able to complete the task well:

- Compromising
- Listening
- Being open-minded

The intent of your questioning sequences, then, should be to ensure that these dispositions and thinking skills are taking place during the activity. That way, you can

pay explicit attention to them with your students so they recognise that not only are these things happening, but they are developing them too.

So, 'Knowing Your Intent' for questioning during a thinking skills activity might be that, 'by the end of the activity, the students will be able to *reason* through the *decisions* they have made in *prioritising* one idea over another'.

When you plan your questioning beforehand, consider how each questioning move encourages reasoning, prioritising, or decision making. Consider how your questioning moves will explicitly take your students toward that goal.

7.1 • DIAMOND NINE

Probably the most well-known form of ranking exercise is the Diamond Nine. It is one of the first thinking skills strategies I ever tried in my classroom. Along with Odd One Out, it seemed a very easy starting point and a good introduction to activities with a thinking skills focus. I was amazed at how quickly it prompted the students to begin talking, sharing ideas, and reasoning. As with many great ideas, the simple ones are often the most effective!

In this strategy, students work with a Thinking Partner or in groups of three to rank nine statements, objects, or images according to importance. This is most commonly done using cards.

Ask the students to place their cards into a diamond shape so that the most important one is at the top and the least important at the bottom. Underneath the most important choice, the students should place two cards that they think are important (but not the most important), followed by three that are of middle importance, then two that are less important, leaving one card (the least important) at the bottom, thus creating a diamond shape (see Figure 22).

▶ **Figure 22: A blank Diamond Nine template, showing the shape the cards should be placed into.**

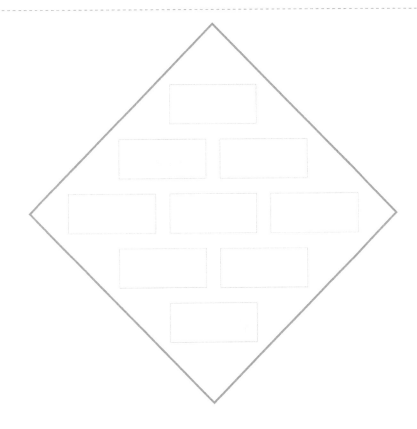

Internet	Aspirin	Plough
©2019 www.challenginglearning.com	©2019 www.challenginglearning.com	©2019 www.challenginglearning.com
Solar Power	Motor Car	Washing Machine
©2019 www.challenginglearning.com	©2019 www.challenginglearning.com	©2019 www.challenginglearning.com
Gun	Telephone	Television
©2019 www.challenginglearning.com	©2019 www.challenginglearning.com	©2019 www.challenginglearning.com

From the cards they have been given, the students will need to arrange them from most important to least important and *give reasons why they have ranked them that way*. The focus of the learning rests on the students' ability to give reasons that explain and justify their decisions, so it is this element that your questioning sequences should aim to draw out.

Placing their cards into a diamond typically takes around 3 to 5 minutes, depending on the age of your students and difficulty (in the students' eyes) of the concepts on the cards. During the activity, your students should engage in dialogue with one another about how to rank the cards, and rehearse the language of reasoning, so they can explain why they have ranked them that way.

Your questioning at the end of the 3 to 5 minutes should intend to debrief the learning, thinking, and language used by the groups during the activity.

In the example in Figure 23, taken from a Grade 7 technology lesson, pairs of students have been given words that relate to what they have been learning about the history of inventions. Ask your students to place these nine cards into a diamond shape from most important to least important.

Have a go yourself, too, or with a colleague. How would you organise these cards? Don't forget to say *why* you would rank them that way!

7.1.1 • Questioning to Debrief the Learning

Following the activity, each pair of students will have a slightly different diamond, according to their conversations. Your task is to draw out from the students the reasons why they ranked the cards that way, so you are encouraging them to:

- Express their understanding
- Make sense of the concepts on the cards
- Listen to, and learn from, the way other students have understood it
- Reflect on their choices, and the choices of others
- Change their mind if they learn something new

To debrief the learning well, it is worth doing the activity yourself and with someone else if possible. This helps you to predict what the students are likely to come up with, and therefore plan your questioning moves to target the learning you want from the activity.

You can use your questioning prompt sheet (Figure 11) to select some questions to ask in the debrief; create a run of three questions to get at how the groups of students have interpreted the thinking differently. But don't wait until the lesson to think of questions on the spot. You are more likely to ask well-placed incisive questions if you have planned them in advance.

Using the Diamond Nine example on inventions (Figure 23), here are some possible questioning sequences to begin the dialogue with your students with the intention of finding out the *reasons* your students have for the *decisions* they made when *prioritising* one idea over another:

Initiate: Which card have you placed as the most important?

Explain: *Why* have you placed that one at the top?

Extend: Does any other pair [of students] have that same card at the top, for the *same reason*? [Encourage the students to extend the initial idea.] Tell me more about your choice.

Extend: Or, does any pair have the same card but for a *different reason*? [Encourage students to add new thinking to the same idea.]

Explore: Does any pair have a *different card* at the top? [Look for a different perspective.] *Why* did you choose that one?

Of course, you can do the same with the bottom card or the 'top three' rather than just the top one; you can play with these variations and extend this opening sequence of questioning to suit the group and the subject content.

Once you have heard some different views, give the students 30 seconds to review their diamond and see if they would change their mind about any cards or reasons. They don't have to move any at all if they don't want to, but giving them the opportunity to models your intent in the session—that you are all learning together, and that reflection is a key to learning. Use the I-R-Explore approach to find out whether your students have changed their mind (with the intent of giving reasons for their decisions):

Initiate: Did you move any of your cards?

Respond: Yes, [this one].

Explore: Why did you move that card [up or down], and what made you change your mind?

And of course, you wouldn't worry if you got the opposite response from your students, would you? Because you know that with a well-planned sequence, you can explore *any* response:

Initiate: Did you move any of your cards?

Respond: No.

Explore: Why did you *not* move any cards in your diamond—what makes you sure of your initial reasoning?

In this way, *all* students are expected to take part in reflection, and you can emphasise that it is OK to hear different opinions and to change your mind. When they do change their mind, it is a useful indicator that the students are making progress in thinking and understanding. If they haven't changed their mind, then they should still have to justify their decision in line with the intention of the questioning.

The success of a Diamond Nine activity in maximising student learning rests not in the activity itself but in the questioning sequence that follows, and its ability to draw out—and make students aware of—their thinking and understanding.

7.1.2 • Extending the Diamond Nine Dialogue

Having placed the statements, images, or objects into a diamond, you will likely want to extend the students' thinking and keep the dialogue moving. Your first instruction in the Diamond Nine, 'to place the cards in order from most important to least important', is quite broad, possibly even vague. The idea of importance and what it means to whom, and when, can make that quite a challenge, as it has virtually no boundaries.

So, you can now narrow down the context or focus of the ranking so that students have to reconsider the order they placed their first diamond in.

Remember that there should always be more than one possible answer, as long as your students can justify their choice. Try to avoid narrowing the focus so much that it frames only one possible answer. And definitely don't frame it so they are all trying to find 'your' answer!

To extend the students' thinking, using the same cards from Figure 23, you could ask the students to rearrange their cards according to these (or similar) new scenarios:

> Imagine you are an 80-year-old lady living on her own. Place your cards in a diamond from most important to least important.

> Rank these cards from those that have improved our quality of life the most to the least.

> Organise the cards from most to least helpful to the environment.

> Which of these cards do you think will be the most important to least important, 100 years in the future?

> Which of these inventions represents the biggest risk? Rank them from highest to lowest.

Choose one of these situations and share it with your students. Using the same cards as in Figure 23, give them another 3 to 5 minutes to rearrange their cards into a diamond shape. As the situation changes, they will find that their priorities and reasons change, too.

Following this extension activity, it is important to again debrief your students' thinking. Having already asked what the students have placed at the top and bottom of their first diamond, you should now take a different questioning line so that you increase the challenge. This encourages them to open up their thinking, go deeper into their reasoning, and build their understanding of the subject content further.

For example, after completing the first diamond using Figure 23 and the debriefing sequence in 7.1.1, we changed the situation to the first one listed ('Imagine you are an 80-year-old lady living on her own . . . '). Your debriefing questioning could now be:

- Which of the inventions *moved* up or down significantly in your diamond, and why?

- What was *different* in this situation compared to your first diamond?

- Can you *add* a new card that might be more relevant to this situation? Why?

These questions focus on how the situation changed your students' reasoning and affected their decision making when prioritising the cards. So the intent remains the same, though the situations look different.

With any ranking activity, it is worth doing the more generic ranking (most important to least important) before adding further situations or scenarios (for example, the 80-year-old followed by '100 years in the future'). Three ranking activities from the same cards, in 25 to 30 minutes, works well to sustain effective dialogue. It also gives you ample time to explore the Learning Challenge Paths!

7.2 • EXTENDING THINKING WITH THE INTENTION TO CHALLENGE

The use of thinking skills activities, with the intention to develop reasoning, provides a very good platform from which to explore the Learning Challenge Paths (see Figure 3) and increase demands on your students' thinking.

Now that your students are actively processing and rehearsing subject-specific language in a context, they are moving into their Learning Zone. The decisions you are asking your students to make—and the reasons for those decisions—are not always clear-cut, especially when the 'situation' they are selecting the priorities for keeps changing. This process of prioritising and reasoning in changing situations creates positive struggle.

You can explore this struggle further through your questioning and create deliberate opportunities for cognitive conflict. Cognitive conflict is the disagreement between two (or more) of the ideas or opinions a person holds at the same time. It is about prompting your students to think more deeply and urgently about their ideas—to seek alternative answers and alternative ways to express their understanding.

The following example questioning sequences demonstrate how you can create cognitive conflict and challenge your students' thinking using the cards as a frame.

7.2.1 • Challenge Intention 1: To Clarify Meaning Using *Similar and Different*

Internet	Telephone
©2016 www.challenginglearning.com	©2016 www.challenginglearning.com

Initiate: You had these two cards on the middle row. Why did you place them there?

Respond: Because they're just for entertainment or for talking to people.

Explain: So are they both the same—for entertainment and for talking to people?

Respond: Yes. Sort of . . . they can both do that.

Challenge: So what makes them different? I can use my phone for the internet and talking to people, and I can go on the internet to talk to people. What makes the phone and the internet different, and what makes them the same?

Interval: Talk to your Thinking Partner. How are these two things the same and different?

Extend: Would an 80-year-old think these two things are the same? Why or why not?

In this sequence, your students are being asked to compare two things that, on the face of it, may not seem worth challenging. But where two ideas are connected but not the same, there is the opportunity to explore interpretation. In the ranking activity, the students placed two cards in the same row and used them to represent the same idea. So the challenge is to clarify the similarities and differences between the two words in the context of the activity.

Doing this encourages your students to use more complex language to express something that would otherwise have remained unconscious.

7.2.2 • Challenge Intention 2: To Challenge the Assumptions Students Have Made and Encourage Them to Rethink Previously Unconscious Ideas

Figure 24 shows a typical diamond that your students might create when given the situation of prioritising the inventions as if they were an 80-year-old lady living on her own. There is no single correct way to position the cards, so there are obviously variations on this placing, but the top three and bottom one are commonly these choices.

▶ **Figure 24: An example of how your students might place their cards in a Diamond Nine shape, showing their priorities for what an 80-year-old lady living on her own would consider to be the most to least important inventions.**

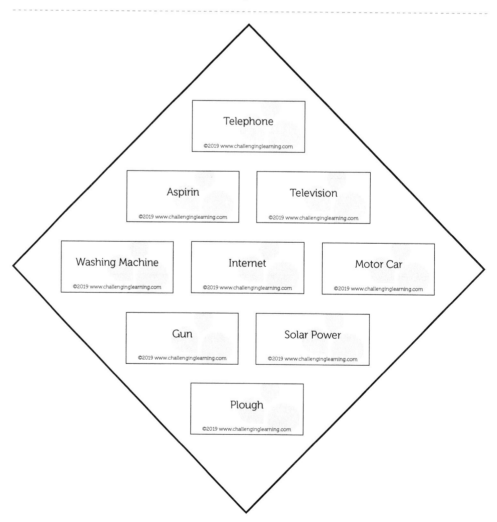

Before we look at what the students often say, have a look at the figure yourself and see if you can predict _why your students_ might place their cards this way.

- **What reasons would they give for the telephone at the top, for example?**

- **Why is the television so important, and why is the plough so low?**

- **What connects the internet and the motor car for an 80-year-old?**

I have used these cards and this 'situation' with hundreds of students all over the world who, for this particular activity, are usually between the ages of 11 and 16. The reasons students give for these placings are often along these lines:

Telephone:	She can keep in touch with family; she can call for help; it can stop her from feeling lonely.
Aspirin:	She might need medicine; she might be poorly more often.
Television:	To keep her company; for entertainment; so she knows what's happening in the news.
Washing machine:	To do the housework; to clean; because she won't want to go to a laundrette or carry clothes.
Internet:	To stay in touch with others; but it's less important if she doesn't know how to use it.
Motor car:	It's less important as she probably won't drive; she can take the bus (for free).
Gun:	She probably won't own one; she might be scared of guns; she might want one, to feel safer.
Solar power:	It's probably not a priority, but if she had it, she could save on energy bills.
Plough:	It's least important because she won't use it!

With any responses students give, there are often assumptions built in, which means you can challenge ideas they hold that they might not even be aware they have!

What assumptions are you noticing in the reasons the students give?

For example, in their picture of our 80-year-old, they might assume that she will be ill a lot (aspirin), be lonely (telephone and television), have few visitors or friends (television and telephone), not drive (motor car), and not be able to use technology (internet and solar power).

It's interesting, isn't it? And yet, many of these students will have grandparents or even great-grandparents who are very active, call them on smartphones, are rarely ill, and are certainly not lonely! So this conflict of ideas (between their personal experiences and a stereotype view) gives you opportunity to put them in the Learning Pit.

You might then use a questioning sequence like this one, taken from a session I did recently:

Initiate:	Why are telephone and television at the top?
Respond:	So she has company.
Explain:	What do you mean?

Respond:	Someone to talk to or people you can see and hear. To keep her company. Like, have people around her.
Challenge:	Does she not have friends?
Respond:	Well, she's living on her own. So . . .
Respond:	And because she's older, she might not have many friends.
Explain:	Why not?
Respond:	Because she doesn't go out as much . . . so . . .
Challenge:	Why not? Can 80-year-olds not go out, be active, or have friends?
Respond:	Well, I guess so. But I don't think of it that way. And it says she's living on her own, so she is.
Challenge:	Does living on her own mean that she can't have friends? Or family living on the same street?
Respond:	She could have, I suppose. Yes. She could, but I dunno.
Respond:	If she was living on her own, she might not be near people she knows really well, or they might live on the other side of town. You know what I mean?
Explore:	Does anyone here have a relative who is elderly and lives close by?

[Several students raise their hands up and nod.]

Challenge:	Do you visit them regularly? Do they have friends?
Respond:	Yes, they do.
Respond:	[She] goes out to things in the social [club], and bingo and stuff like that.
Respond:	My grandma meets my mum every day. She's always 'round for coffee.
Respond:	My granddad, he's not a lady, right? But he does live on his own, and he's 75 or 70-something. He goes to the pub with his mates, and goes to the football every weekend. He plays golf a lot, too. Like, a lot. So he's always out.
Explain:	So why did everyone think that living on your own means you don't have any friends or family to see regularly?
Respond:	Dunno. You get a picture, I guess . . .
Explore:	Go back to your cards. Can you rearrange them to suit the sort of 80-year-old you've just been describing?

What do you notice about the questioning in this dialogue?

How did the questioning help to build a picture of the students' assumptions versus their experiences?

Can you see the patterns of questioning that were used to explain, extend, and challenge the thinking?

How did the dialogue end? Why do you think I planned to do it that way?

What impact do you think this questioning episode had on the students?

I have chosen this example to share with you because it was with a group of post-16 students who were studying health care and who will therefore possibly go on to work with the elderly as a career. Challenging their perceptions of the elderly was really useful for them to get a picture of how they see people and what those people are capable of.

Following their summary of what they changed in the cards (where they started to challenge themselves—for example: 'I can't really say she'd be ill all the time'; 'My gran still drives, so why wouldn't other people?'; 'Maybe a car keeps you young, like having the freedom to get out'), I challenged them around the concept of what it means to be on your own and used the similar–different challenge approach. Here, I have just recorded the questioning sequence without the students' responses so you can see the intent.

Initiate:	How many of you built your first picture of the 80-year-old lady around the idea of her being on her own?
	[Response.]
Explain:	What does it mean to be on your own?
	[Response.]
Extend:	Is that the same as being lonely?
	[Response.]
Challenge:	Can I be surrounded by people and still be lonely?
	[Response.]
Challenge:	So, what's the difference between being alone and being lonely?
Interval:	Talk in pairs and work out the difference.
	[Response.]
Explore:	How would you know if someone was lonely?
	In pairs, you have 5 minutes to research the signs of loneliness. How would you know that someone is at risk?

What do you notice about this questioning sequence?

Can you see where there could be a shift from Comfort Zone to Learning Zone?

Why do you think it would push students into their Learning Zone—what is it that could create cognitive conflict?

As a follow-up to either of these dialogues, you can use the Learning Challenge model as a way to help debrief the learning with your students. Use the questioning sequences we used in 6.5.4 to help plan your sequence. For example:

What did you think at the start of the dialogue?

What do you think now?

What changed in your thinking?

When did you struggle?

What caused you to struggle?

Are you satisfied with where you got to now?

What else might you like to think about more?

7.2.3 • Challenge Intention 3: To Go From Generic to Specific and Test If They Work

In the more generic diamond, your students may use some of the inventions to represent something greater than the item. So, for example, aspirin often goes at the top as it represents medicine and good health. The plough is another common one to place at the top because it can represent food production: 'We all have to eat . . .'

In more specific situations, your students may well take the invention to be more literal. The motor car is a motor car, and the plough is a plough. You can use this 'general to specific' interpretation as a basis to create struggle.

For example, if you notice that your students placed the plough at the top of the diamond in the first activity (because it represents food), you might find it is near the bottom of the diamond for the 80-year-old lady, as she doesn't need a plough.

So, you can now ask why it represented food in the first diamond, but not in the second.

Challenge: Or does an 80-year-old lady not require food?

This type of challenge uses the general and the specific to create cognitive conflict.

In the Diamond Nine activity, you will notice that there are no cards that are wrong, or 'red herrings', to catch the students out. All of the inventions in the example are important, and can be placed anywhere in the diamond, *as long as your students can justify it*. It is this challenge to their perceptions and their ability to reason that makes for deeper long-term learning.

Your questioning can also take place during the activity as you circulate around the pairs, prompting and supporting students' thinking. Whilst circulating, you will get a sense of the common themes in the classroom: those cards appearing at the top and bottom a lot, those cards the students are struggling to place, and perhaps even those cards that the students don't understand. This information will add to the depth and quality of your debriefing questioning.

7.3 • YOUR ROLE DURING THE GROUPWORK STAGE

We have focussed so far on the questioning that takes place after your students have completed their ranking activity, when you are looking to debrief the learning and focus on the intention (to give reasons, make decisions, and prioritise ideas). But your students are not just doing this thinking during the debrief: they are also doing it during the groupwork stage, when they are creating their ranking.

During this groupwork stage, move around the room and pay attention to what your students are saying to one another. There are four key reasons for circulating during the activity: listen, look, intervene for support, and intervene for challenge. Here's why they are useful.

7.3.1 • Listen

Listen to what your students are saying to one another. Listen for interesting ideas that come up in their paired conversations, as you might be able to refer to them in the debrief later. A debriefing questioning stem like 'But this group over here, you were talking about [this], weren't you?' can open up comparisons between the ways your students have interpreted the cards.

You can also listen for subject-specific language that is improving or misunderstood and target this in your debriefing questioning sequences.

7.3.2 • Look

Look for patterns around the room: the cards that are often near the top, and those that are near the bottom. Try to spot a common theme for what is placed as the top card, and then look for students who placed the same card near the bottom, to make a comparison later. For example:

Initiate: Who had [this one] at the top, as the most important card?

Explain: Why did you have [this one] at the top?

Extend: Who else had [this one] at the top? Why?

Explore: But this group over here, you had that one at the bottom, didn't you? Why did you think [the same card] was the least important?

Look for patterns in the reasons given to Thinking Partners: common themes that emerge, assumptions that you could challenge later, or a common misconception.

A top tip is to look for the middle cards: these ones often get least attention, and are often the ones students are uncertain about, so students often place them in the middle row to 'hide' them! So make sure you ask questions about cards in the middle row as well as the top and bottom.

7.3.3 • Intervene for Support

Intervene for support when you listen in to students and think they may be disengaged. This could be because they haven't understood the task, or because they are struggling too much and have 'shut down', or it could just be that they're 'too cool for school' and don't want to talk to each other about learning! So intervene in any of these situations with questions that encourage and make them feel safe to take the first step.

Your questioning here could relate to the encouraging questioning sequence we saw in 6.2 to help place your students into a Learning Zone mindset. Alternatively, a good tip is just to pick up one card and ask them if they think this is a particularly important one. Don't forget to ask for their reasons! Then place it down and pick up a second card. This time, ask if it's more or less important than the last one they placed. Once they are in the habit, you can leave them (and suggest that you return to them in a minute or so, to see how they are getting on).

7.3.4 • Intervene for Challenge

Intervene for challenge when you can see students operating within their Comfort Zones. You can spot this from their body language: slightly off-hand placing of the cards; simple, short reasons given; lots of nods; lots of cumulative talk (where students all agree with each other for a sense of harmony, rather than for learning); or no comments at all.

When you notice this situation, it is useful to intervene for challenge and nudge your students into the Learning Zone. A good way to do this is to highlight one of the cards that is not the top or bottom card and ask them to explain why it is there. Ask them to compare it to another card on the same row: Why is this on the same level? You can then ask them to identify similarities and differences between the two cards—if they are on the same row, is there a connection? Ask them to explain what each of the cards means, ask for examples of each, and encourage them to think of different situations in which this might or might not be important.

In one classroom I worked with, I went to intervene with a pair of students who had turned all their cards face down in the diamond. Thinking they were disengaged, I went to ask them what they were doing, to get them 'back on task', but when I got there, they explained to me that they had put all the cards face down randomly in the diamond shape, and were then going to turn them over and see if they could think of a reason why each card should be in that position! They'd actually increased the challenge for themselves!

7.4 • VARYING THE GROUPWORK TO SHARE PERCEPTIONS

Here, my good friend and Challenging Learning colleague, Richard Kielty, describes an example Diamond Nine he ran in one of his own lessons as a middle school teacher.

Working with a group of Grade 7 students in a citizenship lesson, a question had been raised about the meaning of *democracy* and *monarchy*, and I wanted the group to explore the similarities and differences between the two.

I decided to use a Diamond Nine activity as I wanted to encourage discussion and see if the students could agree on a list of key features of each. The ranking exercise seemed an effective approach as it asks the group to consider a range of priorities and perspectives.

Innovation generally starts with individuals, so I like to build time into the process for students to just be quiet and think for a while.

I then asked the students to get into groups of three for collaborative working. This builds confidence through active involvement, and reticent members can still take part. I wanted to lay the foundations for sharing and contributing to the larger group later. The groups were made up of students who did not normally work together in order to create a range of different perspectives.

Each group received a set of cards marked *M* (for *monarchy*) and were asked to read them together. They then chose the nine most important characteristics of rule by monarchy and organised them into a diamond pattern according to order of importance. Each set contained two blank cards on which the group could write their own ideas if they wished.

Each group placed their completed diamond on the wall so that everyone could see it.

I then asked the groups to merge with another group and explain their selections to each other, before presenting their top and bottom selections to the whole class and briefly explaining how they arrived at this decision. The class then attempted to identify any common choices that most of the groups had selected or rejected.

This activity was repeated with a set of cards marked *D* (for *democracy*). When the activity was completed for both rule by monarchy and rule by democracy, the whole group discussed the similarities and differences between the choices made for each. They looked at the qualities that apply to both, and the qualities that make each rule distinct from the other.

Finally, the students wrote a definition of *monarchy* and *democracy*, using some of the reasons that they had heard from around the classroom and taking ideas from the wall. Each group felt they had greater clarity about the two different systems, and some members of the group said they had contributed to the discussions when usually they would not have done so.

The Diamond Nine encouraged the students to think in ways that they wouldn't normally, and to explicitly develop skills and attitudes for learning in an exploratory environment. And the quality of their written definitions was far better having approached the task using a Diamond Nine and open questioning than it would have been through direct teaching from a textbook.

7.5 • EXAMPLE DIAMOND NINE CARDS FOR DIFFERENT AGE GROUPS

See Figures 25, 26, and 27 for some examples of Diamond Nine activities you could use with your students or adapt to suit the themes of your teaching. They really are very simple to make, too; just think of nine key words you are likely to teach in your current module, unit, topic, or scheme!

▶ **Figure 25:** A Diamond Nine at the elementary school level on evacuees. These cards could be used on a topic of the Second World War, and link in well with books like *The Lion, the Witch and the Wardrobe*. This set can easily be adapted for a theme of 'going on holiday'.

Teddy bear ©2019 www.challenginglearning.com	Writing pen and paper ©2019 www.challenginglearning.com	Gas mask ©2019 www.challenginglearning.com
Wellington boots ©2019 www.challenginglearning.com	Photograph of your family ©2019 www.challenginglearning.com	Your favourite toy ©2019 www.challenginglearning.com
Identity card ©2019 www.challenginglearning.com	A book ©2019 www.challenginglearning.com	Spare clothes ©2019 www.challenginglearning.com

▶ **Figure 26:** A Diamond Nine at the middle school level on movement in science. This one works well with scenarios like 'Which would be most important to consider if you were designing an aeroplane?' or 'Which would you consider most important if you were a Formula One pit crew member?' and 'What if you were on the pit crew and it was a rainy day?'

Friction ©2019 www.challenginglearning.com	Mass ©2019 www.challenginglearning.com	Material ©2019 www.challenginglearning.com
Shape ©2019 www.challenginglearning.com	Wind direction ©2019 www.challenginglearning.com	Power ©2019 www.challenginglearning.com
Drag ©2019 www.challenginglearning.com	Downforce ©2019 www.challenginglearning.com	The surface ©2019 www.challenginglearning.com

Heroism	Hospitality	Relationships
©2019 www.challenginglearning.com	©2019 www.challenginglearning.com	©2019 www.challenginglearning.com
Loyalty	Fallibility	Gods
©2019 www.challenginglearning.com	©2019 www.challenginglearning.com	©2019 www.challenginglearning.com
Searching	Hubris	Family
©2019 www.challenginglearning.com	©2019 www.challenginglearning.com	©2019 www.challenginglearning.com

7.6 • OTHER SHAPES FOR RANKING

7.6.1 • Triangle Ranking

Triangle Ranking operates in the same way as a Diamond Nine, only this strategy does not include a 'least important' choice. It works well for six statements, images, or objects and is most useful in highlighting how some things might be *more* important in different circumstances without deciding on a least important thing. Figure 28 shows a Triangle Ranking you could use in an elementary classroom about being sun safe.

► Figure 28: An example Triangle Ranking exercise on being sun safe.

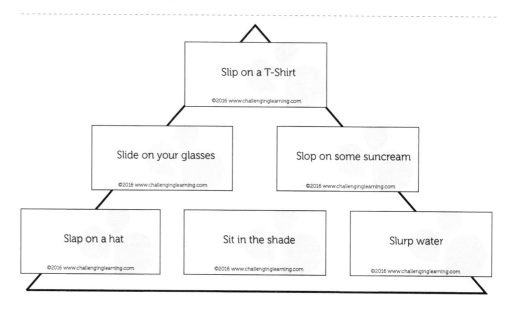

In this sun safety example, we recommend you ask your students questions which encourage them to rank the cards for different situations. So you could ask them to focus on which are the most important cards if they are:

- At the beach all afternoon, swimming in the sea
- At their house, playing in the garden
- At school and it is playtime
- Giving advice to elderly neighbours
- Writing an invitation to a birthday party

This triangle structure is also useful if you want to encourage your students to reflect on learning, especially their skills and attitudes at the end of a lesson, as it doesn't infer that any of the dispositions they have learnt or demonstrated are less valuable; it infers only that they needed different attitudes and skills in different situations.

See Figure 29 for an example.

▶ Figure 29: An example Triangle Ranking exercise to reflect on attitudes for learning.

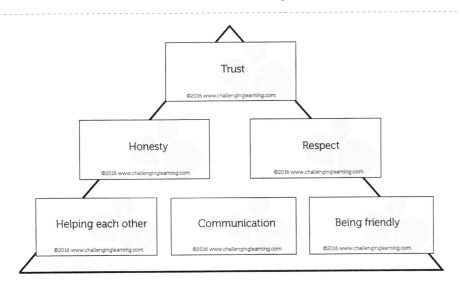

7.6.2 • The Christmas Tree

The Christmas Tree is much like the Triangle Ranking except that with seven cards to use, the students are asked to place one at the bottom as least important, thus creating the 'bucket' under the Christmas Tree! This extends the Triangle Ranking activity so that it has a 'least important' element.

It is worth noting, too, that the phrase 'least important' is deliberate, and doesn't mean the same as 'not important'.

Figure 30 gives an example on healthy living.

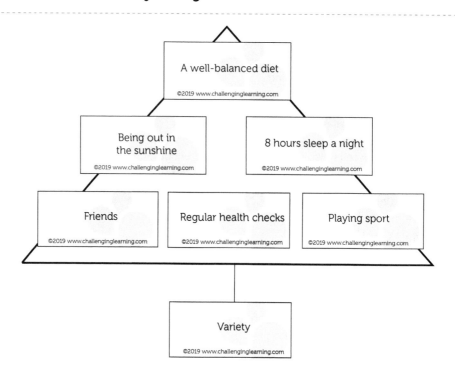

7.6.3 • Line Ranking

This strategy involves placing all of the cards in a line, from left to right or top to bottom. Students place one card to the left of or above the next card so that each one needs to be explained. This allows for a lot more detail in the middle of the line.

However, do be careful that students don't become too overwhelmed with the often very small differences between those cards in the middle. The advantage of the Diamond Ranking is to place some cards on an equal level where distinctions might be more slight. Line Ranking works much better for fewer cards (I recommend four to six depending on complexity).

7.6.4 • Diamond Four

This is the same principle as Diamond Nine but with only four cards, images, or objects. It works much better for infants as, with less 'operational' processing, it focusses on the development of the students' thinking. The open questioning in the Diamond Four can also focus on just the top and bottom cards and why they might be similar or different.

7.7 • REVIEW

In this chapter, we have covered some strategies that encourage your students to engage in collaborative dialogue, giving you the chance to extend their thinking using questioning sequences. The strategies are only really successful as thinking activities if the questioning sequences support reasoning and reflection.

Question your students after they have worked with the ranking tools, to debrief their thinking and share their understanding and perceptions with each other.

You should also circulate around the groups while they are engaged in the ranking exercise. This has many benefits for questioning groups *while* they work, but also in prompting observations, patterns, and interesting ideas during your debrief.

Adding a variety of situations or contexts to your reasons for organising the cards adds an extra level of challenge for your students and often creates the cognitive conflict needed to encourage deeper thinking and longer exchanges.

7.8 • REFLECTION

i. Try a Diamond Nine strategy with your students.

ii. Ask the students to justify their thinking,

iii. Encourage them to move the cards if they change their minds, then ask them which they moved . . .

vi. . . . then question their assumptions.

v. Plan your questioning and use the prompt sheet (Figure 11) to Initiate-Respond-Explore.

vi. Effective questioning models the process of good thinking so that students can adopt the same behaviour and internalise the strategies that will help them learn better.

vii. When you are questioning the students, what is the thinking that you are modelling for them? What are they learning from you about ways of thinking?

The language of classroom dialogue can be used to establish and sustain not just a momentary discussion, but a lasting climate of inquiry.

—Dennis Palmer Wolf (1987)

QUESTIONING FOR CHALLENGE

8

Questioning has been recognised since the time of the ancient Greeks as a method for challenging and engaging learners. To draw out the assumptions, errors, and misconceptions in his students' thinking, the Athenian philosopher Socrates (469–399 BC) developed the skill of questioning as a tool for encouraging his students to think more deeply, express their understanding more fully, and consider alternative ways to think about common concepts and accepted wisdom.

This approach that Socrates took, when applied in the classroom, aims to challenge first responses: to not let students stick with their first idea as an accepted truth, but to disrupt early thinking and encourage positive struggle. I have called that application in the classroom Questioning for Challenge.

The intention of Questioning for Challenge is positive struggle: to deliberately push students out of their Comfort Zones so they experience cognitive conflict. The aim, therefore, is the exploration itself—to improve thinking, understanding, and language.

To connect this intention to earlier chapters, this is extending the Explore step so that your open dialogues become more challenging. You will be able to use all of the tools you have learnt so far, extending your skills of Initiate-Pause-Respond-Paraphrase-Explore to challenge assumptions, consider alternatives, and rethink early ideas. This is the Abstract stage of the IDEAR Framework.

When using Questioning for Challenge, you will be encouraging your students into the Learning Pit as they wrestle with concepts and start to see that their ideas are not always consistent, and that some examples don't fit their current understanding.

In this chapter, I will show you some of the advanced questioning moves that demand more of your students, and really get them out of their Comfort Zones!

8.0 • GETTING INTO THE PIT!

In 6.4, we looked at The Learning Challenge as a model for encouraging deeper thinking, which includes the Learning Pit as a metaphor for wrestling with cognitive conflict.

There are four stages in getting into and then out of the Learning Pit, which we introduced in 6.5. You will notice in Figure 31 that following Stage 1 (identifying the concept), questioning is the key to getting into the pit. Here, your students will experience positive struggle. In terms of your questioning, your intent should be to create cognitive conflict, or uncertainty, about the way in which a concept is currently understood.

8.0.1 Stage 1: Identify the Concept

Working on Questioning for Challenge means first identifying a concept. You can read more about how to do this in *The Learning Challenge: How to Guide Your Students Through the Learning Pit to Achieve Deeper Understanding* (Nottingham, 2017).

As you move from Initiate to Explore in your questioning sequences, concepts (themes or big ideas) begin to emerge. This happens in the shift from *knowing* to *understanding* as your students start to make connections within a topic.

In the questioning sequence about *Jane Eyre* (3.0), the questioning moved from 'What time of day is it?' (fact) to inference from text (concept). And in 1.1, it moved from the name of a city (the capital of Scotland) to understanding 'place' (concept). During the early questioning in a sequence, try to identify the concepts emerging from the dialogue so you can draw them out further.

You can do this when planning your questioning, too. As you predict your students' responses, you will notice the concepts (big ideas) that underpin your students' thoughts. Planning for questioning around a concept allows you to dig deeper and make more connections in the Abstract stage than considering facts in isolation.

You can more easily design a Questioning for Challenge sequence if you are aiming to get your students to understand a concept, rather than state a fact.

Bear in mind that your students need to accept, even if only temporarily, two or more ideas that are in opposition; otherwise, cognitive conflict can't exist. That's why we begin with a concept that your students have at least one idea about. The questioning you do during Initiate-Respond-Explore should help you see the concept: as soon as your students have an idea, you can begin to challenge their thinking.

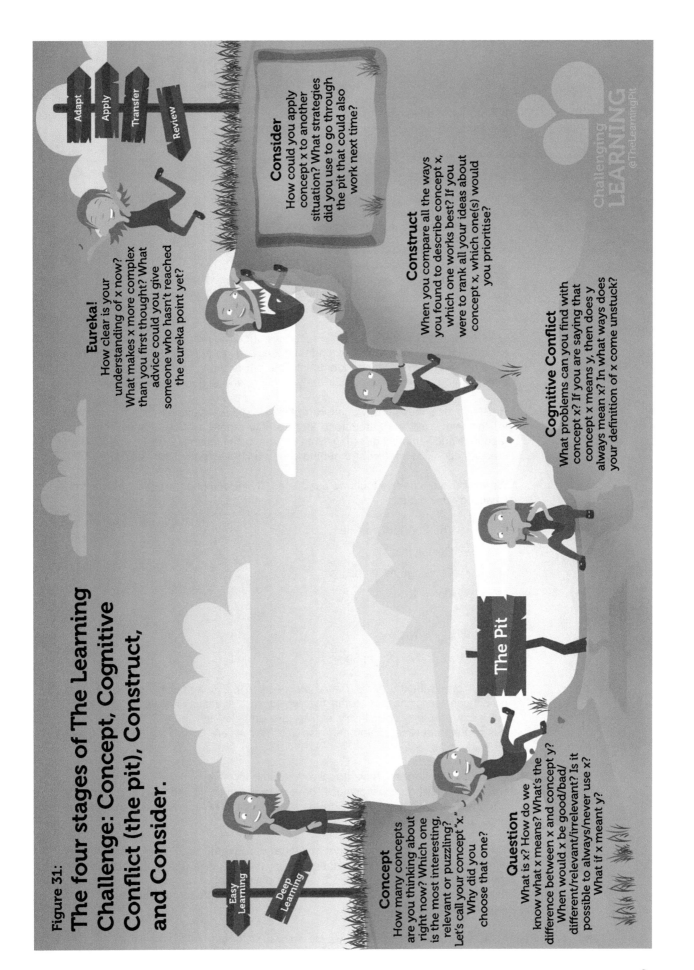

Figure 31:
The four stages of The Learning Challenge: Concept, Cognitive Conflict (the pit), Construct, and Consider.

Concept
How many concepts are you thinking about right now? Which one is the most interesting, relevant or puzzling? Let's call your concept "x." Why did you choose that one?

Question
What is x? How do we know what x means? What's the difference between x and concept y? When would x be good/bad/ different/relevant/irrelevant? Is it possible to always/never use x? What if x meant y?

Cognitive Conflict
What problems can you find with concept x? If you are saying that concept x means y, then does y always mean x? In what ways does your definition of x come unstuck?

Construct
When you compare all the ways you found to describe concept x, which one works best? If you were to rank all your ideas about concept x, which one(s) would you prioritise?

Eureka!
How clear is your understanding of x now? What makes x more complex than you first thought? What advice could you give someone who hasn't reached the eureka point yet?

Consider
How could you apply concept x to another situation? What strategies did you use to go through the pit that could also work next time?

Easy Learning

Deep Learning

The Pit

Adapt

Apply

Transfer

Review

Challenging LEARNING
@TheLearningPit

8.0.2 Stage 2: The Learning Pit

In 4.2, we used my colleague Steve Williams's example about 'teamwork' on Captain Robert Falcon Scott's expedition to the Antarctic to develop questioning that explored his students' ideas about the key concept of communication. We used the Pause-Paraphrase-Explore structure with these five questioning tools:

- further explanation
- clarification
- specific example
- presenting a different perspective
- challenging the response

In that example, we were in the Draw In and Extend steps of the IDEAR Framework. There, we tried to welcome more students into the inquiry, look for reasons, explore the students' perspectives, and develop their language.

These tools can create opportunity for active cognitive processing as your students start to consider new reasons and extend their language to express themselves. However, we have not yet really got the students into the pit! So now we will encourage them out of their Comfort Zones, disrupt their early thinking, and encourage positive struggle.

Here, we use the same Pause-Paraphrase-Explore structure, using the Pause step for think-time and the Paraphrase step to help create a bridge between the students' response and your next question. But this time the intention is Questioning for Challenge: creating cognitive conflict and getting your students into the Learning Pit.

We will build on the five tools we used in 4.2 by introducing these seven Questioning for Challenge techniques:

- The Counter-Example
- Comparisons
- Challenge Assumptions
- Define Extent
- A = B
- Not A, Not B
- What If All, None, Some

We will stay with the same theme we used in 4.2 (communication) so you can see how these tools connect to the five we looked at earlier. Before we get started, the actual cards Steve used in his activity are provided in Figure 32. You will notice that it is a Diamond Nine so you can also see how we are linking together our questioning techniques and tools.

Of course, you don't have to use a Diamond Nine activity when Questioning for Challenge. This could just as easily have begun with the Initiate question, 'What makes a good team?' A whole-class dialogue using the IDEAR Framework could then have been entered into without any card resources.

The same Initiate question, 'What makes a good team?', could have been asked of the whole class and their ideas paraphrased, in writing or on a board or flip chart. Assuming that communication came up in the responses, you could still use the questioning examples we are about to see, but with reference to the list created by your students, rather than cards.

There's always more than one way to enter a dialogue!

Trust ©2019 www.challenginglearning.com	Respect ©2019 www.challenginglearning.com	Communication ©2019 www.challenginglearning.com
Honesty ©2019 www.challenginglearning.com	Helping each other ©2019 www.challenginglearning.com	Humour ©2019 www.challenginglearning.com
A shared goal ©2019 www.challenginglearning.com	A badge or uniform ©2019 www.challenginglearning.com	Being strong ©2019 www.challenginglearning.com

As we introduce the seven tools to support Questioning for Challenge, the opening sequence is always the same so you can make comparisons. In the first tool, the intention is to challenge your students' responses with a *counter-example*.

8.1 • INTENTION TO CHALLENGE 1: THE COUNTER-EXAMPLE

Initiate: Which card have you placed at the top of your diamond, and why?

Pause: [Wait 3–5 seconds.]

Respond: We chose the *communication* card as the most important skill in teamwork because we think that a good team talks to each other, so they can ask each other for help and tell each other what to do.

Paraphrase: So, good teamwork means 'asking for help'.

Explore: But what if someone asks you for help carrying a heavy bag—does that make you a good team?

Now take a moment to consider:

- **What did you notice in this exchange?**
- **What is different in the Questioning for Challenge approach compared to, say, a funnelling sequence?**
- **How do you think your student(s) would react?**
- **What might the student(s) say next?**

In this example sequence, there is a gap in the students' thinking which has created an opportunity to challenge their initial response with a counter-example. Rather than letting your students rest on what is essentially a rather vague explanation, the counter-example encourages rethinking of the response in light of a real situation. This requires rethinking, reframing, and re-explaining on the part of your students.

Notice that the challenge is not aimed at the student; the challenge is aimed at the idea, so remember to 'draw in'. Any student in the class can answer your Explore question, not just the student who answered. So, everyone is being asked to rethink the first response.

List some other counter-examples that you could use to challenge your students' thinking:

- **A student gets stuck in class and asks the teacher for help**

Whichever example you choose to use with your students, it should lead to the next question in your sequence: Is that what you mean by a good team?

Consider Questioning for Challenge to be like taking your journey home from work; you are on 'autopilot' because you make the same journey every day. You (because you are human) take the simplest way home, with the least amount of complication, the shortest length of time, and the least effort required.

But what if your usual route home is blocked?

Then you have to rethink which way to go and take a different set of streets, which takes longer and requires more thought.

But what if that route is also blocked?

Then you have to really struggle with which way to go—how to avoid two roadblocks, look at new alternatives, perhaps even double back on yourself.

And if that route is blocked, too?

You can become frustrated, anxious, or irritated. But you persevere until you get home. And when you do get to the end of the journey, you feel relieved to be back, proud of your efforts, keen to tell others about your experience, and less likely to forget it!

It is the same when your students set off to answer a question. They are also human (they are!), so they will look for the simplest response, the least complex answer, and the one that doesn't take long to explain.

Questioning for Challenge (like the counter-example) provides the roadblock—forcing your students to go a different way and process a new route to their conclusion. Give one answer, rethink, double back, and think again. And once you reach a resolution, all that effort is a reward in itself; you have done the learning yourself, and you are more likely to retain it.

In our first intention to challenge, we used the counter-example. The use of examples and counter-examples is invaluable to support challenge in your questioning sequences. But remember that the expectation is not that you will think of these on the spot during the dialogue: instead, plan your questioning! Considering the dialogue beforehand is essential for challenge, as examples and counter-examples need to be as sharp and relevant as possible: they make the Abstract step more concrete for your students.

In the following examples, we challenge students' responses in different ways but use the same first response (about communication) for each example so we can make comparisons more easily. Notice, as you work with these, that the teacher is paraphrasing different parts of the students' responses in order to bridge to the prepared challenge.

8.2 • INTENTION TO CHALLENGE 2: COMPARISONS

Paraphrase: When you chose communication, you mentioned words like *talking, asking*, and *telling*.

Explore: Are communication and talking the same thing, or are they different?

In this challenge, the teacher has asked for a clarification of how two ideas are similar (compare) and different (contrast). And if you are thinking that sounds like a simple question rather than a challenge, try answering it for yourself! Ask your students to first find some similarities; then, after a short time, ask them to think of differences.

You can develop this line of inquiry further by using Thinking Partners to encourage your students to go deeper and rehearse vocabulary.

This should open up even more possibilities for you to challenge and explore! As with all effective questioning techniques, it is about what you do next—don't accept the first clarification the students give you, but continue challenging instead. That means predicting what they are likely to say in response to the comparison challenge as well so you can then plan your next move.

Here's an example of questioning moves that might follow the first response to the challenge. In each move, I have kept the focus on challenge through comparison:

Compare: Are communication and talking the *same* thing, or are they *different*?

Respond: They're different because communicating also means listening.

Compare: You mean you need talking *and* listening. Which one is *better* for good teamwork—talking or listening?

Respond: Depending on the situation, it might be better to talk, and at other times you might have to be listening. So, they're both important, but it depends when you're doing it.

Compare: Each might be better at different times. So what are the *qualities that make talking good* for teamwork, and what are the *qualities that make listening good*?

You will notice here that comparisons were made using different command words or phrases. For example, the first comparison challenge was based on *similar* and *different*. In the second move, the comparison was based on *better* and *worse*, and in the third, it was comparing the qualities of each.

Comparison challenges can come in several forms:

How are these two similar and different?

Which is better or worse (including good or bad; important or not important; effective or not effective)?

How have these changed over time?

What are the characteristics and qualities of each of these?

What is this like and not like (use of analogy)?

You could paraphrase your students' thinking by writing their responses on a flip chart. From that list, the students will have said something you predicted they would. That allows you to continue challenging.

If you ask your students how talking and communicating are different, what are they likely to say? Write down what your students are likely to list.

Now add in Challenge Intention 1. Can you now think of any *examples or counter-examples* that go against what the students' likely definitions are?

8.3 • INTENTION TO CHALLENGE 3: CHALLENGE ASSUMPTIONS

Paraphrase: You said that a good team talks to each other.

Explore: So are teams always people? What about a 'team of horses'? They can't talk, so can they not be a good team?

Here, the students assumed that the team is a group of humans. So, your questioning provides an alternative perspective that they may not have considered yet: that 'communication' can be more than just talking and that the concept of communication doesn't only apply to people.

In this instance, and depending on the age of your students, you could show a picture of a team of horses pulling a plough or stagecoach to illustrate the example and make the Abstract step more real for your students.

Of course, this makes it even more important to plan your questioning so that you have predicted what is likely to come up and prepared the resources (as much as you possibly can). You will be able to identify assumptions and think of examples much more clearly in advance than if you try to spot them during a dialogue in a lesson!

8.4 • INTENTION TO CHALLENGE 4: DEFINE EXTENT

Paraphrase:	Asking for help is an important part of good teamwork.
Explore:	How often do we need to ask for help to become a good team?
Example:	If I ask you one thing, does that mean we're a good team because I asked for help? No? Two things? How many things do I need to ask you before we're a good team?

In this challenge, the teacher asks for 'how much', 'how long', or 'when does' to define the extent to which the definition applies to the concept.

Defining the extent also brings the idea of too much. The inference in these moves is that, if you need to ask for help a lot, maybe you are not being a successful team. In that case, the challenge question could have been:

If we need ask for help a lot, are we still a good team? [or]

How often is it OK to ask for help and still be a good team?

It is not that you think there is an answer to the question (there is no set number of times to ask for help to become a good team!); it is the process of making sense of your question that prompts your students to refine their thinking about 'a team asking for help'.

Let's put all that together. The intent is to define good teamwork in their module on Captain Scott in the Antarctic. The intent of the questioning sequence is to challenge the students' thinking on what communication means:

Initiate:	Which card have you placed at the top of your diamond, and why?
Pause:	[Wait 3–5 seconds.]
Respond:	We chose the *communication* card as the most important skill in teamwork because we think that a good team talks to each other so they can ask each other for help and tell each other what to do.
Paraphrase:	So, good teamwork means 'asking for help'.
Counter-Example:	So, if someone asks you for help carrying a heavy bag— does that make you a good team?
Respond:	No, you have to work together and communicate with each other, too.
Explore:	What do you mean by 'communicate'?
Respond:	When you talk to each other and tell each other what to do.
Paraphrase:	When you talk to each other . . .
Compare:	. . . are communication and talk the same thing, or are they different?
Respond:	They're different because communicating also means listening.
Paraphrase:	So, you need talking *and* listening.

Compare:	Which one is *better* for good teamwork—talking or listening?
Pause:	[Students spend 20 seconds of think-time with a partner.]
Respond:	Depending on the situation, it might be better to talk, and at other times you might have to be listening. So, they're both important, but it depends when you're doing it.
Paraphrase:	So it's important that we listen and talk, because [another student] said before that 'good teams will tell each other what to do'.
Assumption:	What if our team is a team of horses? They can't talk, and they can't tell each other what to do, so can they not be a good team?
Pause:	[Give students 5 seconds of think-time.]
Respond [uncertainly]:	They can communicate without talking, like through moving and touch. And they might listen to the rider or farmer or whoever.
Paraphrase:	So they communicate without talking.
Counter-Example:	But you said that communicating is listening *and* talking. So what do you mean by communication if it's not talking?
Pause:	Talk to your Thinking Partner and see if you can decide what communication means [in 30 seconds].

Responses were taken from three pairs, but I have only included one here, for the sake of brevity:

Respond:	You don't have to talk, but you kind of have to be able to get what you mean across to someone else. Or something else if you're a horse. So you don't have to talk, but you would need to be able to help each other still in whatever way you can.
Paraphrase:	So a good team helps each other.
Extend:	How often does a team need to help each other?
Example:	If I come and help you once with your maths homework, are we a team?
Respond:	Not really. Not a *good* team. We might feel a bit like a team because we did it together, but a team needs to do it all the time.
Paraphrase:	*All* the time.
Extent:	So if you needed help with your maths *all the time*, and I had to keep telling you what to do, would that make us a good team?
Respond:	Not really, no. But we'd still be a team. Just not a very good one!
Respond:	But you're there for each other, and that's an important bit of teamwork. So you can help, but it would be better if you didn't have to tell someone else what to do all the time.
Reflect:	So, let's think about Captain Scott. They were in the Antarctic, freezing, so it would be hard to talk to each other, or tell each other what to do. And you said that it would be better if they didn't have to tell each other what to do all the time. So, how would they communicate with each other and be an effective team?
	With your Thinking Partner, write down a first thought. Then you have 5 minutes to do some reading and research before we hear back.

A Reflection Section

- **How did challenge add to the students' understanding?**
- **How did their view of communication change through the dialogue?**
- **When do you think the students were in the pit?**
- **How well do you think this dialogue would engage them in the task set in the Reflect step of the IDEAR Framework?**

8.5 • ADVANCED QUESTIONING TECHNIQUES FOR INCREASING CHALLENGE

In this section, we look at questioning techniques that require more planning, preparation, and practice to use really well with your students. They are a great way to get the students into the pit, and a great way to challenge yourself!

Giving examples and counter-examples is key to successful Questioning for Challenge as they make the abstract more concrete. Socrates himself used examples to highlight contradictions in his students' thinking. Of course, they take time to prepare, especially if you're not used to using them yet, but as you develop a feel for it, they become quite natural. You will see this in the scripts below.

8.5.1 Intention to Challenge 5: A = B

Paraphrase:	So, good teamwork means telling someone what to do.
Explore:	Then, if I tell you what to do, does that make us a good team?
Example:	For example, if I tell you to do your homework, are we a good team?

In this questioning technique, the logic runs that if A = B, then B = A. But while that might be true in maths, it is rarely true in language, so your students will feel challenged by the mismatch!

The response from the student is known as A = B and is paraphrased by the teacher. In this instance, idea A is 'good teamwork', and idea B is 'telling someone what to do'. So the teacher paraphrases, 'Good teamwork means telling someone what to do'.

In the Explore step, the teacher reverses these, to ask, 'Is telling someone what to do [idea B] the same as good teamwork [idea A]?'

You will notice that adding an example to support your question makes the question more concrete for your students. As you become more familiar with these techniques, you will be able to make the Explore step sound much more natural, too. Look at the following version, where the teacher has woven the example into the reverse (B = A) to make it sound natural and smooth:

Paraphrase:	Good teamwork means telling someone what to do.
Explore:	So, if I tell you to do your homework, does that make us a good team?

Figure 33 expresses how it works, using an example from another context. What the teacher says is in cells with white backgrounds, while the shaded cells represent the formation (rules) of the questioning technique.

▶ Figure 33: Constructing an A = B challenge probe

Operation	Concept	Operation	Idea
If	**Concept (A)**	**=**	**Idea (B)**
If	sport	is	a contest
Does	**Idea (B)**	**=**	**Concept (A)**
Then is	a contest		sport
For example, is	a quiz show		sport

Consider this Initiate question, and then do your by-now well-honed practice of predicting possible responses. I am picturing a Grade 4 class (9-year-olds) to make my predictions:

Initiate:	What is a tradition?
Possible Responses:	Something you do a lot
	Something people like
	Something everyone does
	Religious festival
	A special day
	Eating turkey
	Something our family does
	Thanksgiving
	Something old
	Holidays
	It's been around for years
	Getting presents

I came up with 12 possible ideas. I'm not expecting to use them all, and I wouldn't expect my students to say them all either! But it's good to have an extensive list to start with, to practise my A = B challenge moves and think of examples that will disrupt my students' first responses.

I've picked a few and put them into the same format as in Figure 33 to plan my questioning moves, as shown in Figure 34.

▶ Figure 34: Constructing an A = B challenge probe on 'tradition'.

Operation	Concept	Operation	Idea
If	**Concept (A)**	**=**	**Idea (B)**
If	tradition	is	something you do a lot
Does	**Idea (B)**	**=**	**Concept (A)**
Then is	something you do a lot		tradition
For example, is	walking to school		tradition

In Figure 35, I have taken out the full scaffold, but created some A = B questioning moves based on some of the other predicted responses.

▶ **Figure 35: Constructing further A = B challenge probes on 'tradition', using a more open template.**

Operation	Concept	Operation	Idea
If	**a tradition (A)**	**is**	**something everyone does (B)**
Then is	something everyone does (B)	a	tradition (A)
For example, is	sleeping	a	tradition (A)
If	**a tradition (A)**	**=**	**a special day (B)**
Then is	a special day (B)		tradition (A)
For example, is	the day I got my cat		tradition (A)

In your classroom, those challenge moves would sound like this:

Teacher:	What is a tradition?
Response:	Something that everyone does.
Challenge:	A tradition is something everyone does. So if we all do it, then it's a tradition? We all go to sleep at night. Does that mean sleeping is a tradition?

I have left the table in Figure 36 blank so you can have a go at planning an A = B challenge for yourself. You can use the example student responses on 'tradition' or choose a concept of your own that you might cover with your class tomorrow. Don't forget to think of an example!

▶ **Figure 36: A blank planning template for an A = B challenge probe.**

Operation	Concept	Operation	Idea
If	**Concept (A)**	**=**	**Idea (B)**
If		is	
Does	**Idea (B)**	**=**	**Concept (A)**
Then is			
For example, is			

8.5.2 • Intention to Challenge 6: Not A, Not B

Paraphrase:	If good teamwork means talking to each other . . .
Explore:	. . . then, if we are not talking to each other, are we not a good team?
Example:	For example, if we are in a synchronised swimming competition, we can't talk, so are we not a good team?

Similarly to Intention to Challenge 5, this method uses 'idea A' and 'idea B' but this time presents them in the negative form. So if A = B, then if it's not B, is it also not A? In our sequence above, idea A is 'good teamwork', and idea B is 'talking to each other'. So, if we are not B (talking to each other), are we not A (a good team)?

The example gives the student a real situation in which the question might occur, so the example becomes what the students process next. It is often the example, more than the question, that creates positive struggle. This is a useful reminder to us that we are questioning, rather than asking questions.

In Figure 37, we have shown how to construct a 'Not A, Not B' challenge using the same table structure as in 8.6.1.

▶ **Figure 37:** Constructing a 'Not A, Not B' challenge probe.

Operation	Concept	Operation	Idea
If	**Concept (A)**	**=**	**Idea (B)**
If	music	is	a tune
Then if it is not	**Idea (B)**	**is it not**	**Concept (A)**
If it	does not have a tune	is it not	music
For example	is a drumbeat	not	music

I have left the table in Figure 38 blank so you can have a go at planning a 'Not A, Not B' challenge for yourself. You can use the example student responses from 8.6.1 on 'tradition' or choose a concept of your own that you might cover with your class tomorrow. Don't forget to think of an example to support your question!

You might find initially that the 'Not A, Not B' move takes a bit more practice. But you will soon get a feel for which student responses lend themselves better to A = B and which work better with Not A, Not B, and they soon start to sound more natural and in flow. In fact, I probably use Not A, Not B now more than A = B: like any skill, they just take time to practise.

▶ **Figure 38:** A blank planning template for a 'Not A, Not B' challenge probe.

Operation	Concept	Operation	Idea
If	**Concept (A)**	**=**	**Idea (B)**
If		is	
Then if it is not	**Idea (B)**	**is it not**	**Concept (A)**
If it		is it not	
For example		not	

8.5.3 • Intention to Challenge 7: What If All, None, Some

Teacher: What is a tradition?

Response: A holiday!

Challenge: What if *every day* was a holiday? What would that be like?

[Response.]

Challenge: What if there were *no* holidays?

[Response.]

Challenge: What if only *some* people were allowed holidays?

This challenge can be really good fun as well as demanding on you and your students! 'What if all, none, some' challenges involve thinking both critically and creatively and having a basis in reasoning and judgement, as well as in speculation and hypothesis. The challenge is to ask what the result would be if 'all, none, or some' of an idea happened.

This kind of challenge requires follow-up with lots of Explore and Extend questioning because the key to the challenge is in predicting cause and effect. So what would the implications be if all of this happened? What would the effect be if none of this took place? What if only some could happen?

All can mean 'all the time'; 'everybody'; 'in every situation'; 'full'; 'permanent'.

None can mean 'never'; 'no one'; 'no'; 'on no occasion'; 'empty'; 'gone'.

Some can mean 'sometimes'; 'a few'; 'occasionally'; 'hardly'; 'infrequent'.

Here's an example from a lesson where Grade 8 students (age 13) are discussing environmental responsibility. The teacher's intent is to challenge her students' thinking so they have to consider cause and effect. We are already a few steps into the questioning sequence when we join the dialogue:

Student A: If people took more responsibility for the environment, there'd be less problems.

Teacher: What can people do to take more responsibility for the environment?

Student B: Not use so much electricity.

Student A: Recycle.

Student C: Not throw away as much plastic.

Teacher: Well, *what if everyone* took responsibility and did all those things?

Student C: There'd be no environment damage.

Student A: Less plastic in the sea hopefully. Which means it would be safer for animals and not threatening endangered species and such. And better for plant life so we're not chopping down trees and then just throwing stuff away.

Student D: The world would be a cleaner place and better for the future with health and better living.

Teacher: Sounds like a better place all 'round. So how could you make *everyone* take responsibility?

Student D: Make it a law.

Teacher: And *what if no one* followed the law?

Student B:	They'd get fined or go to jail.
Teacher:	Then *what if no one* followed the law, *and everyone* had to go to jail?
Student A:	Hmm. Yeah.
Student E:	Bad plan! Maybe they could just get fined.
Student F:	And then use the money to fix the problems.
Teacher:	OK, so we keep the law and use the money to help. *What if* the law was that *everyone* had to take responsibility, which meant *all* cars were banned?
Student F:	You can't do that! We also still need to live a normal life but still try to look after the environment as well, 'cause you can't just stop living in the real world, and it might not even help anyway.
Teacher:	It might not help. Then, what if it were the other way? *What if no one* took responsibility for the environment? What would happen then?

[Talk in groups.]

In this questioning sequence, the teacher used the 'What if . . .' challenge prompt to encourage her students to think of ideas and possibilities but then didn't let the first idea go unchallenged: instead, she prompted them to think critically about the idea of, for example, putting everyone in jail! She then challenged the idea of making it a law at all so that the students couldn't rest on their first ideas. Even reading the transcript, and with small modifications to make it more readable, you can feel the energy in the room and the culture of collaborative inquiry and high expectations the teacher and students worked in.

A Reflection Section

- **What did you notice in these exchanges in 8.6.1 through 8.6.3?**

- **What is interesting about the Questioning for Challenge approach, and what do you think the benefits might be?**

- **How do you think your students would react?**

- **What is the intention of these questioning sequences?**

8.6 • THE ROLE OF THE QUESTIONER: TEACHER STANCES WHEN QUESTIONING FOR CHALLENGE

As you begin a Questioning for Challenge sequence, it is worth deciding on a standpoint (or values) that will best support the development of your questioning. Even if you don't currently act on this standpoint, write it down so you can work toward it.

First, if you have an opinion of your own about the concept you are discussing, *hold on to it lightly*. Try not to let your opinion sway your students' thinking, and don't lead the students to *your* answer. Yours is only one of the possible ways to express understanding, so your students should have time to explore the concept for themselves.

A second value is well expressed by James Nottingham, who uses the phrase 'Not all of our questions answered but all of our answers questioned' to encapsulate his core value in the cognitive conflict stage.

A Reflection Section

- **If you held that same belief as James when initiating a questioning sequence, how might it impact on your actions?**

- **Could you see this stance in action in the examples in this chapter?**

- **What would it be like if you *held onto your opinions lightly*, rather than telling them to your students?**

- **What did you notice about the teacher's stance in this chapter's examples?**

Socrates used four different stances during questioning sequences: the ignoramus, the gadfly, the midwife, and the stingray. These standpoints represent a way of thinking and behaving during questioning sequences and are a fun way to help you plan your dialogues. If you can identify the standpoint you want to take, you are explicitly identifying the intent to challenge in your questioning.

8.6.1 • The Ignoramus

This is Socrates's most well-known stance, often referred to as the Socratic paradox: 'I know only that I know nothing'. The ignoramus standpoint, then, emulates a character who has never encountered the concept being discussed. The intention is to encourage explanation so that by innocently asking, 'But if that is true, why does [this example] not fit?' you ensure that the students have to go another way to reach an answer. As a result, it encourages a broader and more accurate use of language.

Ignoramus questioning can include:

- So you say X is this. But what about this [counter-example]?
- If A = B, then does B = A?
- If A = B, then if it's not A, is it not B?
- Are these two ideas the same then?
- I don't understand how X can be what you say. Can you explain it more?

8.6.2 • The Gadfly

In this role, the questioner mimics the way a gadfly nips away at larger animals. This involves asking lots of short, sharp questions designed to push thinking and clarify ideas, where the student would rather settle on a simple or easy definition.

Gadfly questions might include:

- What do you mean by . . . ?
- Can you give an example?
- What evidence do you have?
- Is that always the case?
- How can you be certain that is true?

8.6.3 The Midwife

The Midwife asks questions that help give birth to ideas. With this standpoint, the questioning is more careful and more deliberate, challenging the students to consider cause and effect and the possible outcomes of their answer.

Midwife questions can include:

- What made you think of that?
- What might happen next?
- What if all, none, or some . . . ?
- If you did that, then what effect would that have on . . . ?
- How might that affect things?

8.6.4 • The Stingray

In this role, the questioner shocks the students' normal line of thinking by asking a question that turns the dialogue on its head, often using a 'reverse' speculation. The purpose is to keep the students engaged with the unexpected, like a stingray unleashing its sting!

Stingray questioning often uses these phrases (after Gershon, 2013):

- What if the opposite to that was true . . . ?
- If this happened instead, what would X be like?
- If Y was not the case, what then?
- How much better/worse would it be if . . . ?
- If X was actually Y, what would that mean?

One of the standpoints that we often hear teachers talk about in questioning is 'devil's advocate'. And often by way of apology! We hear teachers offering a challenge in a questioning sequence, but as soon as the student looks confused or struggles to answer, the teacher blurts out, 'Don't worry, I'm just playing devil's advocate'!

When offering up a challenge or taking a standpoint, you don't need to explain what you are doing: 'I'm just being a midwife' is unnecessary; the students know you are challenging them! The same applies with devil's advocate.

It is also important to avoid the word *playing* as it suggests that you don't really believe in the challenge. As challenge is an essential part of learning, it should always be part of your role to challenge. So definitely don't apologise for doing it or dismiss challenge as 'play'.

Remember—positive struggle is essential, so your role as teacher is to sustain it.

As with all categories and styles, these stances are behaviours which can be learned and developed. So don't choose just one; try them all—even in a single questioning sequence—and flit between them to question the views, opinions, and judgements held by your students.

8.7 • TIME TO THINK WHEN QUESTIONING FOR CHALLENGE

When Questioning for Challenge, students will be thinking on different levels, and in different ways. Like any good dialogue, there will only be one person speaking at any one time. Even with the best intentions of looking to engage a range of students during the dialogue, not everyone will get the chance to speak.

This does not mean, however, that the students who speak out to the whole class are the only ones thinking and learning.

When Questioning for Challenge, the thinking and the learning happen constantly, for those speaking and for those listening: the way a concept is defined can shift quickly, so it is important to make use of think-time to allow students time to process their current understanding of the concept and how it has moved.

Create regular opportunities for these perception checks by utilising Thinking Partners *during* the dialogue. This gives your students the opportunity to rehearse their language and ideas, and you will find that you get more students participating in the dialogue immediately afterwards.

Students talking in pairs or small groups during a perception check often first express a smaller concept, idea, or definition to establish a foundation before linking it to the bigger concept under discussion. You can then draw their perceptions out explicitly through your questioning.

For example:

> Teacher: We are talking about what it means to be 'fair'. Tell the person next to you what you understand by that.

Or:

> Teacher: John said that dangerous situations should be avoided. Talk in pairs and decide whether you agree with this statement or not.

Once they have discussed this in pairs for a minute or so, ask them to connect to the bigger concept again so they keep focussed on the purpose of the discussion and the goal of the lesson.

For example:

> Teacher: Now consider the idea of being fair if you are a king or queen. Do you think it is an important characteristic of being a monarch?

Or:

> Teacher: Is avoiding danger a good way to encourage young children to learn about staying safe?

At, or near, the end of a Questioning for Challenge sequence, you will want to use standpoint think-time (5.5.8) to support your students coming out of the pit and taking a step toward constructing a resolution (moving from Stage 2 to Stage 3 of The Learning Challenge). These reflection times are crucial both to metacognitive understanding and in demonstrating progress in language.

During standpoint time, ask the students to consider what they understand about the big concept under discussion now and how it differs from their first responses. They may not have reached a resolution yet, but they should be able to outline the way their thinking has moved on from their first response at this point in the dialogue.

There are three important questions to ask in standpoint think-time:

1. What do you understand about [the concept] now?
2. How has your thinking developed through the discussion?
3. What is the next thing you need to know/find out to help you learn more?

These questions are a reflection on (1) the students' current understanding, (2) an explicit identification of the progress made in learning, and (3) identification of where to go next. You can read more on working with progress through these three questions in *Challenging Learning Through Feedback* (Nottingham & Nottingham, 2017).

8.8 • REVIEW

In this chapter, we have covered the following key points:

i. Questioning for Challenge is a way of encouraging students into the Learning Pit (Stage 2 of The Learning Challenge).

ii. Questioning for Challenge does to learning what roadblocks do to your journey home—they cause you difficulty and make you think. The effort required is both frustrating and rewarding!

iii. We used seven Questioning for Challenge techniques to encourage cognitive conflict in your students so they experience positive struggle.

iv. Support your questioning with examples to make the challenge concrete for the students.

v. Planning is essential for successful Questioning for Challenge sequences.

vi. Identify your standpoint for improving questioning. Socrates used four: the ignoramus, the gadfly, the midwife, and the stingray.

vii. Use perception checks (5.5.6) and standpoint think-time (5.5.8) to provide opportunity for reflection on learning and progress made both during the dialogue and at the end.

8.9 • REFLECTION

i. Try planning your questioning moves using the ideas in this chapter:

   a. The Counter-Example

   b. Comparisons

   c. Challenge Assumptions

   d. Define Extent

   e. A = B

   f. Not A, Not B

   g. What If All, None, Some

ii. Try practising with one of the four stances. The ignoramus is usually the easiest one to begin with and fits well with a lot of the Explore questions we looked at in earlier chapters.

Then try a different stance. What do you notice about your behaviour and your questioning technique when you wear that mantle?

iii. Remember to use Thinking Partners for regular perception checks during, and standpoint think-time toward the end of, dialogues to encourage reflection on progress.

iv. Review your Questioning for Challenge in practice:

How is it different from your earlier Explore questioning using the funnelling technique?

How do the seven Questioning for Challenge techniques in this chapter build on the five techniques we saw in Chapter 4?

How do the Questioning for Challenge techniques build on the practices you have developed so far?

What is the impact on your students? How did they respond, and what would you like to find out more about from them?

You are probably starting to think that there are likely to be many positives and negatives in Questioning for Challenge. Challenging the students in this way can be, well, challenging! So it is worth reflecting on the positive reasons for challenging students' thinking, and also being aware of possible drawbacks to it. Most importantly, it is knowing the impact you are having on your students' learning. So try to focus on not just the questions you ask, but the impact of your questioning on your students. We have created a table in Figure 39 for you to record some reflections on your experiences.

▶ **Figure 39:** Reviewing your experiences with Questioning for Challenge.

Questioning for Challenge	
Intent (What is the purpose of your questioning?)	

Some Benefits of Questioning for Challenge	Some Possible Drawbacks

Stances I have used and my reflections from trying them:	

The impact I have noticed on my students:	

As with all questioning, the more practised and experienced you become, the more you can plan the right questioning approach for the right moment, to have the maximum impact on students' learning and engagement.

It is also worth remembering that challenging students' thinking should be purposeful. So don't forget your intention! What impact do you hope to have on the students by challenging their responses, and why do you want that?

PART III
STUDENTS
AND QUESTIONING

The questions children ask must be relevant and of potential use to their cognitive development . . . we must see evidence that children's questions help them in some way—that is, that they can ask questions for a purpose, and use the information they receive purposefully to successfully achieve some change of knowledge state.

—M. M. Chouinard (2007)

STUDENTS LEARNING TO ASK QUESTIONS

9

One of the outcomes of purposeful classroom questioning is that students start to ask more—and better—questions that are focussed on understanding. This is because effective questioning models the process of learning and teaches the habits of good thinking. Once they are internalised, students adopt these behaviours for themselves, and a culture of inquiry begins to prevail in your classroom.

In Chapter 6, we saw the importance of cognitive conflict in engaging students in the learning process and positive struggle. Cognitive conflict not only creates better thinking, but it also encourages your students to ask more questions, as they seek resolution to the conflicting ideas or misconceptions they have unearthed.

The purpose of the questions your students raise when they are wrestling with cognitive conflict in the Learning Pit is different from 'typical student questions', which are often procedural (Doherty, 2017). The questions students ask when dealing with positive struggle contribute positively to the process of thinking, and to their learning outcomes, and often have the purpose of:

Seeking resolution

Seeking clarity

Focussing on *how* and *why*

Further investigation

Promoting self-study

Seeking information (to support or counter the prevailing idea)

Beginning or continuing a dialogue

Challenging each other, themselves, or the teacher

In this way, asking questions becomes a strategy for your students to construct new understanding. Being able to ask, and seek answers to, your own questions creates self-efficacy: the ability to effect change. Most people learn best when they have the opportunity to ask questions and therefore *want* to learn. This can also make students' ability to ask questions a powerful strategy at Stage 3 of The Learning Challenge as your students look to come out of the pit.

9.0 • QUESTION STEMS

If you want your students to learn to ask questions to promote their own investigations, then it is important that you explicitly teach them *how* to ask questions. As you have worked through this book, you have developed different types and purposes for questioning. And it is not always easy; despite what we might assume, questioning does not come naturally! If it is hard for you to think about and do well, then you can imagine that it is at least as hard for your students.

We have already seen that think-time encourages unsolicited questions from students: to you and to each other. But in this chapter, we are focussing on the explicit intention to teach students how to question.

The use of question stems is the simplest way to get your students thinking about questioning. I talked about using the questioning prompt sheet (Figure 11) with your students. Put a copy (use a shorter and more focussed version for the topic you are working on) on their desks so they can refer to it during groupwork, during think-time, and when working with Thinking Partners. When your students can rehearse with each other the sorts of questions you are likely to ask them during a questioning sequence, they will also rehearse the target language, and thinking, you set in the Learning Intention of the lesson.

Question stems work in just the same way. You can share these on desks, stick them into workbooks, or post them on your classroom wall. Question stems are a great way to get your students to construct their own questions, to help them investigate concepts and ideas further.

My colleague James Nottingham suggests creating questions at Stage 1, the Concept stage of The Learning Challenge, to encourage your students into the pit using their own concepts:

> [While it can take time, and might be difficult with very young children,] the positive effects can be powerful and long-lasting. Imagine having students who are curious, reflective and able to verbalise their thinking in the form of great questions! That's the impact you can have by working with question stems again and again with your students. (Nottingham, 2017, p. 60)

The question stems in Figure 40 give you an idea of how this works. By mixing and matching some of these suggestions, your students should be able to generate some thought-provoking conceptual questions worth exploring.

► **Figure 40: Question stems.**

Question Stem	Example
What is . . .	What is belief?
What makes . . .	What makes something real?
Would you be . . .	Would you be the same person if someone stole your identity?
How do we know what . . .	How do we know what fear is?
Should we always [or never] . . .	Should we always tell the truth?
What if . . .	What if there was no such thing as curiosity?
Is it possible . . .	Is it possible to be happy and sad at the same time?
When . . .	When is a person an adult?
Who . . .	Who decides what beauty is?
Can we . . .	Can we think without language?
Why do we say . . .	Why do we say 'actions speak louder than words'?
What is the difference between . . .	What is the difference between what's right and what's wrong?

Source: From *The Learning Challenge: How to Guide Your Students Through the Learning Pit to Achieve Deeper Understanding* (Nottingham, 2017, p. 61).

I suggest that you offer your students just three or four of these question stems during their first experiences of working with questioning. As they become more skilful in their use of the stems, you can add one or two more each time until they are familiar with all of the prompts.

Challenge your students to create thought-provoking questions by pairing one of the question stems with one or more of the concepts they have identified. They can then play around with the way in which the question is formed until they are satisfied that they have created a question that is worth exploring.

9.1 • THE QUESTION CONSTRUCTOR

As well as encouraging your students to create the kinds of questions that will lead to engaging dialogue, the Question Constructor strategy, shown in Figure 41, can be good fun, prompt research and self-study, create hypotheses to test, or set up investigations.

The strategy works by asking your students to take one word from each column to create a skeleton question. By using different stems, trailing stems, and endings, they can create questions around the concept they are investigating. In Column 3 (Concept/Idea), I would usually just have the key concepts of the lesson or topic, so there should only be one or two options in there. The remaining columns can have as many or as few ideas as you wish, especially Columns 2 and 4.

The Question Constructor can be used as a table (as in Figure 41) or can be printed out and cut up to make separate cards. If you are printing it to make cards, it works well to make each column a different colour so your students can identify whether their card is a stem, trailer, or ending.

A Question Constructor tool to use with your students to encourage them to create questions of their own for further study or inquiry.

Question Stem	Trailing Stem	Concept/Idea	Question Ending
What . . .	does		mean
Why . . .	is		used/misused
When . . .	could		important/unimportant
Where . . .	if		have in common with . . .
Who . . .	(is it/not) possible		didn't exist
Which . . .	happens	communication	matter/not matter
How . . .	should		change
	can		always/never . . .
	will		affect . . .
	would		seen by others

The example Question Constructor is focussed on the concept of communication. You can ask your students to take a word from each column to create a question. For example:

Question Stem	Trailing Stem	Concept/Idea	Question
What . . .	does	communication	mean

Alternatively, they could create this:

Question Stem	Trailing Stem	Concept/Idea	Question Ending
What . . .	if	communication	didn't exist

Whilst others might create this:

Question Stem	Trailing Stem	Concept/Idea	Question Ending
Where . . .	is it not possible	communication	used

Of course, in this example, your students would need to 'complete' the question so it reads as a proper sentence: *Where is it not possible* [for] *communication* [to be] *used*?

That can often prompt them to look for similar alternatives: *Where is it possible* [for] *communication* [to be] *misused?* And you start to notice that they are creating questions without the scaffold of the Question Constructor each time.

Sometimes, the question stem isn't needed, and a question can be created from the trailing stem. For example:

Question Stem	Trailing Stem	Concept/Idea	Question Ending
	Does	communication	**affect . . .**

In this example, the students chose to miss the question stem and instead use a question that begins with the trailer: *Does communication affect* [success]?

I find that this tool is much more useful to print and cut out as cards. Your students can have endless fun creating questions by placing the cards in different sequences. And, of course, they can add extra words, stems, and ideas for you to keep developing as a class.

It is vital that you make the learning from this activity explicit. Your students are learning how to ask questions, so you will need to spend some time debriefing the Question Constructor activity. I find that questioning students in the following way works well:

What did you create?

What makes that a good question?

What other questions did you create that were good examples?

What makes them good questions for further investigation, discussion, or research?

Were there any questions that weren't so good? Why were they not as good?

Which stems worked best for [this concept]?

Which endings created questions that you think would be most interesting to study further?

If you had to think of a question now, without the Question Constructor, what question would you create?

You don't need to ask all of these to debrief the Question Constructor tool. A well-planned, focussed questioning sequence always works best to ensure your intent in questioning is explicit: to learn how to ask questions for further exploration. Here's an example sequence with that intent:

Initiate: What question did you create?

[Respond.]

Explain: What makes that a good question?

Explore: What does a question need to be like to make it a good one for further investigation?

Conclude: Can you think of another question now, without using the Question Constructor, based on your ideas today?

[Think-Pair-Share.]

This is a strategy widely used in journalism, reporting, media, story writing, and scriptwriting to frame the way information is presented to an audience. It is also a useful tool in the classroom to prompt questions for investigation and to scaffold inquiry.

5 Ws and an H (Who, What, Why, Where, When, and How) allows your students to raise questions by, and amongst, themselves and so supports independent study and research. The purpose is to encourage the process of raising questions from all perspectives and at the same time raise awareness of audience, or the end user of the research. This has the effect of engaging students in the subject you are teaching by creating a 'need to know'.

The tool is very simple, based on an image, text, video, or even statistics to stimulate curiosity and wonder, puzzlement and intrigue. This thinking can prompt questions from your students, which you can ask them to record on the page around the image. They can work in pairs, in groups, or as a whole class to discuss their ideas and questions as they write them.

Figure 42 shows how the tool works with the image in the centre and space around the edge for the question prompts. I usually ask my students to put two or three questions under each prompt, to get them past the first ideas they come up with. Sometimes it works well to ask them to go around all the question stems once, then go around them all a second time, adding further questions.

Once they have created their questions, they can then select the one they think will be best for further study, research, or discussion. See Figure 43 for an example, and Figure 44 for a blank template to use with your students.

▶ **Figure 42:** An example 5 Ws and an H template, with an image to encourage students to think more about the cause and effects of coastal erosion.

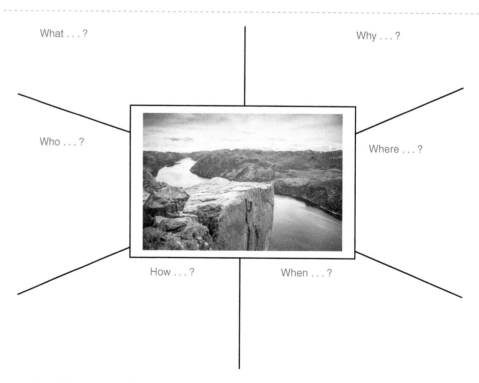

What . . . ?   Why . . . ?

Who . . . ?   Where . . . ?

How . . . ?   When . . . ?

Image Source: iStock.com/cookelma

▶ **Figure 43:** An example 5 *W*s and an *H* template, with text in the centre to encourage Grade 3 students to think more about reading between the lines in a story (after Reed, 2016).

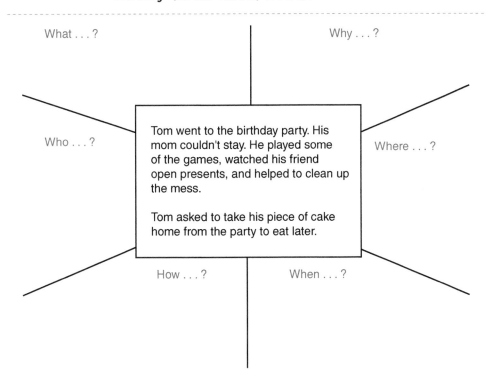

What . . . ?

Why . . . ?

Who . . . ?

Tom went to the birthday party. His mom couldn't stay. He played some of the games, watched his friend open presents, and helped to clean up the mess.

Tom asked to take his piece of cake home from the party to eat later.

Where . . . ?

How . . . ?

When . . . ?

▶ **Figure 44:** A blank 5 *W*s and an *H* template, for use with your students.

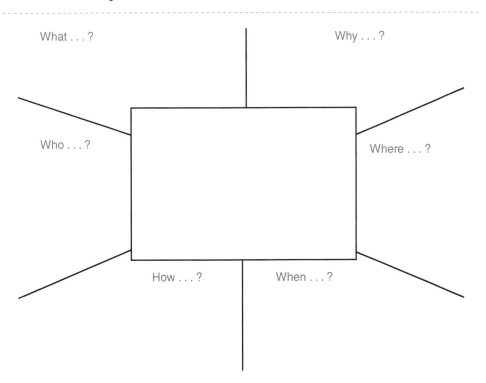

What . . . ?

Why . . . ?

Who . . . ?

Where . . . ?

How . . . ?

When . . . ?

Inference Squares, like the 5 *W*s and an *H* tool, uses a stimulus to encourage thinking around an issue, leading to students asking questions and therefore opportunity for further study or inquiry.

Unlike 5 *W*s and an *H*, though, which is based on question stems, Inference Squares are based on perception and the way we view a situation. This tool presents the idea that not all information is complete and that we often only see a partial view of reality. This can create cognitive conflict between what your students know and what they *think* they know. Inference, then, is the process of making an educated guess based on clues or evidence you can see, and your existing knowledge of the world, to fill in the gaps you can't see.

The tool is built in four steps:

1. What do you know for certain?
2. What can you infer?
3. What do you not know?
4. What questions do you have?

Walking through these four steps teaches your students a strategy for analytical thinking: breaking an event down to look at it objectively. This is best done in pairs or small groups so that there is opportunity for dialogue and shared language along the way. The final step of the Inference Square then creates an opportunity for further study, research, or dialogue so your students can undertake an inquiry based on their own questions.

The Inference Squares strategy is very useful in subjects like the humanities (archaeologists might infer use, design, and age from other similar finds) and in areas like media, advertising, and current affairs; and it can also be used as a means of exploring literature and stories. You can use it with younger students, too: by all means use the word *infer*, but you might also like to add a rephrase at that step, such as 'What can you guess at?' or 'What can you work out?' or 'What might we think this is showing us, even if we don't know for sure?'

See Figures 45 and 46 for examples, and Figure 47 for a blank template to use with your students.

▶ **Figure 45:** An example Inference Squares template, with an image to encourage students to 'read between the lines'. You can print these for students to complete with Thinking Partners, or work on a shared screen together as a class.

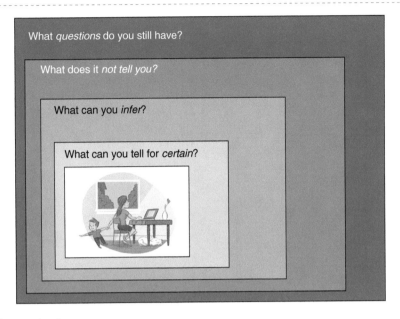

Image Source: iStock.com/darenwoodward

▶ **Figure 46:** An example Inference Squares template, with an image to encourage students to think more about what they know and don't know, and how their knowledge of the world helps them make sense of what they see (perhaps, or probably, differently from what others see).

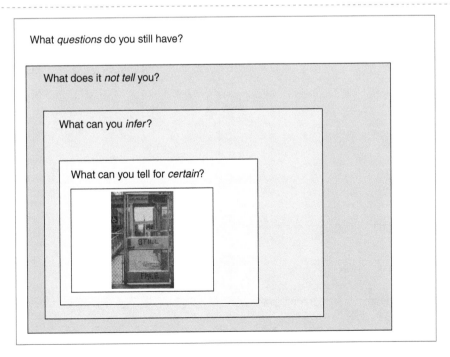

Image Source: Unsplash.com/@nkalil

▶ Figure 47: A blank Inference Squares template, for use with your students.

What *questions* do you still have?

What does it *not tell* you?

What can you *infer*?

What can you tell for *certain*?

For your Inference Squares design, choose an image or text that is open to interpretation and leaves a lot to the imagination. The more there is to guess at, the more your students need to infer. Try to ensure that the steps of inference they take lead them to ask questions relevant to your goal so that their resulting inquiry helps them understand your intention better.

This is what Roberts (2013) refers to as 'framed inquiry'. Challenging Learning consultant Richard Kielty used framed inquiry to design a slightly different approach to teaching inference and deduction with his students:

In this example, I was working with a class of Grade 4 students in a history lesson. The aim of the lesson was to develop our use of sources and interpretation skills to make judgements.

I wanted my students to be able to examine a range of sources and determine what they said about the personality, lifestyle, and age of a person.

We began the lesson by discussing source skills and related this to being a detective, discussing why historians need to be able to use sources effectively. I asked the students to think of how we could discover history without the use of sources.

We discussed the difference between inference and deduction, and I gave two definitions with an example:

Deduction is an understanding based on the evidence we have.

Inference is an idea we create that goes beyond what we can see.

For example, if the police find a dog wandering the streets, we can deduce that the owner is the person named on the dog's collar. We could infer that the dog has run away.

The students were going to play at being detectives, using a range of sources that we had about a person (that person was me, although they didn't know this at the time!).

They were to attempt to answer the question, What do the sources tell us about a person?

They should try and infer from the sources given and reach a conclusion about the person's age, personality, lifestyle, and education.

I placed the students in pairs and gave them each a source from my home. These ranged from old photographs and photocopied exam certificates (partly 'destroyed' to hide my name) to an electric toothbrush and iPod. They then completed an Inference Square using each source, one at a time, building up a picture of the owner.

They had to consider what the source told them for certain (deduction), what the source made them think about (inference), what the source did not tell them (what needs investigating), and questions they would need to ask in order to find out more (inquiry).

They then swapped sources and Inference Squares to determine what they could infer from a different piece of evidence.

We then discussed the usefulness of each of the sources and any conclusions the groups may have reached. We tried to ascertain which sources were most useful for finding out about (my) family and education.

This activity was a powerful way to engage all pupils in generating questions and attempting to arrive at conclusions. It helped determine the criteria for usefulness of sources and the difference between inference and plain guesswork.

And what student wouldn't enjoy playing the role of a detective?

Building on approaches like Richard's, you can debrief the learning from an Inference Square and draw attention to the analytical skill the student has developed in breaking the stimulus down to reach a question:

What did you think you knew to begin with?

What do you think now?

What were you guessing at?

What's the difference between opinion and inference?

What were the clues/evidence that you inferred from?

Why might inferring be important (in other subjects/life)?

Do we ever know the whole story/picture/truth?

Inference is becoming more and more essential, with the advent of short attention-grabbing headlines and social media posts scant on detail, along with the prominence of e-marketing. To filter out what has meaning, students need to learn the thinking skill of inference, to ensure they have the ability to question what they hear or read and think critically, rather than just assuming that everything they see is accurate, true, or beneficial.

9.4 • STUDENTS CLASSIFYING THEIR OWN QUESTIONS FOR INQUIRY

A good way for students to learn about questioning is for them to work with their own questions after they've created them. When any strategy or dialogue generates questions from your students, do take the opportunity to collate the questions and share them. Having a bank of their questions is such a great opportunity to explicitly teach your students *how* to question and help them learn the value of being able to question.

After running the strategies seen in 9.1–9.3, you may well find yourself in possession of many questions raised by your students! You obviously can't use them all for inquiry, dialogue, or research, but you can certainly work with them all to teach your students explicitly about questioning.

Collate the questions your students have raised so you have them in one place. Your students can shout them out for you to write on the board, hand in their papers if they did the strategies on printouts (for you to type up), or use a shared online tool such as Google Docs to type the questions in themselves so they can all see the questions as they are added.

Each pair or group can choose their best three questions, for example, so you get plenty of variety without being overwhelmed! Of course, you will always get crossover: students who chose the same, or very similar, questions. That's fine; either they can choose another one or you can put it up once and put a number next to it to show how many groups said it.

Once you have collated the questions, they might look like the ones in Figure 48. This is from one of my own Grade 8 lessons, where we learn about the concept of *place*: 'to understand geographical similarities, differences and links between places through the study of human and physical geography of a region within Africa' (Department for Education and Skills, 2013).

In this example, the students were studying Kenya and had been asked to work in pairs to first do a search on the internet for some images of Kenya, and then bring five images back to a central table. Each pair had to find images that showed a range of examples from human geography (industry, transport, city, village, people) to physical geography (river, sea, mountains, weather, vegetation).

I asked my students to organise the images into groups that reflected what they now knew about the place. Then, my students were asked what they noticed about the images, and began to look more closely and compare them. I asked if anything surprised them about the images. My students were quite amazed by the wide variety of landscapes and the extremes of wealth on display. When asked what made them surprising, many students responded that they had a preconceived idea of African countries and this didn't completely fit with their view. In effect, they were experiencing cognitive conflict between what they thought and what they were looking at.

Each pair was then asked to go away and write three questions based on what they had seen of Kenya so far. Their questions were collated and are shown in Figure 48.

▶ Figure 48: Student-generated questions on Kenya collated and displayed on the classroom wall in an 'Our Questions for Investigating Kenya' display.

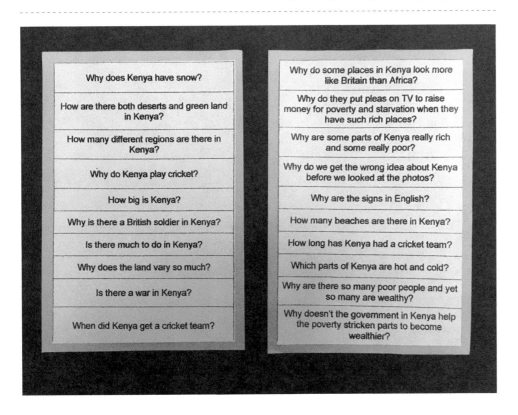

At this stage, my students had raised their own questions, had created a 'need to know', and so were now engaged in thinking about Kenya for themselves. But before being set off to go and find the answers or jump straight into investigation, they worked to understand their questions more deeply.

They were asked if they could spot any 'kinds of questions'. Which questions were similar and different? Would all questions give them the same amount of work to do to find an answer?

By looking at their questions and considering how they would find the answers, my students came up with their own categories of questions. They decided that some questions were *easy to answer* (Does Kenya have large cities? Do all areas have a small population? Do all people live in fields?), some would *need research to be able to answer* (How many people live in the capital city? What is the highest mountain in Kenya? Where does the cricket team play?), and some *either were opinions or had no answer* (Does Kenya make a good holiday resort? Why do we automatically think of poorer areas? Could you have known that all these pictures were of Kenya?).

Using these categories, my students then discussed their questions to decide whether they knew it and it just needed simple research (*easy to answer*), whether they needed to spend time researching it more deeply (*needs research*), or whether they needed to gauge public (well, peer!) opinion and share their own perspectives (*opinion*).

While discussing the questions, they coded them against the three categories. Some used colour, some used symbols, and some used numbers (see Figure 49). The discussion and processing that goes into categorising the questions helps students to learn more about what types of questions support investigations and research, which questions are short and quick, and which questions are more speculative. By doing this explicitly, my students were not only developing a subject-specific language around Kenya and its environs, but also developing a language of questioning.

▶ **Figure 49:** Two examples of coded question sheets on Kenya. Remember that all of these questions were raised *by* students, *for* students. They are working with their own questions.

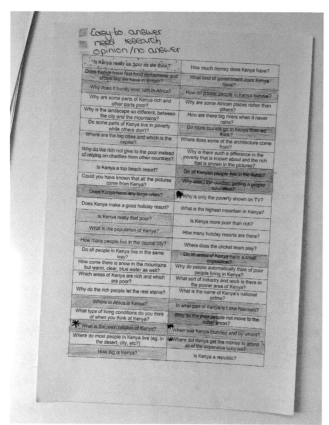
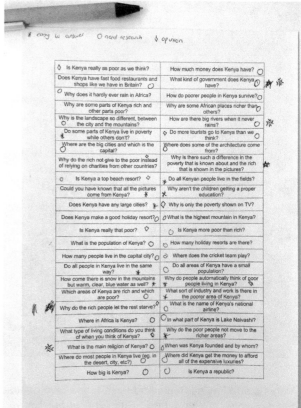

Once they had coded the questions, my students were asked to choose three questions from the *easy to answer* category, two questions from the *needs research* category, and one question from the *opinion* category. These would become their first steps into finding out about Kenya.

My students were engaged, enthusiastic, and already interested in Kenya before they even began researching. They felt like this was their topic, these were their questions, and they were in control of their learning. The use of cognitive conflict at the start and a strategy (questioning) to help them construct understanding had created self-efficacy.

Notice how little direct instruction I needed to give them. Instead, I provided the opportunity for my students to go and learn it for themselves.

Once their research was underway, I provided guidance and ways of getting my students to share what they'd found with each other. For example, they used a 'Research Scaffold' which encouraged them to find out some facts but then still focussed on questioning by asking them what further questions their research created and what other questions their research answered that they hadn't even asked yet!

Figure 50 shows two examples of my students' work on the Research Scaffold.

▶ **Figure 50:** Two examples of a Research Scaffold in use. Notice there are facts that the students have researched and then these facts are taking them into further questions. Students are also learning things that are connected to but not part of their original research: they are learning to look more carefully and make connections in understanding.

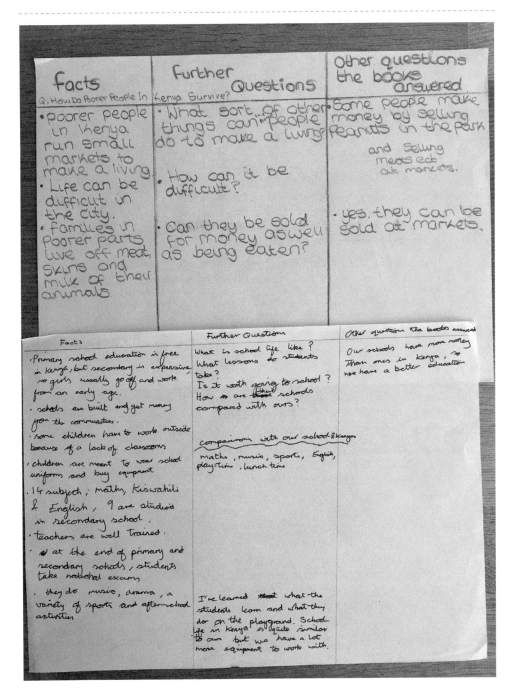

I recently worked with an experienced geography teacher who was more used to using direct instruction. We used this same activity, and as part of our coaching, I asked whether this worked as well as direct instruction for him, and he explained that there was nothing that the students weren't finding out for themselves that he wouldn't have covered with them in direct instruction. Here they were investigating collaboratively, were more engaged, and were able to connect ideas about Kenya in one lesson that he struggled to get across in a whole module!

Of course, this was just one way to get into the questioning. You can do the same exercise with questions you create in the 5 Ws and an H or Inference Squares tool. Once your students have analysed and applied their own questions in the way described here, they will be much more deliberate about the questions they come up with the next time they use 5 Ws and an H or Inference Squares. They learn the value of questioning as part of learning and internalise those thinking skills to become more independent learners.

You might also like to adopt the practice of encouraging your students to keep a reflection book in which they record questions that are of interest to them. This can serve a dual purpose: it can help them to remember earlier questions, and it can also help you identify the progress they are making in terms of the quality of questions they are creating.

9.5 • REVIEW

i. Students asking their own questions has significant implications for engagement in inquiry, research, investigation, and independent or self-study. When students create their own questions, based on a need to know, they will often then engage in wanting to learn the answers.

ii. This approach to framed inquiry involves creating opportunities for cognitive conflict that inspire students to raise questions from the discomfort they feel.

iii. The 5 Ws and an H and Inference Squares tools are a useful way to guide students into the process of asking their own questions and encourage them to share perceptions and ideas that are a spur to action.

iv. Encourage your students to work with questions and dig more deeply into them. When they raise questions, share them with each other to help support a true spirit of collaborative inquiry. With the questions shared, encourage your students to consider the use, intent, and benefit of the questions they have asked: categorise them, challenge them, and take action around them. This can be done with any age of student.

v. Scaffolds for independent inquiry can encourage students to look beyond 'the answer' and raise further questions or extra learning that was not part of their original inquiry.

9.6 • REFLECTION

i. Have a go at getting your students to come up with questions of their own. Try it without a cognitive conflict stimulus first: just tell them the topic title, or the normal text you would use. What questions do your students come up with on their own and without having something to wrestle with?

ii. Then try giving them a stimulus that will make them think more. Have a go at a 5 Ws and an H activity or an Inference Square, using a picture or text that you think will engage them in having to work out what it might mean. Or try using an approach that creates cognitive conflict, like the Kenya example that challenged students' stereotypes.

iii. Then ask your students to come up with questions again. What do you notice compared to the first example? How does curiosity, uncertainty, or cognitive conflict change the questions they ask? Are they different? Are the students engaging differently?

iv. Share the questions as a class and categorise them. Let your students decide how they should be sorted. What makes sense to them? Which questions are they most keen to explore further?

v. Use their questions to start a dialogue or investigation. How do the questions help them understand the topic better? What framework can you use, or create, to help them explore their own questions?

vi. Use their questions to share their learning about the topic. What have we found out about [the topic]?

vii. Create a display of your students' questions or a book of class questions still to explore. Refer to it regularly with your students, and use their questions as a way in to dialogue or as the Initiate step of your questioning sequences.

viii. This approach can start to create a 'community of inquiry', which leads toward more independent learning.

EXAMPLE QUESTIONING SCRIPTS

In this final section of the book, we will take a look at some examples of questioning sequences in action, taken from video and audio recordings. In each example, the teacher or Challenging Learning colleague has been working with techniques from *Challenging Learning Through Questioning*. We have transcribed parts of the dialogue for purposes of professional learning and reflection.

Right at the beginning of the book, we talked about how it is not the question that matters but the questioning process. And that is the same now we reach the end of the book; the questions asked in these sequences are not the most important element. It is how they connect, how they bridge to the next question, how they build on students' responses, and how they contribute to better understanding that matters. Each teacher has drawn from all the elements of questioning and used techniques like funnelling and Pause-Paraphrase-Explore to encourage students into the Learning Zone.

You should start to see patterns emerge, like the IDEAR Framework, because the intention is to challenge first responses and encourage students to go beyond their initial ideas. Pay attention to how the teachers encourage their students to be more focussed, more specific, and more able to reason.

The scripts demonstrate how teachers have used questioning sequences to create sufficient positive struggle to engage their students in thinking. The scripts end, not with a resolution—as we wouldn't expect to reach that for some time after the dialogue—but with the next step of the lesson: the activity that the teacher has planned. This is important for you to picture, because we do not want to think of questioning as a stand-alone exercise; it should enhance the learning activities and accelerate progress toward the goal.

These examples are what can be achieved when you plan your questioning. They have structure and flow, and impact positively on your students' engagement, thinking, and understanding. They are not perfect. They are not expert. But they are real. This, then, is what is possible when you:

- Know Your Intent
- Plan Your Responses
- Stay Silent (and Listen)

Author's Note

Reading scripts never sounds like real life! This is partly because we remove some of the hesitations (*erm*, *err*, *you know*, and so on), replace some of the slang or shorthand, and rephrase what students have said into clear written language that makes sense to the reader. You read in your own voice, with your inflections and accent. All this means it does not quite sound the same as real verbal conversation. To get the most from the scripts, find a partner—or, even better, a group of three—and take the different roles. Read the scripts as if they were a play. It starts to seem more like the real thing, and you will experience *questioning* from a different perspective!

LITERACY LESSON (GRADE 1)

In this example, the class have been looking at stories and talking about the concept of 'what makes something real'. To tie in with the story of Snow White they have been reading, my colleague Jill Nottingham used an apple as a resource. She brought in three apples and placed each one on a separate plate. One is a fruit, one is a plastic apple, and the other is 'invisible' (Jill pretends to place an imaginary apple on the last plate). Her intent is to challenge the students to think about the concept of what makes something real.

TEACHER: So, here are three plates with apples on. What do you think of these apples?

STUDENT 1: You're missing one.

TEACHER: I'm missing one? What do mean I'm missing one?

STUDENT 1: There isn't one on the orange plate.

TEACHER: Let's have a look. This one? That's my invisible apple. Who thinks that we're missing an apple?

[All Students raise a hand]

TEACHER: Why do you think we're missing an apple?

STUDENT 2: You're just pretending.

TEACHER: Pretending?

STUDENT 3: Those apples are real [points to the fruit and plastic apples].

TEACHER: Are you saying those ones are real, but the one on the orange plate is not?

STUDENT 4: Did you make those ones or are they real?

TEACHER: That's an interesting question. Let's think for a moment, how are we going to know if something is real or not?

STUDENT 5: By feeling it... you can feel if it's real.

TEACHER: We can feel it. To know if something is real or not, could we feel it?

STUDENT 1: You can smell them.

TEACHER: Smell them. Right, so you can feel it, you can smell it. What else?

STUDENT 2: Taste it.

TEACHER: So can I feel, smell or taste this [invisible] apple then?

ALL: Nooooo.

TEACHER: Do you not think? If you close your eyes and think about the juiciest, yummiest, most delicious apple you have ever bitten into. Take the apple in your hand [most children grasp their hand] and feel its lovely, nice crisp skin. Then sniff it [most children sniff]. Can you smell that lovely apple-ness?

SOME: Yeeess

SOME: (overtaken by) Nooooo

STUDENT 4: I can't smell anything . . .

TEACHER: Can anybody smell that lovely apple-ness?

STUDENT 1: They taste bad.

TEACHER: They taste bad? Is it a bad apple?

STUDENT 2: Because there's no apple there, you'd probably be eating your hand.

STUDENT 3: You're biting into air.

TEACHER: So, if we can't see something, does that mean that it's not real?

STUDENT 4: Yes.

TEACHER: I've got a pet rabbit at home, but I can't see it right now. Does that mean my pet rabbit is no longer real?

ALL: No.

TEACHER: Why not?

STUDENT 1: Because you left it at home.

TEACHER: But I could have left that apple at home, so does that mean that apple is real or not real?

SOME: Not real.

SOME: Real, real.

TEACHER: Do you know what, my brain is starting to wobble now. Put your hands up if your brain is starting to wobble about whether this apple is real or not.

[Students' hands raised]

TEACHER: So, something can be real, even if we can't see it?

STUDENT 2: Remember it.

TEACHER: So, if you remember it does that make it real?

MOST: Yes

TEACHER: When you had your eyes closed and you were remembering eating an apple did it feel real in your head?

ALL: Yes

TEACHER: So maybe our memories and our thoughts can be real then? Even if we can't see them all the time?

STUDENT 3: You can feel them

TEACHER: How do you feel them?

STUDENT 3: In your head.

TEACHER: Wow! So, forgetting about the invisible apple just for a moment, what about these two apples here then? I am going to pass them around. When you pass it round what I want you to do is just have a feel, have a sniff, have a look at it and then pass it onto the next person. And when you are doing it, I want you to be thinking 'is this real?' 'Is this not real?' And if it is real, why is it real? How do you know it's real? And if it is not real, how do you know it is not real?

[students passing visible apples round]

STUDENT 4: (Whispering to friend) I can't tell.

STUDENT 5: I think that one is real and that one is not real.

STUDENT 6: Look, she [another student] is shaking her head a lot . . .

Following this discussion, the class go on to look at writing in fairy tales that makes things that are not real, real. They use language to describe how things look, sound, smell and feel to make them seem real in the reader's head. The teacher collects in their words and they create a story together.

TEACHER:	Today we are thinking about perimeter and area. What does *perimeter* mean?
DALLAS:	It's the outside of a shape.
TEACHER:	So, if I have a shape, like this [draws random shape on board], the outside is the perimeter?
STUDENTS:	Yes.
TEACHER:	But how is the perimeter different to the shape, then?
KAYLA:	Well, a shape is a 'thing' . . .
TEACHER:	Like this pencil case?
MONICA:	No, that's an object . . .
KEANE:	No, shapes have a name . . .
TEACHER:	So, if it doesn't have a name, it's not a shape? What about my random picture on the board—is that not a shape?
DALLAS:	It is, but we don't know its name. It's just a squiggle. But it's a shape because all the lines join up.
MONICA:	It has to be joined up, or the insides would leak out . . .
TEACHER:	What do you mean, Monica?
MONICA:	Like, if there's a gap in the lines, then the middle bit isn't inside the shape; it's all like, part of, everything [laughs]!
WASI:	It needs to be all joined up with the shape inside.
TEACHER:	This bit *inside* the shape, you mean? I thought that was the area. What's the difference between area and shape, then?
HUEY:	The shape is all of it. A shape has to have area and perimeter to be a shape. And then you can give it a name [laughs] . . .
TEACHER:	So, if there's a gap, it's not a complete shape. And what if I just draw a line?
DALLAS:	[Tuts] Oh, man! My head hurts!
JADE:	Even a line has a perimeter. If it's thick enough, you can measure all 'round the edge of the line.
TEACHER:	Are you saying that you have to measure it to be the perimeter?

The students go on to an inquiry activity, designing gardens for gnomes to a set perimeter of 12 centimetres on graph paper. The gardens can be of any shape, but must have the same perimeter. At the end of the lesson, the teacher returns to the original question: 'What does *perimeter* mean?' The students write their answers down and discuss how their thinking at the end of the lesson is different from their thinking in the discussion.

Standpoint Time

Consider the previous script. After reading it thoroughly, reflect on the process that the teacher and students went through.

What do you notice about the teacher's role?

What do you notice about the teacher's questioning?

What did the teacher encourage the students to think, or rethink?

How is this different from setting up a 'typical' session on perimeter?

Education comes from the Latin verb *educere* meaning 'to draw out'. This fits nicely with this process of questioning, and with the process of *sitting beside* our students to draw out their ideas and understanding.

Asking your students what *they* think, rather than telling them what the answers are, means that they have the opportunity to become more independent, more resilient, and more able to reason for themselves.

POLITICS LESSON (GRADE 10)

Here, the students are being asked to discuss a key concept in politics: democracy. Keep your answers to the standpoint time questions in mind as you read the following script, and see if you can spot the same themes, and variations, in the approach.

TEACHER:	We live in a democratic country. What is democracy?
SAGE:	It means 'rule of the people'.
TEACHER:	OK. So the people rule? But I don't rule, so is it not a democracy? For example, I don't get to make any laws or policies.
VIDYA:	We get to vote for those who do make the laws.
TEACHER:	What if I didn't vote for the people in power—is it still a democracy? For example, Labour makes the laws, but I voted Green Party.
CHANNING:	That's because this is a representative democracy, not a true democracy . . .
ALFIE:	You have the right to vote; everyone has the right to vote.
TEACHER:	Do *you* have the right to vote—aged 15?
ALFIE:	Well, no . . . not yet, but I will . . .
TEACHER:	So, is this not a democracy until you turn 18?
SAGE:	But at 15 you're not responsible enough to vote—you're making decisions that affect everyone in the country.
TEACHER:	So is democracy about responsibility, then?
SAGE:	Kind of, I guess. It's who's responsible for making decisions, like if you vote, you're making a decision.
TEACHER:	And if I *don't* vote?
CHANNING:	That's your choice. You made a decision not to—it was a free choice.
RAY:	You wouldn't have choices, or responsibility, or anything, if you're ruled by a king or queen, or just a person who makes all the decisions for you.
TEACHER:	So, what's the difference between democracy and responsibility?
RAY:	Errrm . . .
BRIDGET:	Well, democracy is to do with politics, but you don't have to be responsible in politi . . . well, actually I suppose you do, so . . . I dunno!
TEACHER:	Talk about that for a minute or two in pairs, then we'll research this further . . .

The students went on to research Athenian democracy, representative democracy, and Republican democracy. Following their research, they completed a 'Most likely to . . .'

activity using the three terms, and at the end of the lesson, they returned to the starting question: What is democracy? The students were then asked to consider how their thinking at the end of the lesson was different to their thinking at the start.

What type of thinking are the students being encouraged to do?

How is this similar or different to your questioning experiences in the classroom?

How are these questioning episodes finishing? What do you notice so far about the final step? Is there a definite outcome? Why or why not?

Consider the three scripts—are there any similarities or differences between the examples?

Key Learning Points

1. The purpose of Socratic questioning is to challenge students' first responses—to encourage them to think more carefully about how they form their opinions.

2. In order to challenge, you need to create 'cognitive conflict'—in other words, set up opposing points of view.

3. Even if you feel that your students have the correct answer, you can still challenge this so that students can clarify their opinions more clearly.

4. Once you have created the conflict, it is important that you prepare questions or activities to help build students' confidence in their opinions. Do not leave them confused!

   PURPOSE: Helps students build *resilience* so that they do not always rely on the teacher to `spoon-feed' the answers to them!

FINAL REFLECTION

Standpoint Think-Time

Now that we have looked at theory, approaches, tools, and frameworks for questioning, we think it is useful to give you some *standpoint think-time* (see Chapter 5) to reflect on your current thinking and your own learning journey.

Right back at the beginning of the book, we shared some common myths around questioning and encouraged you to think about the mindframes you might need to hold if you are aiming to improve the outcomes of questioning sequences in your classroom.

We have placed the myths and mindframes of questioning into Figure 51 as a continuum, to help you consider how far along in your questioning journey you are at this point in time. Underneath each continuum there is also a space to note your patterns of practice and the impact of your questioning on your students: What have you noticed? What have your experiences taught you? And how did you arrive at that perspective?

You can complete the reflection on your own, of course, but as with all reflections, the opportunity to talk to another person is invaluable. Grab your friends or colleagues and share your experiences with them. If they are interested in questioning, too, they can prompt, support, and challenge you. If they aren't yet working on their questioning, maybe your reflections will inspire them to do so!

By taking some time to reflect on, and with, Figure 51, I hope it gives you a sense of where you are with your questioning and makes you feel empowered to take whatever next steps are right for you.

Enjoy the process . . . I hope you find the journey on the Challenging Path a rewarding one!

Martin Renton

July 2019

▶ **Figure 51: Your questioning mindframes. What have you learnt; where are you now, and what are your patterns of practice? A frame for reflecting on your own learning.**

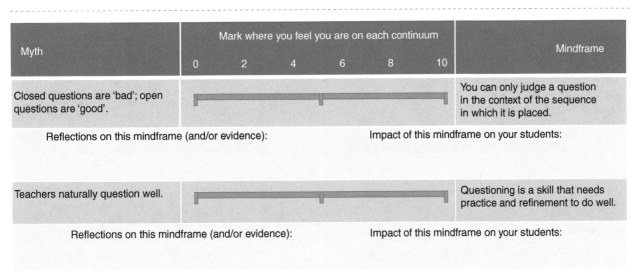

(Continued)

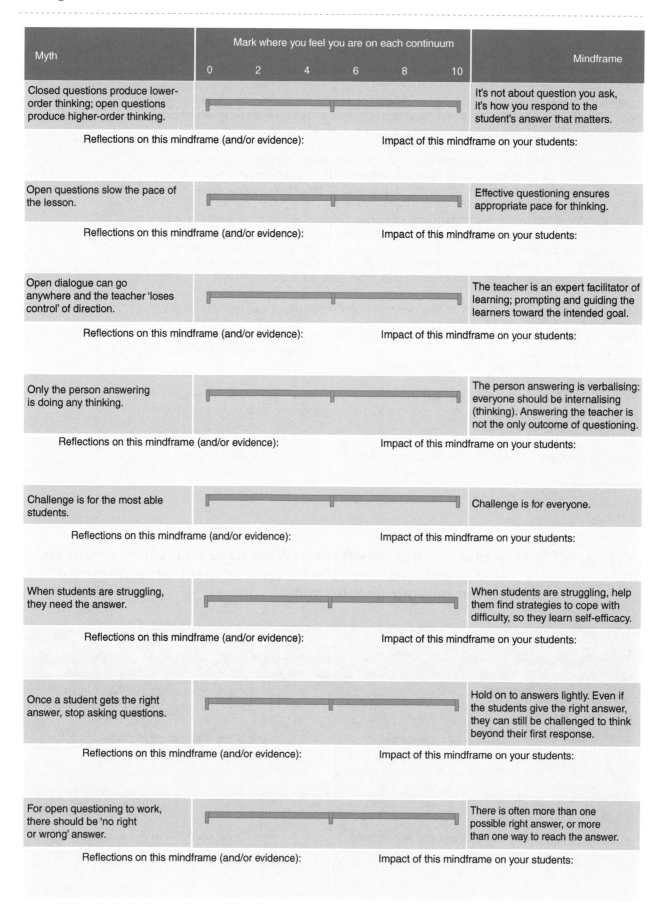

Myth	Mark where you feel you are on each continuum						Mindframe
	0	2	4	6	8	10	
Closed questions produce lower-order thinking; open questions produce higher-order thinking.							It's not about question you ask, it's how you respond to the student's answer that matters.

Reflections on this mindframe (and/or evidence):   Impact of this mindframe on your students:

| Open questions slow the pace of the lesson. | Effective questioning ensures appropriate pace for thinking. |

Reflections on this mindframe (and/or evidence):   Impact of this mindframe on your students:

| Open dialogue can go anywhere and the teacher 'loses control' of direction. | The teacher is an expert facilitator of learning; prompting and guiding the learners toward the intended goal. |

Reflections on this mindframe (and/or evidence):   Impact of this mindframe on your students:

| Only the person answering is doing any thinking. | The person answering is verbalising: everyone should be internalising (thinking). Answering the teacher is not the only outcome of questioning. |

Reflections on this mindframe (and/or evidence):   Impact of this mindframe on your students:

| Challenge is for the most able students. | Challenge is for everyone. |

Reflections on this mindframe (and/or evidence):   Impact of this mindframe on your students:

| When students are struggling, they need the answer. | When students are struggling, help them find strategies to cope with difficulty, so they learn self-efficacy. |

Reflections on this mindframe (and/or evidence):   Impact of this mindframe on your students:

| Once a student gets the right answer, stop asking questions. | Hold on to answers lightly. Even if the students give the right answer, they can still be challenged to think beyond their first response. |

Reflections on this mindframe (and/or evidence):   Impact of this mindframe on your students:

| For open questioning to work, there should be 'no right or wrong' answer. | There is often more than one possible right answer, or more than one way to reach the answer. |

Reflections on this mindframe (and/or evidence):   Impact of this mindframe on your students:

10 TOP TIPS FOR BETTER QUESTIONING

THINK ABOUT *WHY* YOU ARE ASKING THE QUESTION: Will it stretch your students' understanding, engage your students, and make them think?

TAKE THE CHALLENGING PATH: Encourage thinking, reasoning, and better learning by following up first responses with the intention to explore.

PLAN YOUR MOVES: Effective questioning is about how you react to your students' responses. Consider your sequence before the lesson so you are more likely to create exploratory dialogue.

PREDICT WHAT YOUR STUDENTS ARE LIKELY TO SAY: When planning your questioning, imagine what responses you will get. Then prepare focussed questions to explore and challenge.

GIVE YOUR STUDENTS 'THINK-TIME': Wait *at least* 3 seconds to improve the number, quality, and length of your students' responses.

PRACTISE! Don't be afraid to have a 'prompt sheet' in front of you to work from. Share your prompts with your students: this models a process of learning together.

GET COMFORTABLE WITH SILENCE! Give yourself and your students permission to think. Do the least amount possible to encourage them to keep talking, and give yourself processing-time. Some of the best questioning uses questions sparingly.

THINK-PAIR-SHARE: Encourage your students to test out their ideas with another student before answering. This ensures they engage with thinking and language.

TAKE A MEDIATION STANCE: Imagine you don't know the answer yourself. What questions can you ask your students to explore their understanding further and help them be clearer?

DON'T WORRY! However well intentioned and prepared we are, things don't always go to plan! If the sequence doesn't go where you expected, it is better to have made one move to explore than none at all. So just try again—there will be another question to initiate just around the corner.

REFERENCES

This book has drawn on the following texts. You might be interested to find out more by reading:

Alexander, R. (2006). *Towards dialogic teaching: Rethinking classroom talk* (3rd ed.). York, UK: Dialogos.

Bjork, E. L., & Bjork, R. (2014). Making things hard on yourself, but in a good way: Creating desirable difficulties to enhance learning. In M. A. Gernsbacher & J. Pomerantz (Eds.), *Psychology and the real world: Essays illustrating fundamental contributions to society* (2nd ed., pp. 59-68). New York, NY: Worth.

Brontë, C. (2006). *Jane Eyre*. Suffolk, UK: Penguin Classics. (Original work published 1847)

Chouinard, M. M. (2007). Children's questions: A mechanism for cognitive development. *Monographs of the Society for Research in Child Development, 72*(1). Retrieved from https://www.ncbi.nlm.nih.gov/pubmed/17394580. Accessed September 2019.

Costa, A. L., & Garmston, R. J. (1994). *Cognitive coaching: A foundation for renaissance schools.* Norwood, MA: Christopher-Gordon.

Cotton, K. (1988). *Classroom questioning.* Office of Educational Research and Improvement. Portland, OR: Northwest Regional Educational Laboratory.

Council for Learning Outside the Classroom. (n.d.). *Risk, challenge and adventure.* Retrieved from www.lotc.org.uk/why/risk-challenge-and-adventure. Accessed March 2016.

Daniels, H. (2001). *Vygotsky and pedagogy.* Abingdon, UK: RoutledgeFalmer.

De A'Echevarria, A., & Patience, I. (2008). Teaching thinking pocketbook. Alresford, UK: Teachers' Pocketbooks.

Department for Education and Skills. (2002). *Training materials for the foundation subjects (Module 4: Questioning).* London, UK: Author.

Department for Education and Skills. (2013). *Geography program of study: Key stage 3 national curriculum in England.* London, UK: Author.

Dixon-Krauss, L. (1996). *Vygotsky in the classroom: Mediated literacy instruction and assessment.* White Plains, NY: Longman.

Doherty, J. (2017). Skilful questioning: The beating heart of good pedagogy. Retrieved from *Impact: Journal of the Chartered College of Teaching UK* at https://impact.chartered.college/article/doherty-skilful-questioning-beating-heart-pedagogy. Accessed July 2019.

Fisher, R. (2005). *Teaching children to think* (2nd ed.). Cheltenham, UK: Nelson Thornes.

Garmston, R., & Wellman, B. (1999). *The adaptive school: A sourcebook for developing collaborative groups.* Norwood, MA: Christopher-Gordon.

Geldard, K., Geldard, D., & Yin Foo, R. (2016). *Counselling adolescents: The proactive approach for young people* (4th ed.). London, UK: Sage.

Gershon, M. (2013). *How to stretch and challenge your students*. Retrieved from TES Online at https://newteachers.tes.co.uk/content/how-stretch-and-challenge-your-students. Accessed June 2013.

Gray, P. (2015). *Free to learn: Why unleashing the instinct to play will make our children happier, more self-reliant and better students for life*. New York, NY: Basic Books.

Haisch, B. (2010). *The purpose-guided universe*. Franklin Lakes, NJ: Career Press.

Hannel, I. (2009). Insufficient questioning. *Kappan, 91*(3), 65–69.

Harper, D. (2020). Critic (n). Retrieved from *Online Etymology Dictionary* at https://www.etymonline.com/search?q=kritikos. Accessed January 2020.

Hattie, J. (2009). *Visible learning for teachers*. Abingdon, UK: Routledge.

Higgins, S., Baumfield, V., & Leat, D. (Eds.). (2000). *Thinking through primary teaching*. Cambridge, UK: Chris Kington.

Holt, J., & Farenga, P. (2003). *Teach your own: The John Holt book of homeschooling*. Cambridge, MA: Da Capo Press.

Hubbard, E. (1908). *Essay on silence*. Aurora, NY: Roycrofters.

Kagge, E. (2017). *Silence in the age of noise*. London, UK: Penguin.

Kyriacou, C. (1991). *Essential teaching skills*. Hemel Hempstead, UK: Simon & Schuster Education.

Leat, D. (2001). *Thinking through geography* (2nd ed.). London, UK: Optimus Education.

Lipman, M. (2003). *Thinking in education* (2nd ed.). Cambridge, UK: Cambridge University Press.

Levin, T., & Long, R. (1981). *Effective instruction*. Alexandria, VA: Association for Supervision and Curriculum Development.

Luckner, J., & Nadler, R. (1997). *Processing the experience: Strategies to enhance and generalize learning*. Dubuque, IA: Kendall/Hunt.

Marzano, R., & Simms, J. (2014). *Questioning sequences in the classroom*. Victoria, Australia: Hawker Brownlow.

McComas, W. F., & Abraham, L. (2005). *Asking more effective questions*. Retrieved from the Rossier School of Education at http://cet.usc.edu/resources/teaching_learning/docs/Asking_Better_Questions.pdf. Accessed February 2016.

Mitra, S. (2019). Sugata Mitra—Education futurist (#89). Interviewed by Matt Pritchard, the Science Magician, for *Words on Wonder*. Retrieved from https://wordsonwonder.com/2019/10/13/sugata-mitra-education-futurist-89/. Accessed October 2019.

Morgan, N., & Saxton, J. (2006). *Asking better questions*. Markham, ON: Pembroke.

Nottingham, J. (2007). Exploring the pit. *Teaching Thinking and Creativity, 8:2*(23), 64–68. Birmingham, UK: Imaginative Minds.

Nottingham, J. (2010). *Challenging learning*. Cramlington, Northumberland, UK: JN Publishing.

Nottingham, J. (2017). *The Learning Challenge: How to guide your students through the Learning Pit to achieve deeper understanding*. Thousand Oaks, CA: Corwin.

Nottingham, J., & Larsson, B. (2019). *Challenging mindset: Why a growth mindset makes a difference in learning—and what to do when it doesn't*. Thousand Oaks, CA: Corwin.

Nottingham, J., & Nottingham, J. (2017). *Challenging learning through feedback*. London, UK: Sage.

Nottingham, J., Nottingham, J., & Renton, M. (2017). *Challenging learning through dialogue*. Thousand Oaks, CA: Corwin.

Plato. (1969). *The last days of Socrates*. Translated by H. Tredennick. St. Ives, UK: Penguin. (Original work published 399–347 BC)

Reed, D. K. (2016). *Inference making: The key to advanced reading development*. Retrieved from the Iowa Reading Research Center at https://iowareadingresearch .org/blog/inference-making-the-key-to-advanced-reading-development. Accessed July 2019.

Renton, M. (2008a). Creative vocations. *Teaching Thinking and Creativity, 10:2*(27). Birmingham, UK: Imaginative Minds.

Renton, M. (2008b). Thinking in the national curriculum. *Teaching Thinking and Creativity, 8:4*(25). Birmingham, UK: Imaginative Minds.

Roberts, M. (2013). *Geography through enquiry: Approaches to teaching and learning in the secondary school*. Sheffield, UK: Geographical Association.

Rowe, M. B. (1972). *Wait-time and rewards as instructional variables, their influence in language, logic and fate control*. Paper presented at the National Association for Research in Science Teaching, Chicago, IL.

Rowe, M. B. (1986). Wait time: Slowing down may be a way of speeding up! *Journal of Teacher Education, 37*(1), 43–50.

Stahl, R. (1990). *Using 'think-time' behaviors to promote students' information processing, learning, and on-task participation: An instructional module*. Tempe: Arizona State University.

Stahl, R. J. (1994). *Using 'think-time' and 'wait-time' skillfully in the classroom* (ERIC no. ED370885). Retrieved from the Clearinghouse for Social Studies/Social Science Education at http://www.ericdigests.org. Accessed June 2016.

Thomas, D. (2004). *Under milk wood*. St. Ives, UK: Orion. (Original work published 1954)

Tobin, K. (1987). The role of wait time in higher cognitive level learning. *Review of Educational Research, 57*(Spring), 69–95.

Verenikina, I. (2003). *Understanding scaffolding and the ZPD in educational research*. Retrieved from the University of Wollongong at http://ro.uow.edu.au/edupapers/381/. Accessed September 2013.

Vygotsky, L. (1978). *Mind and society: The development of higher mental processes*. Cambridge, MA: Harvard University Press.

Wagner, D. J. (2001–2002). *Introduction to magnetism and induced currents*. Retrieved from https://www.rpi.edu/dept/phys/ScIT/InformationStorage/faraday/magnetism_a .html. Accessed July 2019.

Walsh, J. A., & Sattes, B. D. (2011). *Thinking through quality questioning: Deepening student engagement*. Thousand Oaks, CA: Corwin.

Willingham, D. (2009). Ask the cognitive scientist: What will improve a student's memory? *American Educator*, p. 22.

Wittgenstein, L. (1953) Philosophical investigations. In *Philosophy classics*. Retrieved from www.butler-bowdon.com/ludwig-wittgenstein---philosophical-investigations.html. Accessed July 2019.

Wolf, D. P. (1987). The art of questioning. *Academic Connections* (Winter), pp. 1–7.

INDEX

Helping educators make the *greatest impact*

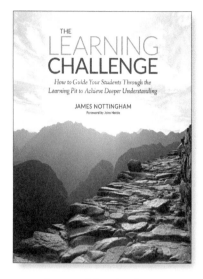

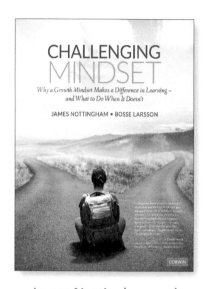

James Nottingham

Dive into the Learning Pit and show students how to promote challenge, dialogue, and a growth mindset.

James Nottingham and Bosse Larsson

Create the right conditions for a growth mindset to flourish in your school and your students.

Jill Nottingham, James Nottingham, Mark Bollom, Joanne Nugent, and Lorna Pringle

For fans of the *The Learning Challenge*, this book provides everything you need to run dialogue-driven challenges so that students develop literary skills critical to ELA standards.

Jill Nottingham and James Nottingham

Twenty compelling Learning Challenge lessons, around topics of current importance, provide teachers with everything needed to facilitate thoughtful, rigorous, dialogue-driven challenges for students.

James Nottingham, Jill Nottingham, and Martin Renton

Use feedback and classroom discussions to teach good habits of thinking and learning.

orwin books represent the latest thinking from some of the most respected experts in eK–12 education. We are proud of the breadth and depth of the books we publish and e authors we partner with in our mission to better serve educators and students.

Sugata Mitra

Discover the results of Sugata Mitra's latest research around self-organized learning environments (SOLE) and building "Schools in the Cloud" all over the world.

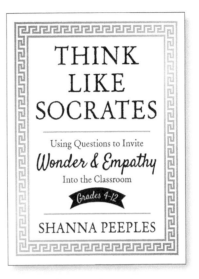

Shanna Peeples

This book reveals the key to creating wonder and empathy in the classroom: Questions!

Kimberly L. Mitchell

Explore the opportunity to do inquiry as you read about it. Learn what inquiry-based instruction looks like in practice through five key strategies.

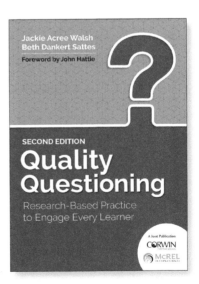

Jackie Acree Walsh and Beth Dankert Sattes

This exciting new book demonstrates how to seamlessly integrate effective questioning strategies into daily practice, thereby energizing teaching and learning.

A SAGE Publishing Company

Helping educators make the greatest impact

CORWIN HAS ONE MISSION: to enhance education through intentional professional learning.

We build long-term relationships with our authors, educators, clients, and associations who partner with us to develop and continuously improve the best evidence-based practices that establish and support lifelong learning.